THE DOWNFALL OF THE SPANISH ARMADA IN IRELAND

KEN DOUGLAS ～

Gill & Macmillan

Gill & Macmillan Ltd
Hume Avenue, Park West, Dublin 12
with associated companies throughout the world
www.gillmacmillan.ie

© Kenneth Douglas 2009
978 07171 4616 1

Maps by Keith Barrett of Design Image
Index compiled by Cover to Cover
Typography design by Make Communication
Print origination by O'K Graphic Design, Dublin
Printed and bound in Great Britain by MPG Books Ltd,
Bodmin, Cornwall

This book is typeset in 11/13.5 pt Minion.

The paper used in this book comes from the wood pulp
of managed forests. For every tree felled, at least one
tree is planted, thereby renewing natural resources.

A CIP catalogue record for this book is available from
the British Library.

5 4 3 2 1

To my family: to my wife Gladys, my son and daughter-in-law Nick and Tricia, and my grandchildren Luke, Clare and Christian, whose love and support mean everything to me.

'... then take great heed lest you fall upon the island of Ireland for fear of the harm that may happen unto you upon that coast.'

MEDINA SIDONIA'S SAILING INSTRUCTIONS TO THE ARMADA

CONTENTS

ACKNOWLEDGMENTS

Although I beavered away on my own for several years, I have also received special help from Seán Nolan of the Ulster Museum. He supplied me with previously unpublished information about *La Trinidad Valencera* and the background to the setting up of the Tower Museum in Derry. He then took on the onerous task of reading my first typescript and made several necessary corrections. His friendship and encouragement were an invaluable support. I also gladly thank Dr Colin Martin of St Andrews University. His distinguished career in Armada research was a continuing inspiration, and more recently he helped me directly by saving me from several mistakes.

I thank the staff at the Belfast Central Library, the Linenhall Library and the Public Record Office, Northern Ireland; they managed to supply me with virtually all the material I needed.

I also owe special thanks to Michael Diggin, landscape photographer from Tralee, Co. Kerry, for his part in assembling a collection of outstanding images of the Irish coast.

And finally I thank my friend Denis Bergin of Dublin, who was instrumental in bringing the book to publication.

INTRODUCTION

Everyone who has read about the Spanish Armada knows that the English fleet defeated it in battle at Gravelines on 8 August 1588. It withdrew northwards, but was still reasonably intact as it sailed between Orkney and Fair Isle, and could hope to return safely to Spain. In order to bring into perspective the magnitude of the disaster that a large part of the Armada then suffered it is essential to learn what happened to it in Ireland. Enemy action is hardly involved. The Armada was instead enveloped by a spider's web of misfortune, in which many complex elements were interwoven. It is the purpose of this book to try to untangle the causes and reveal the many individual incidents that brought catastrophe to the pride of Spanish arms on Ireland's unknown coasts.

More than thirty years have passed since the last general history of the Armada in Ireland appeared. Niall Fallon's book *The Armada in Ireland* was a courageous attempt to collate what is essentially a number of disconnected episodes in many separate locations on the Irish coast. His work is a first-rate compilation of the research material available at that time. Since then new information and revised interpretations have emerged and there is an obvious need to bring the history up to date.

Presentation has always been a problem. There is an inherent lack of unity in so many separate incidents, with the result that they tend to combine to give a confusing picture. It then occurred to me, perhaps belatedly, that the different episodes are unified by time. If they could be presented in the form of a chronicle the general reader might then be able to follow the sequence of events more coherently. Dates are available in the State Papers so it seemed to be a feasible idea. To realize it I have worked directly from original sources and have relied very little on the work of other authors. A by-product of putting things in date order has been to enable interpretations to emerge that were not formerly obvious. For example, on discovering that the date six ships left the Shannon Estuary was the day before three ships appeared in Blasket Sound, it became apparent that these were three of the same six ships.

My aim has been to write in a straightforward, easily accessible way in the hope that the general reader, not necessarily well versed in history, can derive enjoyment from it. I am not a professional historian and so I have tried to avoid the appearance of scholarship I do not possess, while at the same time not compromising on the quality of the historical content. With this in mind there are no distracting footnotes or numbered references. Notes and sources are given at the end of each chapter, and I hope there is enough information there to enable anyone interested to trace my sources. Precedent for this method of authentication exists in the example set by one of the greatest of all Armada historians, Garrett Mattingly, in his inspiring 1959 work *The Defeat of the Spanish Armada.*

There is a great deal of available data relevant to the Armada in Ireland that does not fit into a chronicle format, and I have therefore divided the text into four parts. In part one the action takes place in the North Sea and the Atlantic Ocean as the Spanish decide how they are going to get home and the problems they face trying to accomplish this. Part two is the chronicle of the arrival of Spanish ships in Ireland and their fate. Part three pays tribute to the hugely important role played by divers in the 1960s and 1970s. By producing tangible evidence of the Armada they stimulated widespread popular interest in a subject that had previously been the preserve of scholars. Part four consists of four Appendices giving peripheral information that adds to our understanding. Firstly, a definitive list of ships and men lost in Ireland is necessary. Then follows Captain Cuéllar's account of his journey through Connaught and Ulster. This makes an important contribution to the history of Ireland as well as Armada history. It is disproportionately long, but it is there and cannot be ignored. Aramburu's diary provides a detailed record of the track of the Armada in the Atlantic, which helps to explain why so many ships contacted Ireland when they were specifically ordered to avoid it. Although referred to frequently by historians this is the first time it has been printed in full. And a brief review of Irish History tries to explain the complex combination of population groups that had evolved in Ireland up to the sixteenth century.

A NOTE ON DATING

All dates conform to the New Style calendar.

Dates from Spanish sources disagree with the same day in English and Irish sources by 10 days. Spanish dates have been taken here to be correct, and dates from English and Irish documents have been changed throughout to make them agree. Armada historians have generally adopted this method of dating in recent times, presumably because the Spanish dates are more accurate in relation to the solar calendar.

In western Europe the calendar introduced by Julius Caesar in 46 BC (known as the Julian calendar) had been used for over 1,600 years. Earth orbit of the sun is, however, not a precise number of days and, even allowing for leap years, errors had accumulated. By the sixteenth century the Julian calendar was reckoned to be 10 days behind the true date. Pope Gregory XIII promoted the re-alignment of the calendar in 1582 by eliminating 5–14 October. This became the Gregorian or New Style calendar, which was adopted right away by the Catholic countries of southern Europe. It was resisted on principle in England and other Protestant countries where they continued to use the Julian or Old Style calendar.

The Gregorian calendar was not finally accepted in Britain until 1752, by which time the discrepancy had become 11 days. The uproar caused by the elimination of 3–13 September 1752 is a joy to behold for the connoisseur of human folly. Mobs paraded the streets demanding 'Give us back our eleven days'. City traders refused to pay their taxes on the usual quarter end date of 25 March. They paid instead 11 days later on 5 April, which remains to this day the end of the fiscal year.

NEW STYLE CALENDAR
AUTUMN 1588

	M	T	W	T	F	S	S
August	8	9	10	11	12	13	14
	15	16	17	18	19	20	21
	22	23	24	25	26	27	28
September	29	30	31	1	2	3	4
	5	6	7	8	9	10	11
	12	13	14	15	16	17	18
	19	20	21	22	23	24	25
October	26	27	28	29	30	1	2
	3	4	5	6	7	8	9
	10	11	12	13	14	15	16
	17	18	19	20	21	22	23
	24	25	26	27	28	29	30

Old style dates are ten days behind those in the New Style Calendar. For example, Wednesday 21 September NS is equivalent to Wednesday 11 September OS. Converting between the two, the date changes but the day of the week stays the same.

AUTHOR'S NOTE

For some reason the myth developed, and became established in popular perception, that Spanish Armada ships were 'driven' onto the west coast of Ireland, and crashed to destruction against iron-bound cliffs. The cliffs are there all right, dramatic and threatening, but they were easily avoided by experienced seamen, and there is no record of any Armada ship being lost in these circumstances. The ships struggled to find shelter and for the most part succeeded.

Ironically, and less melodramatically, a critical hazard for big Armada ships turned out to be sand. Several sea-inlets, that at first sight seemed to offer safe shelter, were found to be filled with sandy shoals. And shallow, shelving beaches sometimes stretched out to sea for many hundreds of yards. It was here that some Armada ships met their end, but the crews of grounded ships were usually able to land safely.

There were, however, many factors contributing to the disaster that befell the Armada. It is impossible to generalize and we must examine the situation of each ship or group of ships in their many separate locations to learn the full history of the Spanish Armada in Ireland.

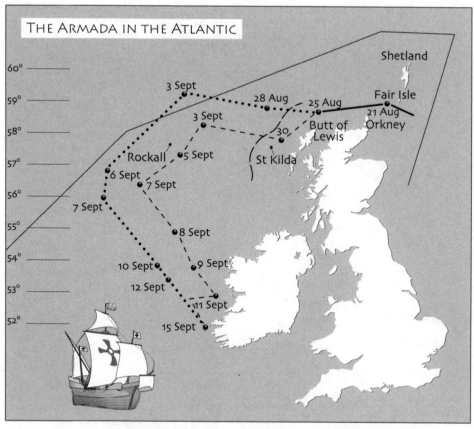

THE ARMADA IN THE ATLANTIC

————————— The course set by the French pilot and directed by Medina Sidonia

———————— The course when the Armada was together from 21 to 25 August

– – – – – – – – – The course followed by Marcos de Aramburu

••••••••••••••• The course followed by Juan Martinez de Recalde

——————— The edge of the Continental Shelf

Two of the ships separated from the main fleet left details of the progress of their voyages in the Atlantic; they were Recalde's *San Juan of Portugal* and Aramburu's *San Juan Bautista*. The crucial period was 21 August to 3 September, when according to their sailing instructions (and basic logic) they should have been sailing south-southwest. On 21 August they came through the Fair Isle Channel at 59° 30'N, yet despite taking courses between SSW and SSE, on 28 August Recalde was still at 59°N, and by September he was actually at 59° 30'N, having made no headway southwards in thirteen days. Aramburu's circumstances were the same except that by September he was at about 58° 30'N. Because of constant southerly winds, ocean currents and leeway they had been held above 58°N all this time.

They calculated that they had at least made sea room by making progress westwards, but even this was wrong. The unknown effect of ocean currents meant they were losing about 20 to 25 miles a day, so that by 3 September, when they at last turned towards the south, they had lost approximately 300 miles, and were consequently that much nearer the Irish coast. When they began to sail courses east of south, they were inevitably heading for Ireland. Other separated ships were affected in the same way.

The main fleet missed Ireland, but not by very much. When they arrived back in Spain they found themselves at Santander, which they thought at first was Cizarga 25 miles west of La Coruña, an error of about 275 miles.

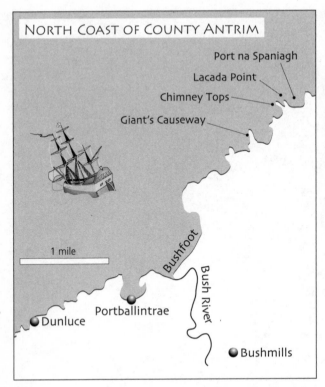

NORTH COAST OF COUNTY ANTRIM

Port na Spaniagh

Lacada Point

Chimney Tops

Giant's Causeway

1 mile

Bushfoot

Bush River

Portballintrae

Dunluce

Bushmills

On 28 October the *Girona* was first seen 'over against Dunluce'. It was much too close to a lee shore and was faced with the problem of avoiding the Causeway and Chimney Tops headlands for which it had to try to sail northeast, close to a strong northwest wind. It only just cleared the Chimney Tops, but was swept into Port na Spaniagh and at midnight was wrecked on Lacada Point.

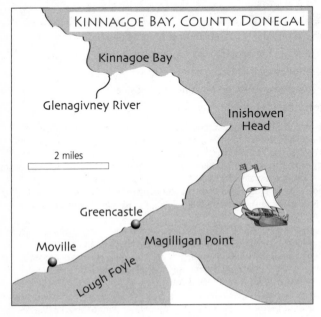

KINNAGOE BAY, COUNTY DONEGAL

Kinnagoe Bay

Glenagivney River

Inishowen Head

2 miles

Greencastle

Moville

Magilligan Point

Lough Foyle

On 14 September *La Trinidad Valencera* was leaking badly and tried to save itself by making for the wide sandy beach of Kinnagoe Bay, four miles west of Inishowen Head. It never reached the beach but mounted a pinnacle of rock about 300 yards off the reef at the western entrance to the Bay. For two days it remained perched on the rock, but then broke in two and sank.

The *Duquesa Santa Ana* had left Blacksod Bay on 23 September with the intention of returning to Spain. She also had on board the survivors from the *Rata Encoronada* including Don Alonso de Leyva. Unable to sail either south or west because of contrary winds, it was eventually decided to head for Scotland, but on 28 September bad weather forced it into Loughros More Bay, Co. Donegal, where it was beached at Tramore Strand about a mile east of Rossbeg. The men landed safely and later marched to Calebeg to join the *Girona*.

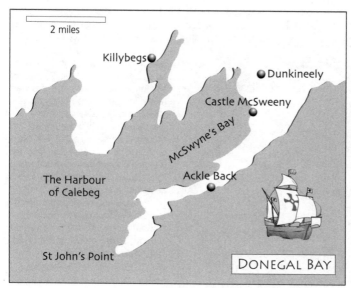

On 15 September the *Girona* and two other unidentified ships crossed Donegal Bay and entered the harbour of Calebeg. This was almost certainly McSwyne's Bay rather than Killybegs because they were entertained by the McSweenys who owned the castle at the head of the bay. On 21 September the two unidentified ships were destroyed by the Great Gale. The *Girona* survived but was damaged. On 10 October Don Alonso de Leyva arrived with the crews of at least two ships. He set to work to repair the *Girona* and on 26 October it sailed for Scotland with 1,300 men on board.

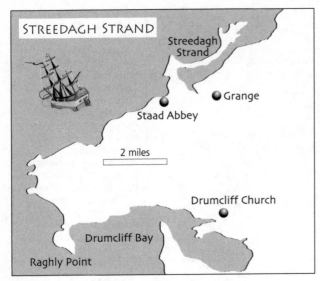

On 15 September three ships, *La Lavia*, *Juliana* and the *Santa Maria de Visón* found an anchorage at the eastern end of Donegal Bay, probably in Drumcliff Bay. On 20 September they sailed west on an easterly wind, but next day they were forced back by the Great Gale and were wrecked on Streedagh Strand.

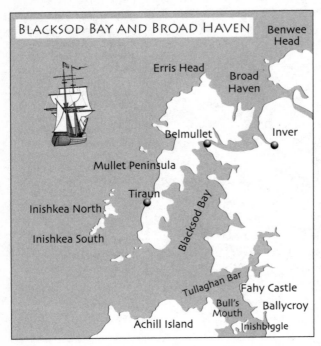

Three ships came into Blacksod Bay about 15 September, but to different locations. The *Duquesa Santa Ana* went north into the bay and anchored at Elly Bay, probably in the north side near the castle. Finding an anchorage anywhere in the area was made difficult because sandy shoals are common. The *Rata Encoronada* went east into Tullaghan Bay, but grounded on the Tullaghan Bar and could not be re-floated. De Leyva got the men off and they sheltered near Fahy Castle. The *Nuestra Señora de Begoña* was said to be at Bealingly, which Spotswood Green interpreted to be Bull's Mouth in the south of the bay, but that is affected by fierce tidal currents, so along the north shore of Inishbiggle is more likely.

The *Duquesa* left on 23 September having taken on board survivors from the *Rata*.

In Broad Haven one ship, possibly the *San Nicolas Prodaneli*, sheltered in an inlet in the south of the bay. It was later lost on a sand bank near Inver. There is a strong probability that the *San Pedro el Mayor* spent time in Broad Haven before leaving at the end of October only to be lost at Hope Cove, Co. Devon.

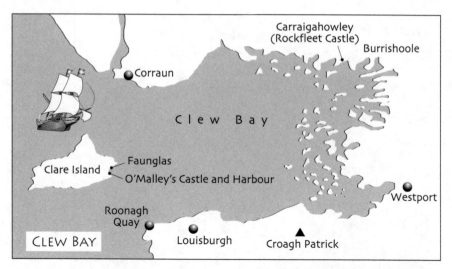

On 16 September a ship was lost among the islands at Burrishoole in the northeast corner of Clew Bay. Sixteen men survived and fell into the hands of a tenant of the Duke of Ormond. The ship has not been safely identified, but may have been the *Santiago*. About the same time the *Gran Grin* also entered Clew Bay and found safe anchorage near the O'Malley castle in the southeast corner of Clare Island. The crew were entertained by the O'Malleys for several days, but the ship was lost in the Great Gale on 21 September. Its remains have never been located.

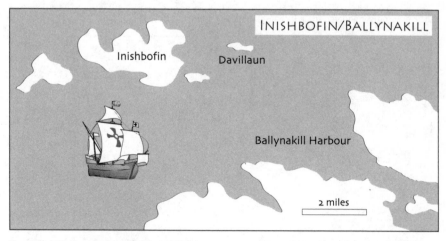

The *Falcon Blanco Mediano* anchored safely somewhere in the Inishbofin, Davillaun, Ballynakill area. The crew of about a hundred came ashore alive and were looked after by Sir Murrough Na Doe O'Flagherty. Later Sir Richard Bingham demanded that all survivors should be surrendered to the English garrison in Galway City. The ship was destroyed in the Great Gale of 21 September, but the site has not been found.

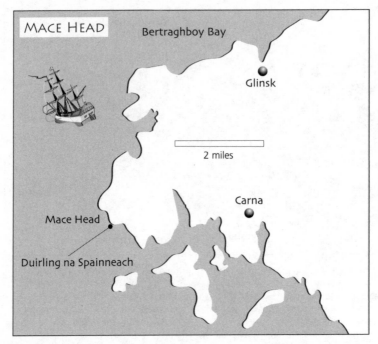

The *Concepcion del Cano* was lost near Mace Head, Co. Galway, probably the rock named Duirling na Spainneach was involved, but no wreck has been located. About twenty Spanish survivors were sheltered by Tadgh Na Buile O'Flaherty for a time before being surrendered to Sir Richard Bingham.

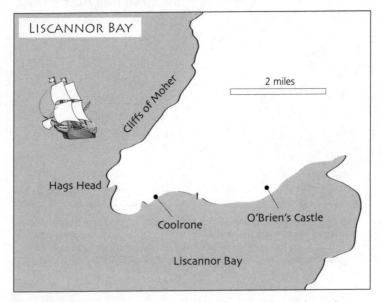

The galleass *Zuñiga* arrived in Liscannor Bay, Co. Clare, on 15 September and anchored at a place about a mile west of Sir Turlough O'Brien's castle, thought to be the rocky bay named Coolrone. This proved to be a secure and safe anchorage, good enough for the ship to survive the Great Gale, and she left Ireland more or less intact on 23 September.

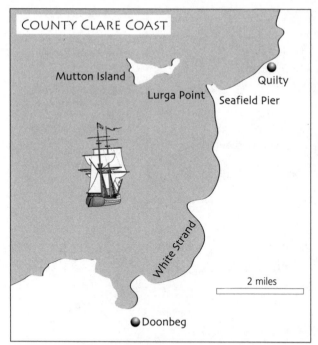

COUNTY CLARE COAST

Mutton Island

Lurga Point

Quilty

Seafield Pier

White Strand

2 miles

Doonbeg

The wreck sites of the *San Marcos* and *San Esteban* have not been conclusively identified, but the documentary evidence suggests that the *San Marcos* was lost between Lurga Point and Mutton Island, and the *San Esteban* on the White Strand near Doonbeg.

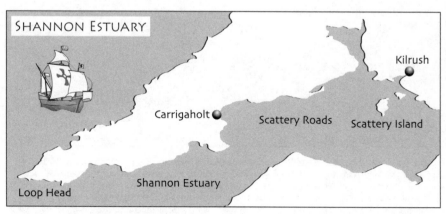

SHANNON ESTUARY

Kilrush

Carrigaholt

Scattery Roads

Scattery Island

Shannon Estuary

Loop Head

Seven Armada ships took shelter in the Shannon Estuary about 15 September. At first they tried to anchor off Carrigaholt, but it was too shallow in that area and they soon moved up river to Scattery Roads, where they were observed by eyewitnesses from Kilrush. The *Anunciada* was unseaworthy and had to be abandoned. An attempt was made to scuttle and burn the wreck, but it drifted ashore somewhere west of Kilrush. The remaining six ships had a favourable east wind on Tuesday 20 September and were able to leave the Shannon.

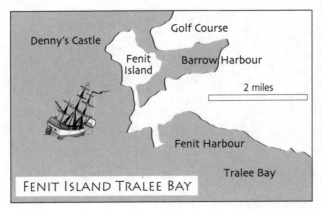

FENIT ISLAND TRALEE BAY

The first Armada ship to be reported was the small patache or zabra in the area of Barrow Harbour near Fenit, Co. Kerry. The ship was probably not wrecked, but 24 of her crew came ashore alive; they surrendered and were held in Denny's Castle by Lady Denny. Later they were killed probably by English garrison soldiers in Tralee.

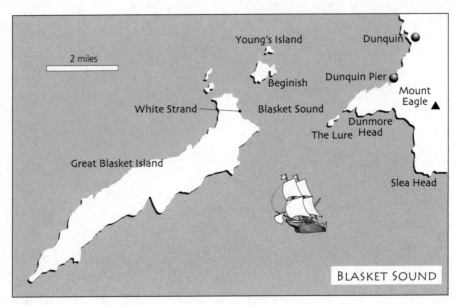

BLASKET SOUND

A major drama was enacted in Blasket Sound, an appropriately majestic theatre for such events. On 15 September two large ships and a patache arrived through the maze of small islands west of Beginish, and anchored off Great Blasket White Strand. One, the *San Juan of Portugal*, was commanded by Juan Martinez de Recalde, senior admiral of the entire Armada. The other had on board Marcos de Aramburu, who kept a detailed diary of his voyage; his description of the Great Gale of 21 September is priceless. On that day two of the ships from the Shannon entered the Sound badly damaged by the gale. The *Santa Maria de la Rosa* hit a submerged rock in the southern entrance to the Sound and sank with all hands except for one small boy. The other, the *San Juan of Fernando Horra*, had to be abandoned. An attempt was made to sink it, but it seemed to survive for a time; its location has not been found. Both Recalde and Aramburu left the Sound about 23/24 September and returned safely to Spain.

PART I
The Armada Sets Course for Disaster

Chapter 1 ∾

| 12 TO 21 AUGUST 1588
WHERE WILL THEY GO?

The Spanish Army bare away with all the sails they were able to make.

(SEYMOUR, WYNTER AND PALMER)

THE ARMADA, HOMEWARD-BOUND

On 18 August 1588 a bark of Southampton was fishing about 36 miles southeast of Sumburgh Head, Shetland, when the crew sighted the Spanish Armada approaching from over the horizon to the south. As they watched,

> … they descried a very great fleet of monstrous great ships, to their seeming being about 100 in number, lying just west, with both sheets aftward, whereby their course was to run betwixt Orkney and Fair Isle, Shetland lying North and by East of Orkney 21 leagues …

'Lying just west with both sheets aftward' meant sailing westwards with a following wind from the east or northeast.

There is a similar statement in Spanish sources based on the report of Scottish fishermen. It confirms that the Armada passed between Orkney and Shetland. It was estimated that there were 120 ships in the fleet. Apparently the Spanish took all the fishermen's dried fish and paid well for it. They also took some 'shipmasters and pilots', though qualified pilots are unlikely to have been out earning their living fishing. Likely it meant men familiar with local waters around the Northern Isles.

The Southampton crew stopped fishing and, after the Armada had passed, the bark headed south. The only method they had of reporting the news was to deliver it in person. It was important because it confirmed that the Armada was returning to Spain by sailing round Scotland. But the Southampton fishermen were delayed by winds from the south. It took them seven days to reach the Moray Firth, and it was 1 September before their report arrived in London.

The intervening news blackout aroused anxiety in the English fleet. They had tracked the Armada up the east coast, but on 12 August broke off around Tyneside and returned to station off the North Foreland. 'About noon we headed west to recover our coast, the enemy going NW and by N as they did before'. Two pinnaces were sent to follow the Armada, but no news had come back from them as yet.

What was the Armada going to do? Technically it was still a threat. Out of the original complement of 130 vessels it had lost only six great ships and a few pataches had been sent off on communications duties, so there were roughly 120 ships left with the best part of 30,000 men on board. They were a menace and could not be taken lightly. Although all the ships had battle damage, the Armada was capable of being repaired, and could possibly return to the Channel to continue the fight.

The English captains were not slow to speculate and offer their opinions:

The only thing that is to be looked for is that if they should go to the King of Denmark, he is a prince of great shipping and can best supply their wants which now the Duke of Medina Sidonia standeth in need as great anchors, cables, masts, ropes and victuals. What the King of Spain's hot crowns will do in cold countries for mariners and men you can best judge thereof.

(FRANCIS DRAKE in the *Revenge*)

… they have no place to go withal but for the Scaw in Denmark … I verily believe they will pass about Scotland and Ireland to draw themselves home.

(THOMAS FENNER in the *Nonpareil*)

… in my conscience, I speak it to your Honour, I think the Duke would give his dukedom to be in Spain again.

(WILLIAM WYNTER in the *Vanguard*)

There was some alarm on 26 August when Henry Seymour received a report that the Armada was in the Moray Firth. No one seemed to be sure whether the Firth was big enough to hold the ships. But they were just passing through.

The Southampton fishermen established beyond doubt that the Armada was on its way home, but the news had been 14 fractious days in coming. The immediate danger had passed, and there was a practical understanding that the ships should get home safely from there. There was hardly the remotest suspicion that Ireland might become involved.

All the English captains used tremendously vivid language in their letters, not only Howard, Drake and Hawkins, but also Wynter, Seymour, Frobisher, Fenner, Palmer and others. Often they wrote several letters every day. They all exhibit an underlying energy that communicates vitality even over the centuries. They had the same controlled aggression in battle; if not always attacking the enemy, then at least they were threatening them. They were always at them, showing relish for the fight. They had attitude. They were all characters.

Howard, the Lord Admiral, summed up the English spirit when he wrote:

> … notwithstanding that our powder and shot were well near spent we set a brag countenance and gave them chase.

When old seadogs routinely illuminated their letters with such lively imagery it is not surprising that the same generation produced William Shakespeare.

Martin Frobisher, a Yorkshireman, had no time for Drake's antics in taking the *Rosario* at night when the rest were laid to. 'He thinketh to cozen us of our shares of fifteen thousand ducats, but we will have our shares … He hath used certain speeches of me which I will make him eat again or I will make him spend the best blood in his belly'. If their internal rivalries were capable of generating so much heat, the enemy had better look out.

When it came to the serious fighting off Gravelines it was this confidence in their superiority that defeated the Armada. The English naval guns of the time were not capable of sinking large wooden ships. They battered them, destroying masts and rigging, and hitting hulls hard enough to cause leaks. But the English were disappointed with their results: they expected to sink Spanish ships or at least smash them to pieces. In October an English master gunner, William Thomas, wrote a lengthy report to Burghley in which he lamented:

> What can be said but our sins was the cause that so much powder and shot spent, and so long time in fight, and in comparison thereof so little harm?

Although only six great ships were lost, English gunners had done enough to convince the Spanish that they could not win here. Medina Sidonia's letter to King Philip on 21 August seems so abject in the way it accepted defeat:

> This Armada was so completely crippled and scattered that my first duty to your Majesty seemed to save it, even at the risk we are running in

undertaking this voyage, which is so long and in such high latitudes … experience has shown how little we could depend on the ships that remain, the Queen's fleet being so superior to ours in this sort of fighting, in consequence of the strength of their artillery and the fast sailing of their ships.

'Brag countenance' was their secret weapon.

ON BOARD THE SPANISH FLEET

On Friday 12 August at 2 o'clock in the afternoon, the Spanish watched the pursuing English fleet slacken sail and put about. They were at 55°N, just north of Newcastle, but apparently over the Dogger Bank because they were drawing only nine fathoms. The Armada faced a quandary about what to do next, a quandary that exercised the English captains at the same time.

The leading generals and admirals were summoned to a council headed by the Duke of Medina Sidonia on his flagship the *San Martin*. Most senior were Don Alonso de Leyva and Juan Martinez de Recalde, but there were also Miguel de Oquendo, Don Diego Flores de Valdés, Don Francisco de Bobadilla, Martin de Bertondona and, very wisely, several pilots and seamen. Bobadilla had been Medina Sidonia's consultant tactician throughout the voyage. There was some farcical posturing from Oquendo who declared that he was going to return to the battle and 'fight and die like a man'. Diego Flores de Valdés thought that it might be possible to return to Calais. But presumably the sensible advice came from the pilots. It was resolved that the Armada should set its course for Spain even though they were all made aware it would be a laborious journey and would take them round Scotland and Ireland, '750 leagues through stormy seas almost unknown to us'. It seems the Spanish pilots were already prepared to experience navigation difficulties in unfamiliar waters.

Next day, 13 August, it was recorded that Medina Sidonia offered 2,000 ducats to a French pilot if he would guide them to a Spanish port. Later that same day he issued his sailing orders for the voyage ahead. It is almost certain that these were based on advice from this French pilot since, as it had already been acknowledged in the Spanish fleet, these waters were almost unknown to them. No one else would have had the experience to prescribe such detailed directions as to courses and latitudes, certainly not the Duke himself. The orders were copied to every ship in the fleet, and one of these copies was recovered in Ireland in the possession of one of the men taken prisoner, most likely Don Luis de Cordoba. It read:

The course that is first to be held is to the north-northeast, until you be found under 61 degrees and a half; and then to take great heed lest you fall upon the Island of Ireland for fear of the harm that may happen unto you upon that coast. Then parting from those islands and doubling the Cape in 61 degrees and a half you shall run west-southwest until you be found under 58 degrees; and from thence to the southwest to the height of 53 degrees; and then to the south-southwest (sic), making to the Cape Finisterre, and so to procure your entrance into the Groin or to Ferol, or to any other port of the coast of Galicia.

This would have been translated from the Spanish in Ireland (or as they said then 'Englished') and later transcribed by various secretaries. It appears to have been taken in Galway where David Gwyn was acting as an interpreter. Not only was he an unreliable translator, he was also a bombastic showman and was soon in serious trouble when he purveyed scurrilous accusations against Francis Walsyngham. His involvement is a pity, because the published version of this important document in the Irish State Papers contains at least one glaring mistake—the final sailing direction obviously should have been 'south-southeast', not 'south-southwest'. The similarity between 'este' and 'oeste' perhaps makes it understandable, but it should surely have been corrected at an early stage. References to Ireland leave an impression that the French pilot did not really know where Ireland was, or he would not have been warning the ships to 'take great heed' of it when they were at 61° 30′N, bearing in mind that Malin Head, the most northerly point in Ireland, is at 55° 23′N. The advice was clear enough however: Ireland was to be avoided.

On Thursday 18 August when the Armada ships cleared the Scottish mainland they found they had an unusually favourable wind from the northeast. It was therefore a perfectly sensible decision to take advantage of it and make their way through the Fair Isle Channel out into the Atlantic. Fair Isle is at 59° 30′N, well south of the '61 degrees and a half' directed by the sailing instructions issued only five days previously. It was, nevertheless, an important accomplishment to have turned the whole Armada westwards into the Atlantic without mishap.

This took three days, and it was on Sunday 21 August that Medina Sidonia felt relieved enough to write to King Philip and send him what he thought was good news:

We have therefore run through the Norwegian Channel and between the Scottish islands, and I am at present in this place, whence I have set my course for La Coruña so as to make the voyage as short as possible.

He seems to be saying that he consciously disregarded his own orders to go to 61° 30′N in order to take advantage of a favourable wind and in the interests of curtailing the voyage, which was fair enough.

Some of the men, however, thought they had indeed been as far north as 61° 30'N, and gave estimates of their later positions that were wildly inaccurate. Others cannot have failed to notice that the sailing orders were first breached by the Duke himself.

These sailing instructions have acquired a disproportionate importance in some Armada histories. For most of the twentieth century it was axiomatic that the Armada followed the course laid down for it, even to the extent in many cases of showing it going round the north of Shetland. Virtually every historian accepted and used the map of the course drawn by W. Spotswood Green in 1906, and presumed it to be correct. It seemed they could not contemplate anything other than that Medina Sidonia's directions would be obeyed to the letter. Unfortunately the map makes a bad start by getting the first part of the course wrong, and then goes on to a position in the Atlantic that fails to explain why so many Armada ships came in contact with Ireland. It will become apparent that these sailing instructions were less sacrosanct to the Spanish captains, who were aware that they were only the recommendations of a Frenchman.

The truth is that, other than for a few miles in the North Sea, the Armada *never* followed the course in the sailing instructions— neither the main fleet nor those ships that were separated from it. The instructions are interesting, especially as they emphasize the order to avoid Ireland, but they have proved to be a prodigious red herring for Armada historians. How tempting to find the actual route of the Armada! What a gift! Unfortunately it just did not happen that way. But there are some clues to the actual course followed and, if assembled systematically, they can lead to a more realistic interpretation of the Armada voyage. These clues are examined in detail in the next chapter.

THE SPANISH LEADERSHIP

There have been some eccentric choices for military command throughout the course of history, but the appointment of the Duke of Medina Sidonia to lead the Spanish Armada must stand out as one of the strangest.

Don Alonso Perez de Guzman El Bueno was the 7th Duke of Medina Sidonia. The family estates were (and still are) at Sanlúcar de Barrameda in Andalusía on the south bank of the Guadalquivir where it widens into a sea estuary. In January and February 1588 the Duke had been involved in helping Armada ships to fit out with men, munitions and victuals, while they were sheltering in the Guadalquivir prior to moving round to their eventual rendezvous at Lisbon. He was a conscientious administrator and carried out his responsibilities well.

The designated leader of the Armada was the Marquis of Santa Cruz, an admiral experienced in seafaring and in fighting Drake. The King's decision to put him in charge was belated enough, and not finally confirmed until 4 September 1587 when Santa Cruz was returning from a voyage to the Indies. In January 1588 he became ill, and it was apparent that he was not going to recover. Even before Santa Cruz died King Philip had decided to put Medina Sidonia in his place. The King's Secretary, Idiaquez, wrote on 11 February to advise the Duke that 'His Majesty had fixed his eyes on him to take charge of the expedition'.

Medina Sidonia was panic stricken. On 16 February he replied to Idiaquez pointing out reasons why he was unsuitable for the task. It was a formidable list:

- I have no experience of seafaring or of war
- I have not the health for the sea. I become seasick
- I possess neither the talents nor the strength necessary
- I have no knowledge of the Armada or the persons taking part in it
- I have no intelligence of England or acquaintance with the ports there
- I would have to be guided by the opinions of others of whose qualities I know nothing.

He begged that the King would 'not entrust to him a task of which he would certainly not give a good account'. He kindly suggested that the 'Adelantado' had much better qualifications for the job. Once before he had managed to escape military service. In 1581 he had been made captain-general of Lombardy, but he had pleaded poverty and ill health and was exempted.

His objections were all true, and if the King had had any sense he would have accepted them. The only conceivable reason for Medina Sidonia's appointment could be one of nobility of rank. If someone says that he does not want the job and could not do it anyway, it is the height of folly to insist on going ahead with the appointment. But King Philip had only a tenuous connection to the real world. He buried himself in his chambers in the Escorial, controlled an empire by voluminous correspondence, and believed that his devotion to God would vindicate all his desires.

His plan of campaign for the Armada was worked out, and was communicated to his officers in the smallest detail. It was completely impractical and impossible to carry out. It involved the Armada positioning off 'Cape Margate' (North Foreland). From there it was to protect the barges of the Duke of Parma as they crossed the Channel from Dunkirk with an army on board. Neither the weather nor the English fleet were ever going to allow that to happen. But the plan was capable of being adapted; 30,000 men arriving in Kent might have had a chance. A culture of obedience, however, stifled that kind of initiative.

The King brushed aside Medina Sidonia's application *not* to be appointed, and replied to him: '… in a case so entirely devoted to God … there is no reason for you to trouble about anything but the preparation of the expedition and I am quite sure you will be diligent in this respect'. Is he really saying that all Medina Sidonia had to do was see to the preparations for the voyage and God would provide the leadership during it?

What else could the poor man do but acquiesce and try to do his best? And to be fair to him, he was always a diligent and conscientious administrator. But what a contrast there appears between those animated English captains and this quiet, dutiful, decent man, without a trace of aggression, charisma or leadership in him.

The Armada, staffed by many experienced admirals and generals, by some quirk of Spanish tradition was commanded by a man, at that time only 37 years old, who by his own admission had no knowledge of the sea or of warfare. Maybe the King wanted a leader who would unquestioningly carry out his neurotically meticulous designs. A previously successful commander in battle, either at sea or on land, might have been tempted to improvise. He had to have a plan, but he would be ready to react to changing circumstances. In fact he should expect changing circumstances and have alternative plans in mind. This situation actually did arise on two occasions during the voyage up the Channel. On Sunday 31 July Juan Martinez de Recalde, vice-admiral of the fleet, wanted to attack Plymouth. Then on 4 August he advised taking the Isle of Wight to provide a secure anchorage for the Armada at Spithead while awaiting news from the Duke of Parma. Both suggestions were ignored by Medina Sidonia as he stuck rigidly to King Philip's plan. Recalde took umbrage at the way his advice was dismissed and later refused to attend council meetings because 'his opinions counted for nothing'.

King Philip had designated Diego Flores de Valdés as Medina Sidonia's adviser. Diego Flores de Valdés was well qualified for the task with long experience of command at sea, most recently with the elite Indian Guard escorting Atlantic treasure fleets. However, he was hindered by an irascible temperament and was not reconciled to what he regarded as babysitting an inexperienced commander-in-chief. His appointment was not a success. Far from supporting Medina Sidonia, he actually undermined him. To be treated with disdain by one of his closest advisers cannot have helped the Duke's already fragile self-esteem.

This deficiency was to be compensated for by one of the professional soldiers. During the course of the voyage Don Francisco de Bobadilla gradually assumed the position of a kind of Chief Executive Officer to the Duke. He was Colonel-in-chief of the regiments of soldiers and had many years experience. Bobadilla had been on the *San Marcos*, but at La Coruña he was ordered to come on board the flagship *San Martin*, and from that time onwards he shadowed Medina Sidonia closely, not only in council, but also in the day-to-day running of affairs. He was able to supply qualities that the Duke himself lacked, particularly the capacity to command. According to one officer, Bobadilla was 'the man who gave orders in the Armada and everything was managed by him'. In some ways this was a strange appointment. The senior officers had obviously become aware of the Duke's imperfections as a leader and of Diego Flores de Valdés's unsuitability as an adviser. It seems that this was their way of sidelining them both to ensure that the business of command could continue efficiently. Correspondence emanated from the council over the Duke's signature, but it is doubtful if he was responsible for all of it.

All was not well in the Spanish high command.

After the fight in the Channel and the obvious failure of the expedition, the Duke, unable to carry the stress any longer, gave way to depression and withdrew to the seclusion of his cabin. When they arrived back in Santander, the Duke left to Bobadilla the unenviable task of reporting to King Philip. He languished in his bed, 'unable to attend to anything, truly at my last gasp', and begged for permission to go home. There is no doubt that by this time the Duke was showing indications of acute depressive illness, not uncommonly experienced by a person overwhelmed by a difficult situation. It is clear that he had been reduced to a state of inertia. He appeared after they had been in port for six days, but only when he and his entourage had dressed in black, a typically obsessive reaction by someone in the depths of a breakdown. Perhaps on Bobadilla's advice, Medina Sidonia was granted licence by the King to leave the fleet and return home. Would it be too much to hope that the King was man enough to acknowledge that the mistake was his?

The Duke's heart was among the vineyards, olive groves, Stone Pine woodlands, Cork Oaks and orange trees that dress the landscape in his beloved, sunny Andalucía. Will Wynter was right: he would have given his dukedom, and much more, to be home again. Once there his cure could begin.

He eventually did recover well enough to enjoy twenty-seven more years of quiet life at the family estate in Sanlúcar de Barrameda—an innocent victim of King Philip II's irrational disregard for the realities of naval warfare.

SOURCES

The great majority of the references in this chapter are from original sources, and the intention is that they will be used whenever possible. Quotations from other writers will be kept to a minimum in order to try to present a fresh analysis of the History of the Armada in Ireland.

We are fortunate that so many original sources have been transcribed and collected by nineteenth-century historians. The English letters were collected and edited by J.K. Laughton and published by the Navy Records Society in 1894 in two volumes under the title 'State Papers Relating to the Defeat of the Spanish Armada'. References are noted as 'Laughton' together with the volume and page number.

Spanish sources originated in the Spanish Archives of Simancas, some of which are now preserved in the Archives Nationales in Paris. They were transcribed and edited by Martin Hume and published by the Public Record Office in 1899 under the title 'Calendar of Letters and State Papers Relating to English Affairs Preserved in or Originally Belonging to the Archives of Simancas Volume IV Elizabeth 1587–1603'. Although entitled a calendar, most of the letters are transcribed in full. References are noted as 'Hume' and the page number.

Most references from Irish sources are from the 'Calendar of State Papers Ireland—Elizabeth Volume 137'. Irish State Papers are more often summarized in the calendar, but full texts of the original documents are available on microfilm in the Public Record Office in Belfast. References are noted as 'CSPI' together with the page number. When full texts are used they are noted as the relative microfilm number and document number.

NOTES AND REFERENCES

The quote from Seymour, Wynter and Palmer is in Laughton VOL. II p. 95.

The sighting of the Armada in the Fair Isle Channel is in Laughton VOL. II p. 137 and Hume p. 434.

Drake's comments are in Laughton VOL. II p. 98, Fenner's on p. 40 and Wynter's on p. 13. Howard's 'brag countenance' comment is in Laughton VOL. II p. 54 and Frobisher's outburst is on pp 102–103.

The Spanish report of the turning back of the English fleet is in Hume p. 447, and the decisive council meeting is on p. 393.

William Thomas's report to Burghley on the effectiveness of English gunnery is in Laughton VOL. II pp 258–260.

Medina Sidonia's deal with the French pilot and the subsequent publication of 'orders for the future voyage of the Armada' are part of Calderon's account in Hume p. 447.

The sailing directions are in CSPI OCT 1 (10) 1588 pp 49–50. The map was first published by W. Spotswood Green in the *Geographical Journal*, May 1906, VOL. XXVII p. 431. He labelled the map correctly as the 'Course in the sailing orders given by the Duke of Medina Sidonia'. He did not point out that right from the start it was not the course followed by the Armada; later historians were guilty of *presuming* that it was. He picked up Aramburu's *San Juan Bautista* on 25 August far to the west of Rockall, which was not correct. Medina Sidonia's letter to the King is in Hume p. 393. Some of the basic details of his biography are from the Internet.

The appointment of Santa Cruz is in Hume p. 136. Santa Cruz's death and Medina Sidonia's appointment are in Hume pp 207–209. A brief summary of King Philip's battle plan is in Hume p. 187.

Recalde's suggested variations to the plan are in the 'Diary of a Soldier …' reproduced by Geoffrey Parker in *The Mariner's Mirror*, August 2004, pp 328 and 330.

The emergence of Bobadilla as the Duke's Executive Officer is in Hume pp 321, 348, 350, 403 and 433. And Diego Flores de Valdés's failure as an adviser is in Martin and Parker, *The Spanish Armada*, 1988, p. 24.

Chapter 2 ❧

21 AUGUST TO
10 SEPTEMBER
WHERE WERE THEY?

We sailed without knowing whither

(CALDERON)

Marcos de Aramburu was Inspector General and Paymaster of the squadron of Castile. He sailed aboard the galleon *San Juan Bautista*, vice-flagship of the squadron. From 24 August he assumed responsibility for the command of the ship, presumably because the principal seamen on board were either dead or seriously ill. He was a soldier, not a navigator, but he had pretensions to nobility and that may have been enough to qualify him for command. He carefully compiled a diary of each day's events, which was so detailed that it could only have been selected from the ship's log. Perhaps he was preparing for the time when he might have to justify his stewardship.

His entire diary is fascinating, but there are a few entries that provide vital information from which it is possible to make deductions about the course the Armada was following:

On 28 (August) … we took soundings and found ourselves in 120 brazas (108 fathoms) with a gravel bottom
On 30 (August) we took a reading of the sun in latitude 58°N, 95 leagues from the coast of Ireland in 125 brazas (113 fathoms), a rocky bottom without sand or gravel
On 9 September we took the latitude in 54°N 100 leagues from the land of Ireland, running with a moderate southwest wind easing gradually; the course was SE¼S
On 10 September we held the same course with a light wind and did not take a latitude reading
On 11 September we sighted land two hours before dawn. We were on a fresh southwest wind steering southeast, the weather was misty and we did

not see it until we were only one league from it ... We turned out to sea with a southwest wind and headed west.

The soundings taken on 28 and 30 August tell us a lot. First of all the fact that Aramburu was able to find bottom at around 100 fathoms confirms beyond doubt that the *San Juan Bautista* was still over the Continental Shelf, which drops away steeply to over 1,000 fathoms around 30 miles west of St Kilda. His estimate of '95 leagues from the coast of Ireland' while at 58°N makes no sense and emphasizes how shaky the Spanish were on the geography of Ireland. Secondly, since no further soundings are mentioned in the diary, we can presume that by 31 August or 1 September they were finding no bottom, and therefore that was when they had crossed the edge of the Continental Shelf. Soundings were sometimes taken as a matter of safety and, although they were by that time on the open ocean, they may have been within sight of some of the Scottish offshore islands, perhaps the Flannen Islands or even Sulisker and Rona. They were probably just north of the St Kilda group.

On 27 August they had been within sight of the rest of the Armada, although they were delayed by a damaged foresail and lost position from then onwards. The main fleet, however, could not have been all that far away to the west. This enables us to estimate the Armada's position on 31 August to within 50 miles or so of 58½°N and 8°W.

Aramburu's diary entries for 9, 10 and 11 September are even more revealing. On 9 September at latitude 54°N the pilot's calculated position was '100 leagues from the land of Ireland'. The Spanish league was equivalent to 3.68 miles, so he was saying 368 miles west of County Mayo. On 10 September they were 'on the same course with a light wind' and would have made only modest progress. Then on the morning of 11 September, two hours before dawn, they sighted land. The pilot thought it was the islands Bull and Cow; other suggestions were the Isles of Quelmes (the Skelligs) and Dursey Island.

These islands are off County Kerry and County Cork at around 51½°N, which was too far south considering that only 36 hours earlier they had been at 54°N. The Armada ships seemed to average about 60–65 miles a day, and so, given that on 10 September there were only light winds, a better estimate of their position on the morning of 11 might be somewhere off the entrance to Galway Bay, perhaps near the Aran Islands.

They were, nevertheless, in no doubt that the land was Ireland.

It is astonishing that Aramburu allowed to pass without comment the fact that they were some 368 miles east of their calculated position on 9 September. It was of massive significance in relation to the record of navigation in the first part of his diary. All his previous estimates of distance from Ireland were obviously wrong. Why could he not say so?

And it is of cosmic importance for Armada history, because it provides the key to understanding why so many Armada ships came in contact with Ireland.

For the *San Juan Bautista* there are two locations that can be accepted as reasonably accurate. One is the sighting of islands on the Irish coast on the morning of 11 September at around 53°N. The other, on 31 August, is the sea area at about 58½°N 8°w when the Armada crossed the Continental Shelf. In between we have an almost complete record of the courses that were steered each day. Working backwards from Galway Bay on 11 September and plotting in reverse the courses set and the relative latitude readings for the previous 12 days, it is possible to construct a tentative estimate of the track of the *San Juan Bautista* from its position on 31 August. The pilot's estimates of distances from Ireland have to be ignored. Other factors also need to be taken into account. For example it is apparent that for several reasons the ship often failed to make good the courses set, and between 3 and 11 September the ocean current would have caused a slight drift to the east.

This map has been drawn and, although the daily courses are estimated, the positions on 31 August and 11 September are quite conclusive. It gives a general view of the track of the *San Juan Bautista*. And, because the main fleet was never very far away to the west, it shows roughly where the rest of the Armada was too.

A letter from Medina Sidonia to the King on 23 September after arriving in Spain establishes his position:

> I continued on my course to Cape Finisterre with a westerly wind. We ran down to 43½°, and on 21 at two o'clock we sighted land, which was said to be the island of Cizarga seven leagues from La Coruña. The wind then fell calm, and one of the little caravels belonging to the Armada came to us from towards the land and cried out that we were lost as we were off Santander.

He was east of Cape Finisterre by 350 miles and east of Cizarga, his calculated position, by 275 miles. The main body of the Armada missed Ireland, but came too close for comfort.

The explanation for misjudgment on such a scale by all the Armada pilots hinges on a combination of three principal elements—the weather, the limitations of sixteenth-century navigation and the fact that ocean currents could not be determined at that time.

'CONSTANT STORMS, FOGS AND SQUALLS'

Thanks to the Climatic Research Unit at the University of East Anglia in Norwich we have a fairly coherent account of the weather during the whole of the Armada summer of 1588. This is based partly on weather observations extracted from letters and reports relating to the Armada in both Spanish and English sources. The Danish astronomer Tycho Brahe also kept weather records at his observatory on the island of Hven in Copenhagen Sound, and they were added by the staff at the Unit. These observations were of interest to Professor Hubert Lamb, director of the Climatic Research Unit, because they were the longest continuous record of weather during the onset of the Little Ice Age. He developed the research for publication and it was printed as Climatic Research Paper no.6.

The period from 21 August to 3 September was of crucial importance for the Armada, when it was heading out into the Atlantic and trying to turn towards the southwest. The Armada ships had had a favourable northeast wind in the Fair Isle Channel, and Medina Sidonia's letter of 21 August was optimistic that they would soon be home. It did not continue, however.

Almost at once the wind swung round to the south and for the next 13 days remained unrelenting at points between southeast and southwest. What happened was that an anticyclone developed over Scandinavia as it often does at that time of year. It was large enough in extent to cover the northwestern approaches of the British Isles for the next five days. It was also strong enough to obstruct the normal southwest to northeast movement of Atlantic depressions, which were consequently deflected northwards. The depressions carried frontal systems over the western edge of the anticyclone. So not only was there a constant push of wind from the south, it was frequently accompanied by gales, rain and fog. One of the Spanish correspondents, Pedro Coco Calderon, wrote:

> From 24 (August) to 4 September we sailed without knowing whither, through constant storms, fogs and squalls. As this hulk could not beat to windward it was necessary to keep out to sea, and we were unable to discover the main body of the Armada until 4 September, when we joined it.

The fronts produced no change of wind direction, but the strength of the southerly airstream varied. Just as the speed of a convoy is only as fast as the slowest ship, its track is only as straight as the most cumbersome. There were several Baltic hulks and other cargo vessels in the Armada, and if Medina Sidonia wanted to hold them all together the galleons would have had to 'keep out to sea' with the hulks. In other words they would all drift northwards when the wind was strong from the south but come back closer to the wind when it was light—a zigzag course.

On 27 August the wind changed briefly north-northeast, indicating that wave depressions were beginning to break away to the east, as the Scandinavian anticyclone slipped south and west to cover southern England. This was of no assistance to the Armada, because wave depressions soon move away and the main low pressure centres stayed firmly to the west.

By 1 September the anticyclone was beginning to decline and, over the following two days, it moved firstly to the north and then to the east, eventually allowing one of the main low pressure centres to travel northeastwards. On its western side the winds at last came around to west and then to northwest. So on the night of 2 September all the ships were able to sail south for the first time. Aramburu recorded that on 3 and 4 September he sailed courses between southeast and south-southwest. Medina Sidonia wrote to the king on 3 September:

We have had, on four separate nights, heavy gales with strong head winds, thick fogs and rain. This has caused 17 vessels to separate from the Armada. By God's mercy, yesterday at noon, the wind shifted to the west, somewhat more in our favour. We were therefore able to sail in a southerly direction, and are now in 58 degrees north latitude, having counted 95 sail during the day. The wind has now veered to the west-northwest with a more favourable appearance.

If it took most of a day's sailing to get them to 58°N, the Armada ships must have been at about 59°N on 2 September. During nearly two weeks they had made no progress southwards; all they were able to do was to keep working their way west, which should at least have given them adequate clearance to avoid Ireland. Everything depended on the accuracy of the calculation of the distances they had travelled. This was one of the pivotal points in deciding the fate of the Armada. The pilots thought they had sailed far enough to the west to begin to steer courses east of south. It would transpire that they had not.

They deserve credit for one achievement: it was a remarkable performance to have kept 95 vessels together after 13 days of appalling conditions.

Southwards at last

From 3 to 6 September the depression moved away northeast and filled, maintaining a west or northwesterly airflow over the Armada. It was close enough to the low pressure to be typically unstable and gave rise to showers and periods of strong winds. Aramburu sailed wsw¼w for a short time on the 5th but the presumption was that he had sufficient sea room to steer generally east of south, which is what he did.

On 7 September a light southwest wind and a gentle sea heralded four days of fine weather. An anticyclone to the east was extending ridges of high pressure over the ships. Aramburu steered SE¼s on 8 and 9, and was still heading southeast in misty conditions on the morning of 11 September when he encountered the islands on the Irish coast and turned out to sea.

The weather was one of the instruments of disaster for the Armada crews. For 13 days, from 21 August to 3 September, they had been imprisoned above 58°N by southerly winds. By the time they were able to turn south they did not know where they were.

THE ART OF NAVIGATION

The Spanish pilots were good. They were formally trained at the Casa de Contratacion in Seville, and they had a textbook, *Arte de Navegar* by Martin Cortes published in 1551. Navigation was a highly cultivated art in the sixteenth century and, for all normal circumstances, the Spanish pilots had mastered it. The difficulty for the Armada was that, in its voyage round the north of Scotland and into the Atlantic Ocean, the circumstances were not normal. The art of navigation in the sixteenth century had its limitations, and the proposed Armada voyage was exposed to them.

Experience

One of the most important tools of the navigator was experience of the journey they were undertaking. The focus of Spanish pilots was on the regular trading voyages their flotas made to the Americas. These followed a pattern that used the trade winds. To go westwards they first sailed south to about 15°N. Then, with the northeast trade wind to help them, they crossed the Atlantic staying strictly on the same latitude until they sighted land in the Caribbean. The voyage back to Spain used the soutwest trade wind in the same way at about 35°N. The pilots were also familiar with the trading ports of northwest Europe and the Mediterranean. The Atlantic Ocean off north and west Scotland was unknown to them, as they predicted while they were still in the North Sea.

Knowledge of Ireland was a real problem. Only Recalde had genuine experience, from taking part in the Smerwick escapade in 1580. He made use of this in 1588. Some Spanish records exhibit depressing ignorance of Ireland. For example Aramburu's pilot twice recorded his position as 'leagues from Ireland' when he was at 58°N! But then he showed surprising familiarity with the names of Kerry and Cork offshore islands. For the most part the only place on the Irish coast many of them seemed to know about was Cape Clear, and they freely referred to nearly every headland either as Cape Clear or as an estimated distance from it. For practical purposes it is safe to assume that the Spanish on the Armada had no experience of Ireland whatever. Any knowledge they had seemed to be confined to names on maps and charts, and at that time even English maps of the west coast of Ireland were quite useless as an aid to mariners.

Latitude

Astrolabe rings were recovered from some of the Armada wreck sites in Ireland. The sea-astrolabe was used for taking the altitude of the sun at midday, and the angle measured gave the latitude. It was reasonably accurate and most of the latitude readings recorded in surviving documents can be taken as reliable. Caution is needed, however, as the astrolabe was not easy to use on a moving deck. Pilots preferred to go ashore to take the latitude, but naturally that was not possible on the Armada.

Some latitudes quoted in Armada histories are unfortunately wrong. They invariably come from reports originating with ordinary seamen or soldiers rather than navigators. One appears in a transcript of interviews with men from the galleass *Zuñiga* in which they claim to have been as far north as 63½°N on 8 September. This is clearly wrong. The *Zuñiga* was in company with the flagship on 2 September at 58°N, after which they were steering southerly courses. Another quote from a prisoner captured at Dingle from Recalde's ship, *San Juan of Portugal*, claimed that the whole fleet went as far north as 62°. This looks like a case of believing that the sailing instructions had been followed and that the Armada had been at 61½°N before turning west.

It can be taken as certain that neither the Armada as a fleet nor any of the ships separated from it were ever further north than 60°.

Longitude

In the sixteenth century longitude could not be found at sea. The English navigator William Bourne wrote:

> I would not any seaman should be of the opinion that they might get any longitude with instruments—but let them keep a dead reckoning.

Longitude was not, therefore, a factor in the navigation of the Armada, apart from the reality that pilots could not fix their position when out of sight of land. They had to use other methods of navigating.

Dead reckoning and the problem of distance run

'Let them keep a dead reckoning' meant that they had to calculate (or guess) the distance travelled each day, and record it on a chart. Dead reckoning was far from being sloppy guesswork. The ingenuity that went into it and the skill applied to allowing for known variables made it into a genuine art, one that is in danger of being lost to 'progress' in the form of satellite navigation.

Every half-hour the pilot estimated the way the ship had gone, taking account of her average speed, the compass course steered, the effect of the wind and the leeway characteristics of the ship. This was recorded on a Traverse Board by inserting pegs into holes aligned with the compass course. 'They keepe an account how many glasses (half-hours) they steer on every point'. After every watch the direction and distance run were transferred to a chart, and the Traverse Board was cleared for use by the next watch. English pilots used log and line to estimate speed; the Spanish pilots did not.

The technique of 'latitude sailing' evolved as an attempt to compensate for lack of longitude calculations. The pilots found the known latitude of their destination and then sailed towards it along that latitude as accurately as possible. They took soundings when they were within soundings and kept a careful watch. It became the practice to overestimate slightly the distance run—'to keep their reckoning before their ship and so to sight land after they sought it'.

From 21 August to 3 September the Armada fleet was effectively latitude sailing, making as much headway westwards as it could. A tendency to overestimate distance run would work against it in this case.

Yet the carefully calculated records of distance run turned out to be wrong by a huge amount—almost half. Something was interfering with the progress of the ships, something they did not know about—ocean currents, the North Atlantic Drift, the Gulf Stream.

THE POWER OF OCEAN CURRENTS

Mariners were conscious of coastal currents and tidal streams close to shore. They kept notebooks of all the information they gathered about the various hazards to be expected in the ports they used.

The existence of an east-flowing Atlantic current had been suspected by Spanish navigators as early as 1512, but all they knew about it was that west to east crossings at around 35°N could be unpredictable. Without the ability to calculate the longitude at sea it would remain impossible to measure ocean currents for another 200 years. In 1588 nobody appreciated that there was a relatively powerful current in the northeast Atlantic.

By the time the waters of the Gulf Stream reach the northeast Atlantic they comprise several complex elements. The contours of the sea floor play an important part in influencing their speed and direction. West of the edge of the Continental Shelf the North Atlantic Drift is moderately strong. It becomes the Continental Slope Current at the edge of the shelf where it is at its strongest, and then weakens as it becomes the Continental Shelf Current closer to land. At its strongest it is about 0.5 knots.

An additional factor is the Surface Layer Current, which is the result of friction caused by the wind. This is reckoned to be 2 per cent of wind speed and can at times amount to very little. For the critical period between 21 August and 3 September, however, the wind experienced by the Armada was constantly strong and always from the south. If the average wind speed was approximately 20 knots the value of the Surface Layer Current could have been as much as 0.4 knots.

Taking both currents into account the Armada was losing almost a knot, which was the equivalent of 20 to 25 miles, a day. The cumulative effect over these 13 days would therefore be around 250 to 300 miles, which corresponds very closely to the discrepancy in the calculations of both Aramburu's pilot and the pilot on the *San Martin*.

Understanding the predicament of the Armada when it was out of sight of land is therefore a complex puzzle, in which all the factors played a part. The weather held them north of 58° for 13 days, during which time they could only fetch as far as possible to the west. The limitations of sixteenth-century navigation meant that they were unable to check their positions and so mistakes went undetected. And, unknown to them, they were pushing against a strong ocean current, which nullified part of their apparent progress, again without the opportunity to discover that something was going wrong. What has presented difficulty for historians is the fact that mistakes never seem to be acknowledged in official documents. Surely Aramburu and Medina Sidonia owed their colleagues at least some kind of explanation for the fact that they were 300 miles out of position.

The story is not yet complete, however. Although they did not miss Ireland by much, the main body of the Armada that stayed with Medina Sidonia did get back to Spain. Thirty-eight ships made contact with Ireland, and they can be accounted for only by the fact that they were not with the main fleet. They were stragglers.

THE STRAGGLERS

As the Armada passed through the Fair Isle Channel it numbered approximately 120 vessels. All the ships were well together. During the flight up the North Sea, the Duke had taken special care to put the galleons in the rearguard to protect the weaker ships from the English fleet, and this had the added effect of making sure that none of them dropped out of formation.

Out in the Atlantic, however, the stress of heavy weather soon began to take its toll. Some ships had been so badly damaged in the battles in the

English Channel that they could not keep pace with the rest. On the first day of fighting Recalde's *San Juan of Portugal* had taken two shots through the foremast. It did not fall but it was unable to carry sails. The strong southerly winds were too much for it, and it dropped away to the northeast. Other battle-damaged ships included *La Rata Encoronada* of Don Alonso de Leyva, the *San Marcos*, the *Santiago* and *La Trinidad Valencera*. At Gravelines the *Duquesa Santa Ana* became isolated and was attacked, and the *San Juan de Sicilia* was 'so much damaged as to be almost unable to offer further resistance'.

The hulks and Levanters were especially vulnerable. The hulks were high-sided Baltic cargo vessels and were prone to lose position because of leeway. Calderon wrote that his *San Salvador* 'cannot sail to windward'. The Levant squadron were built for the Mediterranean trade, not for the seas of the North Atlantic. Their seams split; they took on water and became progressively slower. Battle damage affected them more severely than the galleons.

On 26 August the *San Juan Bautista*, under the command of Aramburu, had a damaged foresail. The repair delayed them for about six hours during which time the main body of the Armada passed onwards. The ships were still in sight well to windward as darkness fell, but on the next morning they had disappeared. Aramburu never saw the fleet again. But he did fall in with other stragglers, Recalde's *San Juan of Portugal* and the ship *Trinidad*.

The galleasses *Girona* and *Zuñiga* had badly designed sterns. Their rudders were exposed and overstressed. In rough weather they constantly broke the rudder thole pin; it could be repaired but it took time and they lost position as a result.

From 21 August a situation gradually emerged in which the main body of the Armada steadily diminished and a string of stragglers fell away for 50 miles or more to the east. Mostly they were in small groups, because if they had company they tried to stay together, but some were alone.

On top of the 300 miles they were already out of position this left the stragglers poised to descend on Ireland. None of them took a conscious decision to head for Ireland; they simply encountered it over a period of four or five days at widely scattered locations.

It is worth reflecting that by 10 September the Armada had lost no ships since the Battle of Gravelines on 8 August. The voyage round Scotland and out into the Atlantic had been a hectic experience. Heavy weather had battered them and frustrated attempts to make good southerly courses, but it had not sunk any ships. Despite the dispirited tone in most of the Spanish correspondence, they should still have been able to return safely to Spain. The disasters that befell the Armada all occurred in Ireland. Four times the number of ships and men were lost in Ireland than in the fighting in the

Channel. Even in Ireland ships were destroyed by the weather on only one day, 21 September. Others may have perished because of leaks and accidents, but the effect of bad weather has tended to be exaggerated.

Where were they? The answer is that they did not know where they were, and until recently historians did not know either.

ADDITIONAL SOURCE

Marcos de Aramburu's diary is printed in Spanish in C.F. Duro, *La Armada Invencible*, 2 volumes, Madrid 1884–1885. An English translation is given in Appendix 3.

NOTES AND REFERENCES

The quotation from Calderon in the chapter heading is in Hume p. 448.

Medina Sidonia's account of his arrival in Spain is in Hume p. 432. On page 433 he tells how he has withdrawn to his bed and is unable to do anything. He begs the King to grant him license to return home, and is apparently at death's door. Although he has continually pleaded ill health, he appears to have been one of those creaking gates that somehow survive. He returned to his estate in Sanlúcar de Barremeda and lived until 1615, when he died aged 65—a man who genuinely desired obscurity but had fame thrust upon him.

All the weather details are published in K.S. Douglas, H.H. Lamb and C. Loader, 'A Meteorological Study of July to October 1588: The Spanish Armada Storms' (University of East Anglia, Climatic Research Unit, Paper NO. 6: Norwich 1978).

Pedro Coco Calderon's long exposition is in Hume pp 439–450.

Medina Sidonia's letter to the King dated 3 September is in Hume p. 411. It gives an account of the weather experienced by the Armada between 21 August and 3 September.

All the information about sixteenth-century navigation is from D.W. Waters, *The Art of Navigation in England in Elizabethan and Early Stuart Times* (London 1958). This book is an art treasure in itself. It is, unfortunately, now long out of print, but it would surely be worth reprinting.

Information about the ocean currents was compiled from *The Climatological and Oceanographic Atlas for Mariners*, US Dept of Commerce and US Dept of the Navy. And also from B. Hansen and S. Østerhus, *Progress in Oceanography*, 1959.

There are many references in Hume to the damage sustained by the ships that became stragglers—pp 351, 373, 394, 397, 398, 401, 411, 448.

The calculation of the course followed by the Armada is in K.S. Douglas, 'Navigation: the Key to the Armada Disaster', published in the *Journal for Maritime Research* by the National Maritime Museum, Greenwich, 2003.

PART II

September to November 1588
The Spanish Armada on the Coast of Ireland

Chapter 3 ༷

11 TO 20 SEPTEMBER ARMADA SHIPS ARRIVE IN IRELAND

... they fell with the coast of Ireland, not knowing where they were, but resolved to return for Spain ...
(THE CREW OF THE SHIP AT TRALEE)

... the galleass wherein this bearer was, what for want of meat and water, and partly through error for lack of pilots, did come to such perilous place ...
(PETRUS BAPTISTA ON THE GALLEASS ZUÑIGA AT LISCANNOR,
COUNTY CLARE)

DESCENDING ON THE IRISH COAST

Thirty-eight Armada ships were in contact with Ireland or were just off shore. None of them arrived before 11 September and there were no new arrivals after 16 September. The locations were widely dispersed, from out at sea off the north coast of County Donegal to Dingle Bay in County Kerry—a spread of about 300 miles. In terms of sixteenth-century transportation they arrived virtually simultaneously. Despite frequent references to Cape Clear in Spanish accounts, none of the ships coming from the northwest would have been able to see the island as it is tucked in behind Mizen Head.

The sailing orders issued by the Duke of Medina Sidonia were revealed during the examination of Don Luis de Cordoba in Galway City, probably under the supervision of Sir Richard Bingham, about the end of September. They are enclosed by the Lord Deputy in his letter to Lord Burghley of 10 October, along with a report from Bingham and a copy of de Cordoba's examination, in which he actually refers to them. We have already seen that the navigation directions never even came close to being fulfilled; now the order to 'take great heed of the island of Ireland' was apparently being flouted with equal abandon.

Two of the men on the Irish coast were Don Alonso de Leyva, second in command of the whole expedition, and Juan Martinez de Recalde, senior admiral of the fleet. It is clear, therefore, that this was not widespread mutiny. History has attached too much importance to these sailing instructions. A commonsense explanation has to be that they were simply overtaken by events and the pressure of immediate necessity. When the pilots thought they were 350 to 400 miles out in the Atlantic, they did not 'decide' to head for Ireland. That journey would have taken the better part of a week.

The *San Salvador* and Aramburu's *San Juan Bautista* were the only ships to turn out to sea as soon as they realized they were on the Irish coast, and the *Bautista* came in towards the coast again four days later. All the others spontaneously tried to find shelter and relief supplies, and no one seemed to be concerned that the Duke's orders were not being obeyed. It seemed to be common knowledge throughout the fleet that the sailing directions were the work of the French pilot and did not therefore carry the same authority as they would have done if they had been conceived by the Duke himself.

The quantity and quality of evidence describing the arrival of the Spanish is very variable, but we have to be grateful that so much information has survived and is in many cases surprisingly detailed. Sometimes just an isolated fact is enough to enable a logical interpretation to be made. It is possible to identify 14 different locations where the ships were, and they can be brought into focus to be examined at some length.

CALM DAYS, WINDY DAYS

The weather during these 10 days has to be judged to be good by the normal standard of mid-September on the west coast of Ireland. The previous week had been settled under the influence of an anticyclone, and on Saturday 10 September some of the ships had almost calm conditions. This situation broke down only slowly with a freshening wind from the southwest on the afternoon of 11 September, and it was late on the afternoon of 12 September before a southerly wind blew up into a storm with rough seas, rain and mist. This lasted only until dawn of the next day when the wind veered to northwest and moderated, a normal enough Atlantic depression. There followed two more days of good sailing weather with a moderate northwest wind. On 15 September the wind backed westerly around dawn, and the ships were able to steer south for a time. It continued to back during the day, and by evening it was blowing hard from the south. This was another Atlantic depression, which passed through on the night of 15 September, but again it was clear by the following morning. A ridge of high pressure then settled the weather over the next four days until 20 September, when an easterly breeze sprang up.

There was nothing in the weather at this stage to suggest that the Armada ships were being 'driven' onto the Irish coast. Those that were seaworthy were able to make a successful approach and find safe, secure anchorages. Any that decided to turn out to sea again were able to do so. The favourable conditions during the four days following 16 September allowed the ships' boats every opportunity to work back and forth with the shore to transport casks of water and food.

Not all the ships were seaworthy, however. A few of them succumbed as a result of leaks and accidents, but none because of sea conditions at this time.

———

No. 1 At sea off northwest Donegal

Five ships comprising two Levanters and three hulks were bearing down towards the northwest corner of County Donegal. They were *La Trinidad Valencera*, *San Juan de Sicilia*, the *Gran Grifon* the flagship of the squadron of hulks, the *Barque of Hamburg* and the *Castillo Negro*. They were all in bad shape with water in the hulls and pumps not able to cope.

The evening of 10 September was almost flat calm. The *Barque of Hamburg* was in danger of sinking and could go no further. Small boats were able to take off the crew and transfer them, part to *La Trinidad Valencera* and the rest to the *Gran Grifon*. The *Barque of Hamburg* sank during the night. Also missing next morning was the *Castillo Negro*. She disappeared without trace and was not seen again. She is presumed to have foundered with all hands off the north coast of County Donegal. The *San Juan de Sicilia* headed towards Scotland and eventually arrived in Tobermory Bay on the island of Mull.

The *Gran Grifon* turned away from the Irish coast and, according to a report written very much later, steered southwest with the intention of returning to Spain. She needed favourable sea conditions because she too had a lot of seawater in her hull. The rough seas of the night of 12/13 September were enough to put her in danger and all she could do was run northeast on the southwest wind. This took her as far north as 57½°, but at that point a northeast wind allowed the crew to try for Spain again. She rode out all the gales at sea, apparently obliged to run downwind to reduce the risk of taking more water in the bows, thus proving that it was much safer to be at sea in a gale than anchored close to shore. Despite all her twists and turns, by 26 September she was within sight of the Orkney Islands. There is a suspicion that the report laboured too much in order to sound convincing about the efforts being made to return to Spain. The *Gran Grifon*'s homeport was Rostock in the Baltic, and to find herself back in the Fair Isle Channel again in the middle of the last week in September suggests that the crew might 'accidentally' have discovered themselves heading homewards. She could go no further, however, and on 27 September anchored in the lee of Fair Isle at Swartz Geo, intending to beach there next morning. But during the night she drifted ashore into Stroms Hellier from where the crew were able to scramble to safety.

La Trinidad Valencera seemed to try to avoid the Irish coast, and on 12 September was still wallowing around off the north of County Donegal.

———

No. 2 Kinnagoe Bay, County Donegal

The strong winds of the night of 12/13 September were the last straw for La Trinidad Valencera. It became obvious that her only hope lay in finding a safe anchorage or at least a place where she could be beached. It has been calculated that she had seven feet of water in her bows. Coming down the north coast of Donegal, the prospect is one of high cliffs enclosing large sea inlets—not very inviting! She seems to have spent all of 13 September looking vainly for a suitable harbour, drifting between Malin Head and Inishtrahull Island, and along the Inishowen Peninsula. On the morning of 14 September the crew sighted the wide sandy beach of Kinnagoe Bay just four miles from Inishowen Head. It is doubtful if this was much of an improvement on what had faced them the previous day, but the situation was now urgent, and it offered them a chance.

As they headed in towards the beach but were still some 300 yards from the shore, they were very unlucky to strike a submerged, isolated rock. The bow rode up onto the rock leaving the stern embedded in sand. The ship stayed in this tilted position for two days, giving the crew plenty of opportunity to bring everyone on board safely ashore.

First to land was a small party of soldiers under their commander, Don Alonso de Luzon. They were lightly armed but their rapiers were not needed because they were well received by four or five local people. The ship's boat was damaged but serviceable enough to bring men ashore in small groups. Later they hired another boat from the Irish chieftain of Inishowen, Sir John O'Doherty. Soon more 'wild men', as the Spanish referred to them, appeared and they were able to purchase some basic food, just butter and ponies, which they killed and ate. The 'wild men' regarded it as their right to help themselves to any valuables they could find, but there was not much the Spanish could do about it.

All the men were ashore and should have been safe, but they started to try to recover as much as they could from the ship. Continuous tide and wave action and the bad weather of the night of 15 September caused more damage. On the morning of Friday 16 September the keel of *La Trinidad Valencera* suddenly shattered and she quickly sank. There were about forty men working on her at the time—some of them Irish, apparently on board looking for plunder. They were all, unfortunately, drowned.

An estimate of the number of men now stranded on the beach at Kinnagoe must realistically be put at about 350 to 400. There were just over 400 in the *Corunna* muster and sixty or more were taken off the *Barque of Hamburg*. The original number would have been reduced by losses during the fighting and through sickness. Don Alonso de Luzon was colonel of the regiment of soldiers and seemed to have assumed command. In his examination at Drogheda on 23 October he put the figure much higher, at around 600, plus 100 from the *Barque of Hamburg*, but this number seems unlikely.

It was still an imposing force of mostly well, if lightly, armed experienced soldiers. Their problem was one of supplies; they could not keep on eating the local horses, and there was nowhere to acquire food nearby. For the next three days they marched south along the west shore of Lough Foyle towards Sir John O'Doherty's castle at Illagh. Although he was a traditional Irish chieftain with no reason to fear the Spanish, he still felt vulnerable and on 16 September he had written to Castle Burt just seven miles west of Illagh to inform the garrison of the arrival of Spanish soldiers on his territory, and to ask for assistance.

Castle Burt was occupied by Richard and Henry Hovenden together with Sergeant John Kelly and about 150 Irish mercenaries. They were in the service of Hugh O'Neill, Earl of Tyrone, but also carried the Queen's ensigns. It is doubtful whether they were under the direct control of the Lord Deputy in Dublin, though he probably bore the cost of maintaining them. The area around Castle Burt is very remote, even today, and it is hard to find a rational explanation for a force of this size being there in 1588.

The Hovendens immediately responded to O'Doherty's request and joined him in time to face the Spanish when they arrived at Illagh. After a parley the Spanish agreed to lay down their arms. De Luzon described what happened:

> ... he and the whole company yielded themselves within 6 or 7 days of their landing, to the captains that carried the Queen's ensigns, on condition that their lives should be saved till they came to the Viceroy ...

They were promised that, if they surrendered their weapons, they could retain their other possessions. De Luzon complained bitterly that the promises were not kept and that 'the soldiers and savage people spoiled them of all they had'. The worst spoiler was John Kelly whom they termed sergeant major. They were left naked and kept out in the open all night.

Next morning the officers were separated from the rest of the men, who were then taken into an open field where they were attacked with arquebuses and lances in an attempt to kill them all. It was a ruthless but fairly inept massacre. Many were simply able to run away. Others were wounded and subsequently cared for in O'Doherty's castle. A Catholic bishop, Cornelius, who was staying in the area, provided a guide to take survivors to O'Cahan's country on the east side of the Foyle. There they were well treated, fed and clothed and, after three days, taken on to the Macdonnell stronghold at Dunluce Castle on the north coast of County Antrim. They stayed there for 20 days and were well looked after. The Macdonnells had family connections with Kintyre just a short sea trip away. And so more than a hundred survivors from *La Trinidad Valencera* escaped to Scotland. They eventually gained passage on four boats that were travelling from Edinburgh to France. By a final irony the Scottish ships were forced into Great Yarmouth by bad weather, but the Spanish were lucky to be able to proceed unmolested.

In October Don Alonso de Luzon and about twenty captains and ensigns were forced to walk to Dublin. Some died on the way and others were killed. Only Don Alonso de Luzon and one Don Rodrigo de Lasso were alive three years later, living in London and waiting to be repatriated.

Although this is one of the best documented episodes of the Armada saga in Ireland, there are still a few unanswered questions. What were the Hovendens doing with a relatively large force in a remote castle on the Inishowen Peninsula at a time when there was a severe shortage of manpower in the rest of the country? And how can the roll played by Sir John O'Doherty be explained? Being from the Gaelic Irish tradition his sympathies are bound to have been with the Spanish forces, yet he offered them very little help, in contrast with the O'Cahans only a few miles away across the Foyle, who sheltered and clothed them.

No. 3 Inner Donegal Bay

There is only one reliable source for the arrival of Armada ships in the inner part of Donegal Bay, but it is an absolute gold mine of information. This is a letter from George Bingham, at that time occupying a fortification at Ballymote, 13 miles due south of Sligo town. It is dated Tuesday 15 September and the relevant part reads:

… this morning John Fetigan came out of the Barony of Carbrie and doth declare for certainty that he and divers others of the country saw three great ships coming from the southwest and bearing towards O'Donnell's Country. And one of them being some league or two before the other two, bore in towards the Barony of Carbrie and at an island being six miles below Sligo towards Ballyshannon, there did strike sail, staying for the other two, which as soon as they were come right with him but further off at sea a great ways, he then hoisted up his sails again and veered about the island and so went to the others, and took their course right to the harbour of Calebeg as he thinketh … He saith that that ship was a very great one yet the other two being further off at sea seemed to be far greater. There be some of the country say that they saw yesterday about Aringlass in Treragh six great ships …

At this point there is a note in the margin by way of explanation, presumably by George Bingham: 'Aringlass, an open bay in O'Dowd's Country in the County of Sligo'. Aringlass is shown on early maps as Ardneglasse. Treragh was the name of the barony covering the Sligo coast from Killala Bay in the west to Ballysadare Bay, and was marked on old maps as O'Dowd's Country.

The Barony of Carbrie was that part of the coast of County Sligo north of Sligo town from Lackmeeltaun to Mullaghmore Head. The island off shore is Inishmurray.

O'Donnell's Country is literally the whole of modern County Donegal, referred to then as Tyrconnell. But there were a number of subservient families who owed him allegiance, including the O'Boyles around Donegal Town and there was an O'Boyle castle west of Killybegs, O'Doherty on Inishowen and three branches of the McSweeneys—McSweeney Banagh around Dunkineely, McSweeney Na Doe near Ardara, and McSweeney Fanad on the north coast. They were descendants of Scottish mercenaries known as gallowglasses who had settled in Ireland many years earlier.

'Taking their course right to the Harbour of Calebeg' suggests that they were acting under the friendly advice of local people, perhaps picked up the day before. The Harbour of Calebeg was not just the modern port of Killybegs. A contemporary map indicates that it also included the broad sea inlet enclosed by the long peninsula running south from Dunkineely to St John's Point known today as McSwyne's Bay. This is the place in which three large ships, new to the area, would most likely choose to shelter. The entrance to the port of Killybegs is narrow and partially blocked by a small island, while at the head of McSwyne's Bay, MacSweeney Banagh's castle gave promise of a generous welcome. These three ships were the galleass *Girona* and two others that have not been identified. The Spanish party must have contained at least

1,000 men, destined to put a severe strain on McSweeney's resources.

'Six ships seen yesterday (i.e. 14 September) about Aringlass in Treragh'—an open bay in O'Dowd's Country—must have been an eye-opener. This is the bay just east of Aughris Head, which is indeed exposed. It is five miles west of Ballysadare Bay, itself an unsuitable anchorage, because it empties at low tide. The remains of O'Dowd's castle can still be seen close by.

Finding a safe harbour was proving to be a problem.

Three of these six ships had crossed Donegal Bay to find refuge in the 'Harbour of Calebeg'. The other three moved round the coast and on 16 September were reported by George Bingham to have 'cast anchor in the Bay of Sligo'. The sandy estuary opposite Sligo town would have had the same tidal difficulties as Ballysadare Bay, but a better anchorage was available in Drumcliff Bay, and that is probably where they stopped. Bingham's report said that 'they sent men aland for fresh victuals who said they were Frenchmen and not Spanish, but in the end it was perceived and known that they were Spanish'. They would have received the relief they needed from the people of the area in return for payment. George Bingham had only a small force and he was keeping well out of the way in Ballymote. They had four days to procure supplies and ship them on board. These three ships were *La Lavia*, *Santa Maria de Visón* and *La Juliana*.

It would be easy to get stuck in Donegal Bay. Winds from the west and southwest can last for a long time at the entrance to the bay, leaving no opportunity to head out into the Atlantic and back to Spain. On the afternoon of 20 September, however, a most unusual easterly breeze sprang up. This was a chance to get under way and the ships hurried to leave the anchorage in Drumcliff Bay. In Bingham's Report it is stated '… the said three ships upon the change of wind hoisted up sail and put to sea'.

The details in George Bingham's letter of 15 September allow the interpretation of one final item of information. If the six ships were as far up the bay as Aringlass on 14 September then it is reasonable to suppose that they arrived in Donegal Bay not more than two or three days earlier, giving their arrival date as 11 or 12 September at the latest.

———

No. 4 Tirawley, County Mayo

West of Killala Bay on the north coast of County Mayo the land was divided into two baronies. The Barony of Tirawley was the smaller of the two and extended only as far west as the Keerglen River. William Burke was the Irish chief of the barony, which he ruled from his home at Ardnaree, on the

Port na Spaniagh, Co. Antrim. Lacada Point is the long low finger of black rock sticking out from the bottom of the cliffs. The *Girona* was impaled on the end of it, and it can be seen why so few men survived. The vertical cliffs, over 400 ft high, meant that no one could escape by climbing out; the only access is by sea. (*Luke Douglas*)

The mouth of the Bush River, the Bushfoot, with the Rock of Bunboys, which was thought for years to be the site of the *Girona* wreck, until 1967 when Robert Sténuit found the actual site. Since the *Girona* was clawing its way along the coast it might well have been seen in the bay here. (*Luke Douglas*)

Dunluce Castle, Co. Antrim. This was the home of Sorley Boy and James MacDonnell, and was the conduit to safety in Scotland for survivors from *La Trinidad Valencera* and the few men from the *Girona*. (© *Michael Diggin Photography*)

Dunluce graveyard, Co. Antrim. We are told that about 260 bodies were recovered from Port na Spaniagh, and tradition has it that they were given a Christian burial here. (© *Michael Diggin Photography*)

Kinnagoe Bay, Co. Donegal. The remains of the wreck of *La Trinidad Valencera* were discovered on 20 February 1971 by members of the City of Derry Sub Aqua Club. The rocky promontory just below the car park extends as an underwater reef for about 300 yards and, a few yards beyond that, an isolated rocky mound was where guns and other debris were found. (*Luke Douglas*)

Possibly the most spectacular Armada artefact seen to date, this 7¼ inch cannon has been mounted on a newly built gun carriage, and is on display in the Tower Museum in Derry. (*Courtesy of the Harbour Museum, Derry*)

West Light, Tory Island, Co. Donegal. In the sea area behind, two Armada ships were lost on the night of 10/11 September 1588. The *Barque of Hamburg* was waterlogged and abandoned, the crew having been transferred to other ships. The *Castillo Negro* disappeared overnight, and neither the ship nor the crew were seen again. (© *Michael Diggin Photography*)

McSweeny's Castle at the head of McSwyne's Bay, Co. Donegal. Up to 2,000 Spaniards were camped near the castle for several weeks, fed and cared for by the McSweeny family. Eventually, 1,300 of them left on the *Girona* only to be lost at the Giant's Causeway. Another 500 or so walked overland and were shipped to Scotland through the north coast. The McSweenys had frequent contact with relations on the Out Isles, and smaller boats probably took some more survivors this way. (*Luke Douglas*)

Letter from George Bingham to Sir Richard Bingham, 15 September 1588. 'It may please your lordship, this morning John Ffetigan came out of the Barony of Carbrie, and doth declare for certaintie that he and divers others of the country, saw three great ships coming from the southwest and bearing towards O'Donnell's Country. And one of them being some league or two before the other two, bore in towards the Barony of Carbrie, and at an island being six miles below Sligo towards Ballyshannon (Inishmurray) there did strike sail, staying for the other two, which as soon they were come right with him but further off at sea a great ways, he then hoisted up his sails again and veered about the island and so went with the others and they took their course right to the Harbour of Calebeg as he thinketh.' 'Calebeg the next haven to Donegal northwards in O'Donnell's Country'. (*Courtesy of the Public Records Office of Northern Ireland*)

Extract of Spanish document giving correct spelling of *Santa Maria Vison*. This extract, dated 24 June 1588, is from a list of ships that still had not joined the main fleet in La Coruña. The eighth ship shows the correct spelling of *Santa Maria de Visón*, which was at that time as far east as Laredo between Bilbao and San Sebastián. (*Courtesy of the General Archive of Simancas*)

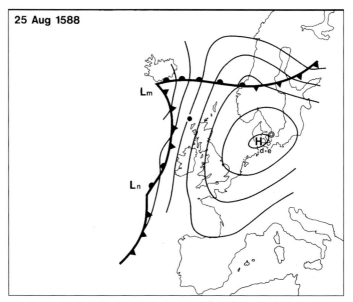

This is typical of the weather situation for the period 21 August to 3 September and shows how constant southerly winds held the Armada above 58°N for thirteen days. (*Climatic Research Unit, Norwich*)

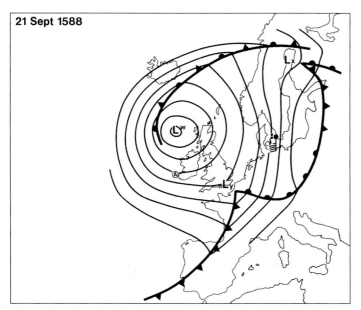

The weather chart for the Great Gale, which destroyed fourteen Armada ships on the Irish coast. It tracked ssw to nne over the two days 20 and 21 September, beginning with strong easterly winds on its northern side, followed by hurricane-force winds from the west. (*Climatic Research Unit, Norwich*)

The Mullet Peninsula with Blacksod Bay, Co. Mayo in the background. The Armada ship *Duquesa Santa Ana* sheltered in Elly Bay behind the Mullet. It survived the gale of 21 September, and left two days later, having taken on board the crew of the *Rata Encoronada*, lost nearby on the Tullaghan Bar. (© *Michael Diggin Photography*)

West Cliffs, Clare Island, Co. Mayo. The imposing features of the island can be seen to guard over the entrance to Clew Bay. *El Gran Grin*, a Spanish galleon of the Biscay squadron, sheltered in the lee of the island near O'Malley's Castle. (© *Michael Diggin Photography*)

opposite bank of the Moy River to the modern town of Ballina. The remainder of the northwest corner of Mayo was the Barony of Erris, a huge area and very remote. Even today there are many places where there are no roads. The chieftain of Erris was Richard Burke, often referred to as 'The Devil's Hook'.

These are the demarcations shown on a contemporary map, but of course there is no guarantee that references in the State Papers adhered exactly to them. George Bingham did not venture further west than Killala Bay, and the remote areas of Erris were not visited by garrison troops at that time.

News from the north coast of County Mayo travelled slowly if it travelled at all, and there are in fact no reports in the period up to 20 September. We know that a ship was in Tirawley, but we do not know its name or where it was, and we can do no better than guess.

The logical place for a ship to find shelter along this part of the coast would be in Killala Bay; under the high ground on the west side of the bay would be a sensible choice of anchorage. There are sandy shoals in the south and east of the bay that have to be avoided. We do not know the date of the ship's arrival.

As to the ship's name, it has been worked out by a process of elimination that it was most probably the *Ciervo Volante*, one of the squadron of hulks. But this is just one of those situations about which, up to 20 September at any rate, we are starved of information. There are no references to its name in any of the documents.

———

No. 5 Broad Haven, County Mayo

Broad Haven is a very wide sea inlet in the extreme northwest corner of County Mayo, between Benwee Head in the east and Erris Head in the west. A long, narrow channel runs south from it, down to Belmullet, which almost succeeds in cutting off the Mullet Peninsula and turning it into an island. There is a small port on the east side of this channel called Inver about a mile south of the point where it narrows. Another even narrower channel called Sruwaddacon Bay runs southeast for five miles until it melds into a huge marsh. Almost at its entrance is Ross Port. Erris Head is the most northerly point of the Mullet Peninsula; it is wild and remote. The majority of sea inlets on this part of the coast are filled with sandy shoals.

There is very little information in the State Papers that relates to Broad Haven and nothing at all before 20 September. No correspondent visited the area and so there are no eyewitness accounts. It was known that at least one ship was sheltering close to Inver, and the crew would have had several days to collect food and water without the threat of interference from an English garrison. And they would have learned from the local people of the presence of other Spanish ships, especially the *Duquesa Santa Ana* less than 12 miles away at Elly Bay, which would have been near enough to enable them to make contact by walking overland.

There is a possibility that the ship at Inver could have been the *San Nicolas Prodaneli*. And there is a further possibility that the hospital ship *San Pedro el Mayor* was somewhere nearby.

——

No. 6 Blacksod Bay, County Mayo

Blacksod Bay is the general term applied to the complex of sea inlets enclosed by the Mullet Peninsula and Achill Island. Blacksod Bay is properly that section of the bay running north inside the Mullet. On the map it looks like a Norwegian fjord, but the surrounding land is mostly low-lying. Due east of the entrance is Tullaghan Bay, which bends northeastwards and becomes very shallow. Achill Sound, in the southern part of the bay, divides Achill Island from the mainland. It is almost blocked off by the island of Inishbiggle except for a narrow entrance known as the Bull's Mouth, through which a fast tide flows four times a day.

Three Armada ships arrived in the Blacksod Bay area. They must have come in separately and at different times, because they ended up at separate locations well isolated from each other. The three ships were the *Duquesa Santa Ana*, which anchored in Elly Bay in the lee of the Mullet Peninsula, the *Rata Encoronada*, which headed east into Tullaghan Bay, and the *Nuestra Señora de Begoña*. The latter's anchorage is not known; the only reference to it is given as 'Bealingly' and that is thought to be somewhere in the south of the bay near Inishbiggle.

In the period from 15 to 20 September there is no mention in the record of either the *Duquesa Santa Ana* or the *N.S. de Begoña*. That probably means they would have had four or five days to replenish their water and victuals unmolested by any English garrison soldiers. There is, however, a brief note relating to an incident on the *Duquesa* shortly before she arrived in Ireland. One of the passengers was a young Irishman called Maurice Fitzgerald said to be the son of James Fitzmaurice Fitzgerald, revered as leader of an abortive rebellion in Munster in 1579. He died at sea just off the Irish coast and 'was cast into the sea in a fair cypress chest with great solemnity'. He cannot have imagined when he joined the Armada that he had much expectation of seeing

Ireland, but it was a poignant occasion nonetheless.

By contrast there are surprisingly detailed accounts of the fate of the *Rata Encoronada*. The first reference to it is in a letter from Sir Richard Bingham to the Lord Deputy dated 18 September in which he writes:

> This morning I had news brought me that the Devil's Hook a notable malefactor of the Burkes in Mayo, hath of late taken a dozen skiffs or small boats with certain kernes into the islands there, by which should seem that they have knowledge of some foreign enemy to land thereabouts ...

The *Rata* had grounded on the Tullaghan Bar, a sandy shoal at the entrance to the inner part of Tullaghan Bay, either as it entered the Bay or soon afterwards on a falling tide. It would appear that the Devil's Hook was intent on plundering the wreck. The ship must have come in at least two days earlier, placing its arrival at around 15 or 16 September.

It was later discovered that the *Rata* belonged to one Horatio Balanzine. It was an Italian ship and the crew were Italians, but the Spanish had requisitioned it to carry a large regiment of soldiers under the command of no less a figure than Don Alonso de Leyva, second in rank only to Medina Sidonia in the whole Armada. The Italian crew were just ordinary seamen pressed against their will into the service of Spain.

The ship's master, Giovanni Avanici, and 15 mariners took the cockboat and went ashore, allegedly to find out where they were, but they set off inland and 'travelled through the country to save themselves'. They were seized and 'spoiled by certain of the Burkes'.

Don Alonso now had a problem. The *Rata* was stranded about 600 yards from the shore and could not be moved. The ship's boat had been abandoned on the beach and, without it, the remainder of the crew could not be rescued. 'Don Alonso was compelled to send men aland upon empty casks and other devices to fetch it again, whereby they saved themselves from drowning when their ship was distressed'.

Sir Richard Bingham's informant, who might well have been one of the Italian captives, impressed on him the significance of Don Alonso de Leyva. He wrote that he '... was a special man of attempt of the enemy, landed with 600 men at Ballycroy in Irrus and began to fortify there ...'

Ballycroy is about four miles inland, and the Spanish actually set up their camp on the coast around Fahy Castle. It was too small to accommodate the whole party. Six hundred men seems to be an overestimate of the numbers involved. At the Lisbon muster the *Rata* had 84 mariners and 335 soldiers, a total of 419. At La Coruña this had risen to 448—93 mariners and 355 soldiers. Allowing for the usual attrition from fighting and sickness, the *Rata* would have been lucky to have 350 to 400 still alive. Many of the soldiers were in fact young noblemen, 'the flower of all the aristocratic families of Spain', who were attracted to the patronage of de Leyva, seeking honour and glory in military service. This was the first of three shipwrecks the young noblemen would experience and so they would have been able to save only their small, precious possessions.

At some stage the three ships must have become aware of each other's presence, but we are left to wonder just how much communication there was among them. The *Duquesa*, in Elly Bay, was 10 miles away and out of sight of the *Rata* behind the Doohooma Peninsula. A lot depended on the local people. The Spanish usually paid generously in return for food, water and assistance. Local boats could have played an important part in the subsequent course of events. The favourable weather on the days from 16 to 20 September meant that full use could be made of them.

―――――

No. 7 Clew Bay, County Mayo

Clew Bay in the south of County Mayo provides as dramatic a feature as could be wished for. It is eight miles wide throughout its 16-mile length. In the middle of the entrance Clare Island seems to stand guard with its western cliffs and its steep mountain rising to over 1,500 feet in the northwest of the island. Achill Island is the northern sentinel, and in the south the sacred mountain of Croagh Patrick overlooks it all. The eastern end of the bay is sprinkled with dozens of small islands—sunken drumlins that are a relic of the last Ice Age. They are as effective as a minefield to unwary shipping, and in places there are other islands just below the surface.

The area enclosed by Clew Bay is vast and is capable of hiding any number of shipwrecks. And that is what it has done, because, despite the ingenuity and efforts of different diving teams over the past 35 years, no trace of an Armada ship has ever been found. But they are in there somewhere and one of these days …

Two Armada ships were in Clew Bay, according to documentary evidence.

The first reference is a letter dated 20 September from a Galway merchant, George Wodloke, to the Mayor of Waterford, Alexander Brywer:

> I have seen a letter bearing the date 16 September being the present month of the arrival of one of the Spanish ships at a place called 'Borreis' which is to the northward of Galway 20 leagues, which place belongs to the Earl of Ormond. The same ship is cast upon the shore and past recovery, so as

the most part of the men are lost and cast away. There is come ashore of them 16 persons alive, and apprehended in the hands of a tenant of my Lord of Ormond who dwells upon the same land, they report of certain that the ship was of the burthen of 1,000 tons, and had in her 50 pieces of brass, besides four great cannon, so as the ship is past recovery.

Alexander Brywer immediately sent a copy of this letter off to Walsyngham in London. The source of the information was 'a credible man, whose name is James Blake', presumably an eyewitness. Its meaning is fairly clear: a place called 'Borreis' … which belongs to the Earl of Ormond' can only be Burrishoole in the northeast corner of Clew Bay.

The date is significant. The letter by James Blake is said to bear the date 16 September, so the ship must have been wrecked that day or the previous day. The night of 15 September was wet and windy but it was not a ship-smashing gale. It was enough to finish off *La Trinidad Valencera* on Inishowen, and it suggests that this ship must have been in the same sort of condition, with leaks that could not be controlled. Probably it was trying to find somewhere to beach safely.

The maze of islands between Burrishoole and the open part of the bay presents an almost insuperable challenge to anyone searching for the wreck site. It will require a colossal piece of luck and we can only wish that someone experiences that luck some day. The reference to it being 'cast upon the shore' suggests that it did avoid the islands and came to land, but then some evidence of it should surely have been found.

The second Armada ship to come into Clew Bay was *El Gran Grin*, a huge Spanish galleon, a fighting ship and vice-flagship of the Biscay squadron. It appears to have arrived about 15 September, because it is referred to by Gerald Comerford in a report to Sir Richard Bingham, which he received in Athlone on 17 September. It says simply: '… that a great ship of 800 tons lay at anchor at the Isle of Clare'. Eight hundred tons is a serious underestimation of the size of the *Gran Grin*. In the Lisbon muster it is registered as being of 1,160 tons.

The place where the *Gran Grin* 'lay at anchor' is revealed in a list of ships sent by Geoffrey Fenton to Lord Burghley in which he states 'In Fynglas, O'Males Country … one ship'. Faunglas is the name of the district on Clare Island that encompasses the harbour, O'Malley's Castle and the main settlement area in the southeast corner of the island. Nothing is more logical than that the *Gran Grin* should anchor there, easily accessible for obtaining supplies, and well sheltered on the lee side of the island.

It takes little imagination to picture, over the next four or five days, frequent exchanges between ship and shore. Given the traditional trading relationship the O'Malley family had with Spain and the shared customs of seafarers, the Spanish would without question receive all reasonable assistance. On the evening of 20 September it seems that some of the crew of the *Gran Grin* were on land, possibly enjoying O'Malley hospitality.

————

No. 8 At sea off the coast of County Galway

Pedro Coco Calderon, purser of the squadron of hulks, sailed on the *San Salvador*, vice-flagship of the squadron. He wrote a long account of the events on the voyage, and in it he briefly records that they sighted Ireland:

> On the west coast of Ireland this hulk found herself near an island 10 leagues in extent, the sea running strongly towards the land to the great danger of the hulk. The purser [Calderon himself] ordered her to tack to the northwest, which took her 30 leagues distant, and it is believed that the rest of the Armada will have done the same. If not they will certainly have lost some of their ships, as the coast is rough, the sea heavy, and the winds strong from the seaward.

He gives neither date nor latitude for the sighting of the Irish coast, but it appears in his statement between entries dated 10 and 14 September, on which date he claimed to be at 51°N. 'Winds strong from the seaward' suggests that it was on either 12 or 13 September, in which case he was probably about 53°N, or somewhere off the coast of County Galway. There are no islands 30 miles long on the Irish coast, but from some angles the Aran Islands at the mouth of Galway Bay could look like one island. He turned out to sea and never saw Ireland again. The *San Salvador* was one of those ships that had a near miss.

It is worth noting that he must have been reasonably close to the coast, because he used the words '… this hulk found herself *near* an island …' It does not seem like a distant view from the horizon.

No. 9 County Galway

Three Armada ships arrived in widely separate locations in County Galway. Again we have only the date on which Bingham received the report of them, not the date they arrived.

> And upon Monday 19 September he was advertised from the Mayor of Galway that a great ship arrived and cast anchor within that Bay and three in Iar Connaught, commonly called O'Flaherty's Country.

Allowing two days for the report to reach Bingham in Athlone and, in addition, taking further time into account for news to come in from the outlying sites, the ships must have arrived about 15 or 16 September.

The 'great ship that cast anchor within the Bay' was the vessel included in Fenton's List of Ships as 'In Galway Haven one shipp which escaped and left prisoners 70'. This ship has never been identified, but it has traditionally been believed to have anchored close to Barna, just six miles from Galway City. The prisoners were taken by the townspeople themselves, and unfortunately no examination of them has been preserved. The prisoners captured in the west of Galway have been the only source of information as to the names of the other ships involved.

The Mayor of Galway wrote to Bingham asking what he should do:

> ... 70 of her men came aland to take fresh victuals, which were apprehended by the townsmen and detained prisoners. The Captain and the rest of his company did offer to yield their ship and goods so they might have their lives saved ... the mayor was content that they should have their lives ... but the Captain, seeing how disorderly the townsmen handled such of his men as came aland, departed to seaward. The said ship had a great leak and lacked victuals and such water whereby in his extremity he might never recover Spain, but must needs perish and sink by the way ...

The prospects did not look good for her, but there is nothing to suggest that she became an Irish shipwreck. Judging by the sequence of events it seems to have left on one of the days before 20 September.

Three ships in Íar-Chonnacht seems like one too many, because only two have been identified. It has been suggested that the third might have been a small patache, or that it may have been one of the ships on the border of County Galway, possibly one of those seen around the Aran Islands.

The *Falcon Blanco Mediano* was anchored close to Inishbofin Island, off the north coast of Connemara. There is no certain location for it as nothing has ever been found. One of the crew was Don Luis de Cordoba, whose life was spared because of his seniority. In his examination before Sir Richard Bingham in Galway City at the beginning of October he said that his ship was 'a Flemish hulk called the White Falcon'. And it was he who had in his possession a copy of the Duke of Medina Sidonia's sailing instructions.

The second ship in Connemara tried to find shelter close to Mace Head, a remote area to the south of Bertraghboy Bay. A member of the crew was taken prisoner; he was Don Diego Sarmiento who was listed as the commander of a company of soldiers on the ship *Concepcion* of the Biscay squadron. There were two ships of that name in the Biscay squadron, each recognized by the name of the respective captains. This was the *Concepcion del Cano*.

The Mayor of Galway's report simply refers to the fact that these two ships 'arrived and cast anchor', and there is no reason to believe that they were lost before 20 September.

Íar-Chonnacht was a general name for the western part of the Connemara peninsula. The areas where these ships found themselves fell under the control of two different clans of the O'Flahertys. In the north, the *Falcon Blanco Mediano* was in the country of Sir Murrough Na Doe O'Flaherty. In the south the *Concepcion del Cano* lay at anchor within sight of Ards Castle, the home of Tadgh Na Buile O'Flaherty.

———

No. 10 The coast of County Clare

For ships coming from the northwest the dominant feature of the coast of County Clare is the Cliffs of Moher. From just south of Doolin to Hag's Head they stretch for a distance of five miles and present a sheer cliff face over 600 feet high. Any vessel finding itself on a lee shore here could be lost without trace. Running firstly due eastwards for six miles from Hag's Head to Lahinch, the Clare coast then turns southwest again, creating Liscannor Bay. It is four miles across and is exposed to winds from the southwest, but it does offer shelter of a sort. From the top of the Cliffs of Moher the three Aran Islands can be seen lying across the entrance to Galway Bay, angled from northwest to southeast.

The sheriff of Clare, Boetius Clancy, seems to have maintained a lookout, for on the evening of 15 September he reported that he had seen two ships about the Islands of Aran. They were on the seaward side of the islands and were in for an uncomfortable night, because there was rain and wind through the dark hours until dawn next day. Nevertheless, they survived.

The galleass *Zuñiga* also arrived on 15 September and on the next day Clancy gave an eyewitness account in a letter to Sir Richard Bingham:

> … in truth one ship is anchored in an unusual harbour about a mile westward from one of Sir Turlough O'Brien's houses called Liscannor … they offered to land last night in one of their cockboats, which they could not do by reason of the weather and the harbour. I do here watch with the most part of the inhabitants of the barony.

We know that the weather was rough on the night of 15 September, but they would try again to land the following day. Sir Turlough O'Brien's house at Liscannor still stands, and 'a mile' west from it suggests that the anchorage of the *Zuñiga* was at a small cove known as Coolrone. It is actually closer to two miles west of Liscannor. A stream of fresh water runs down from the fields and across a rocky beach at the western end of the cove. The wind was westerly early on the 15th, but it backed to southerly strong in the evening. The *Zuñiga* had a firm anchorage and, even though Liscannor Bay is vulnerable to winds from this quarter, she seems to have endured it without too much difficulty.

On board the galleass they were understandably anxious about their position on a lee shore. Surviving a stormy night is one thing, but putting to sea again against a prevailing wind would be well nigh impossible. One member of the crew was later captured. He was the 'scrivener', and his name was recorded as Petrus Baptista. He gave his statement in Latin, so, as his home was in Naples, he was probably Pietro Baptista. He told how they came to Liscannor and how he was taken:

> … what for want of food and water and partly through error for lack of pilots did come to such perilous place that it is hard for them to escape if the westerlie wind should blow. One of their boats slipped away and being blown to land the sheriff did cause it to be burned fearing lest they should recover the same again. Shortlie after did set another boat wherein this examinee was sent with others peaceablie without weapons faining themselves to be merchants, in hope the rather to get flesh and water for monie without suspicion … they that were ashore presentlie laid hands upon the said examinee …

The crew of the galleass were then compelled to send an armed party ashore to seize whatever food and water they could. Both Boetius Clancy and Sir Richard Bingham were intent on showing how well they had discharged their duties, and reported that the raiding party had been beaten back to their boats and forced 'to leave their prey behind'.

Juan de Saavedra, captain of the Neapolitan Regiment on the galleass, tells a different story:

> We were at this time in such dire need of food that nearly 80 of our soldiers and convicts died of hunger and thirst, the inhabitants refusing to allow us to obtain water; nor would they sell us food. We were therefore forced by our necessity to take up arms and obtain by force the supplies, which have lasted us until this 4 October.

In County Clare at least there was no welcome for the Spanish from the Irish population; in fact they were shown outright hostility. De Saavedra commented that: '… The inhabitants are rustic savages, devoted to England, with a few officials amongst them'.

That certainly sums up the situation. The local people were either unwilling or unable to help them, especially with Boetius Clancy buzzing about being the 'sheriff'. It is hard to believe that, given a free hand, they would not gladly have exchanged supplies for money, and even harder to believe that they were 'devoted to England'.

The two ships that had spent a night off the Aran Islands were probably persuaded by the rough weather of 15 September to look for anchorages on the coast. On the 18th Sir Turlough O'Brien reported to Bingham that there was a ship at Tromra in Ibracane; this was almost certainly the *San Marcos*. Tromra was another of Sir Turlough O'Brien's houses south of Quilty and close to Lurga Point. Offshore from Lurga Point to Mutton Island is littered with rocks and small islands so it was a hazardous enough anchorage to choose, but Sir Turlough O'Brien's report is quite specific and he knew the area. Just further north, Spanish Point has always appeared to be misnamed, because there seems to be nothing to connect it directly to the Armada.

A further report of a ship in the bay at Doonbeg would have been the *San Esteban*. The truth is that along this part of the Clare coast there are no anchorages offering safe shelter from the westerly winds. By the merest chance the *Zuñiga*, in the cove at Coolrone, had found a niche that provided a modicum of protection.

No. 11 The Shannon Estuary

The man on the spot on the coast had been Boetius Clancy; in the Shannon Estuary it was Nicholas Cahan. He was a coroner and one of the commissioners appointed to act in County Clare on behalf of the Council of Connaught in the current emergency. Clare in those days was part of the province of Connaught; today it is in Munster. Cahan was responsible indirectly to Sir Richard Bingham.

As early as 15 September Cahan wrote to Boetius Clancy that seven Spanish ships had 'come into this haven before Caryge-e-colle', that is Carrigaholt on the northern shore of the estuary, only seven miles from Loop Head. The previous day four ships had been seen on the seaward side of Loop Head, so it looks as though the seven ships did not arrive together.

The ships were the *Annunciada*, the *Santa Maria de la Rosa*, the *Barque of*

Danzig, the *San Juan* of Fernando Horra plus three patches, one of which was captained by Miguel de Aranivar; the other two patches have not been identified.

Eight men tried to come ashore from the ships, but Nicholas Cahan, Owen MacSweeney and 'the rest of the country kept them yet from the land'. Cahan spoke to them, but they claimed they could not understand English. He surprised them, however, by being able to address them in Spanish. 'They then confessed that they were of the King's Armie coming from Flanders and Spain'. It appears that they gave up at this point and returned to their ships.

The southerly wind of the night of 15 September caused some of their anchorages to slip. There were in any case dangerous shoals in this part of the bay, and on the next day they moved up river close to Scattery Island where they had better holding. Cahan moved with them and took up residence in Kilrush, from where he could keep them in sight.

The *Annunciada* was in a bad way. She had suffered from leaks ever since they had left Calais and had up to five patches attending her all the time in case the crew had to evacuate in a hurry. They would have to leave her behind, and over the following days the men were transferred to the *Barque of Danzig* and the patches.

They were still in desperate need of water and, according to Bingham's Report, they offered 'a butte of wine for every butte of water or so much monie as should be required for it, which being not accepted they proffered to give one of their ships with the goods and munition for licence to take in as much fresh water as would supply their wants, which in no sort would be agreed to'. How much of this selfless devotion to duty can be believed is open to question. Naturally no official was going to put on record that he had supplied the water and taken the money. In any case, enterprising local citizens are unlikely to have overlooked the trading opportunities presented by wealthy Spanish ships on their doorstep, even if they had to avail of them in the middle of the night.

The *Annunciada* was set on fire after being evacuated and the wreck drifted ashore. On Tuesday 20 September an easterly wind came up. This was an unusual chance to get away. The prevailing westerly wind could have made it difficult for them to leave the Shannon. The three remaining great ships and the three patches set sail in the hope that they were at last on their way back to Spain. Cahan's eyewitness report written in Kilrush said: '… those ships that were here went forth a Tuesday'. The same easterly wind had enabled the three ships in Drumcliff Bay to hoist their sails and leave their anchorage. These, along with the ship at Barna were the first ships on the coast to attempt to depart for Spain before 21 September.

Nicholas Cahan tried to advise the Mayor of Limerick of the departure of the Spanish, but he could find only a young boy to take the letter. He complained bitterly that 'only by much ado could he get him to go, for all men be about the ship that is lost'. Despite the fire on the *Annunciada* there was apparently much plunder still to be had.

————

No. 12 Tralee Bay, County Kerry

At the northern entrance to Tralee Bay the little port of Fenit stands about seven miles from the town of Tralee. Behind Fenit there is a large, shallow, sea inlet with a narrow entrance called Barrow Harbour. This virtually empties at low tide, although a river runs across the sands. On the northern shore of Fenit Island at the entrance to Barrow Harbour the remains of a sixteenth-century tower house can still be seen. This was the home of Sir Edward and Lady Denny, English settlers and important landowners in the area.

About 15 or 16 September 1588 a small Spanish vessel with 24 men on board arrived somewhere in this area; the exact location is not known. A few men swam ashore, but all landed safely. No one was drowned and none was injured, implying that this was not a shipwreck. It is very probable that the ship was saved and retained by the Denny family. Sir Edward Denny was away at the time and so Lady Denny was saddled with the responsibility of attending to the survivors. It would have made sense for them to be transferred to Tralee where there was an English garrison. There they were questioned and a composite record of their examination gives some useful information. They said:

> … they fell with the coast of Ireland, not knowing where they were, but resolved to return for Spain … they say that they lost the Duke by tempestuous weather about 18 days since, the which they think to be now somewhere about this coast.

The tempestuous weather about 18 days since was the period of southerly winds they experienced between 21 August and 3 September. This also acknowledges that they were not able to keep track of their position, and that the main body of the Armada was not very far away.

After the examination they were all killed 'because there was no safe keeping for them'. Thomas Norreys in Cork was annoyed by the killings; he probably felt that more information should have been had from them. We can presume that the killings were not done at the instigation of Lady Denny, although in most histories they are attributed to her. To carry out these interrogations required the services of a Spanish speaker and a secretary to summarize and transcribe them, facilities that would have been available in Tralee.

There is one more interesting comment. Of the 24 men, two were supposed to be the Duke of Medina Sidonia's personal servants and two were 'little boys'. This appeared in a report by the Lord Deputy and Council of Ireland to the Privy Council in London, and was passed on to Spain by a spy in London who obviously had access to some fairly sensitive documents.

The fact that the Duke's servants were on board has led some commentators to deduce that the ship might have been one of the zabras attached to the squadron of Portugal, the *Augusta* or the *Julia* perhaps. The men declared they were from Castile and Biscay, and in the Biscay squadron there was a patache, the *Nuestra Señora del Socorro* with a small crew which just possibly could have been the ship at Tralee. But naming these pataches and zabras on the basis of such flimsy evidence is a fruitless task. One of their duties was to act as mobile service boats so they could literally turn up anywhere, although some were attached to flagships to carry stores of food, water and ammunition. The great majority of them had crews of 40 to 60 men, and for the complement of the Tralee boat to be reduced to only 24 probably represents a severe rate of attrition.

———

No.13 Blasket Sound, County Kerry

The Blasket Islands are off the tip of the Dingle Peninsula. From Tralee to Dingle is about 50 miles of beautiful but tortuous roads through mountains and valleys, and it is a further 10 miles round Mount Eagle and Slea Head before you can overlook Blasket Sound. At 10° 30' w, it is the most westerly point in Europe. It is remote. The Sound is formed by the mainland of the Dingle Peninsula and Great Blasket Island. It is narrow at the southern end, constricted by Dunmore Head with its offshore rocks known as the Lure pointing westwards from the steep cliffs of Dunmore Head and in the west by the southeast corner of Great Blasket. Begenish and numerous rocks and islets surround the northwestern approaches and look to be an impenetrable maze. There is a clear entrance to the Sound close to the coast from Clogher Head southwards, but that would entail skirting a lee shore. An almost vertical path leads down to Dunquin Harbour, a modern construction which adheres to the bottom of the cliffs. The village of Dunquin is about a mile north of the Harbour, and here there is now a Visitor Centre.

On 11 September, after Aramburu in the *San Juan Bautista* had his brush with islands on the Irish coast, he turned out to sea on a south-southwest wind and headed west. In chapter 2 we have seen how Aramburu's pilot was able to suggest possible names for these islands. He mentioned Los Quelmes (the Skelligs), Dursey Island and the Bull and the Cow. It appears they were referred to in a document known as the *Derrotero*, which had been distributed throughout the fleet. This seems to have been a kind of rutter for the British Isles rather than a map. Certainly no reliable map of the west of Ireland existed at that time in either Spanish or English sources. Although the pilot was able to put forward these names he did not have an accurate idea of where they were. On 11 September at around 53° N he was much too far north to see them.

He kept on the same course all day on 12 September until the evening when the strong wind they had experienced during the day blew up into a storm. He was joined for a time by the ship *Trinidad*. They hove to with both mainsails furled, but by morning the *Trinidad* had disappeared.

At dawn on the 13th the wind veered to northwest and the seas began to go down. At that point the pilot took a strange decision: he set a course s¼se. He must have known that they were still off the Irish coast and that any course east of south would risk putting them in danger again. Even allowing for the fact that they had sailed west for a day and a half, the correct course was due south. The truth is that knowledge of the geography of Ireland was poor at that time; no one seemed to know how far west it came.

On the 14th they continued on the same course on a northwesterly wind. At midday they sighted to leeward a big ship and a patache sailing together, and they headed over towards them. In other words they moved even further east. Aramburu claimed to have been within a league of them as darkness fell, but he seemed to get no response from them. The ships were the *San Juan of Portugal*, Recalde's flagship, and his attendant patache.

The next morning, Thursday 15 September, Aramburu was heading south on a westerly wind. He claimed he was standing away from land, but in fact he must have been drifting eastwards, because at first light he had two large islands straight ahead, and he could see the mainland off to the east. He turned towards the northwest to escape, although that must have been tight on a westerly wind, and immediately came across the *San Juan of Portugal* and the patache. He had no idea where he was, but he followed Recalde, who rounded one of the islands and headed east. Aramburu must have been horrified, for they were now sailing towards the maze of small islands with the bulk of the mainland and Mount Eagle looming behind. The only option for him was to keep close behind Recalde, and he comforted himself by observing that Recalde seemed to know what he was doing. Sure enough, he kept on towards the mainland, 'and got into the Port of Vicey through an entrance between low islands no bigger than the length of a ship'. It sounds hair-raising even now, but all three ships came safely into Blasket Sound and dropped anchor.

Much has been made of Recalde's intimate knowledge of the area and the fact that he had been part of the ill-fated force that landed in Smerwick in 1580. Smerwick is just around the corner on the northern side of the Dingle Peninsula. This is probably justified, since it was the practice of navigators to make notes and sketch maps of every place they visited and retain them for possible future use. Recalde was old and ill; he suffered from arthritis and had spent much of the voyage in his bunk, but he had revived sufficiently to come on deck when he was needed. Certainly no one else could have accomplished such a remarkable feat of seamanship, although it is possible that he was assisted by a Scottish pilot captured off Orkney.

A chalup from the *San Juan* with eight men on board was sent over to the mainland to reconnoitre, but as bad luck would have it there were English soldiers waiting for them and they were captured. Although this is a remote place there was a garrison stationed at Dingle, possibly as a result of the Smerwick invasion eight years earlier. Four of the men were later examined in Dingle and their statements are printed in the State Papers. Three were Portuguese and one was from Flanders but with an Irish name, 'Pierre O'Carr'. Unfortunately, all were killed.

The afternoon and evening of 15 September blew up into a storm, but by that time Aramburu and Recalde were safely tucked up in the shelter of the Great Blasket.

On the 16th they exchanged anchors and cables which would later prove to be lifesavers. Recalde gave Aramburu two cables and an anchor, while Aramburu was able to supply Recalde with a heavy anchor of 30 quintals.

On the 17th Recalde again tried to make a landing. He sent over a longboat with 50 soldiers in it. They took a linguist to treat with the Irish for water and meat, and they were obviously prepared to fight to get it. But they could not find a landing place; they said they 'found only wild cliffs beaten by the seas and about 100 soldiers marching along the cliffs carrying a white flag with a red cross on it'. It is fairly certain that the English did not have anything like 100 soldiers available, but it sounds like a successful bluff.

On 18, 19 and 20 September Aramburu simply records that they remained in port without being able to sail: 'Juan Martinez managed to get some water, but I, without a batel or chalup could do nothing. He got little and that with much effort'. There is still a small spring on Great Blasket giving little with much effort! In fact we learn from the report of a soldier on Recalde's *San Juan of Portugal* that on 19 September members of his crew were able to fill 14 casks of water, some of which were later shared with Aramburu.

———

No. 14 Valencia Island, County Kerry

On 28 August Aramburu in the *San Juan Bautista* had found a companion in the ship *Trinidad* and they stayed together for two days. At dusk on the evening of 29 August they were only half a league apart, but next morning she had gone. She reappeared briefly again on 2 September, but with the sea mist Aramburu lost sight of her almost at once. As the mist cleared in the afternoon there she was again quite close. Aramburu hauled over towards her within hailing distance and the crew of the *Trinidad* said that they had to stop as she was taking a lot of water forward.

He did not see her again until 12 September, but that night a storm blew up and they were separated once more.

On the morning of 15 September, when Recalde was taking the light from Aramburu's eyes entering Blasket Sound, he recorded that he saw another ship to leeward close to the mainland. 'God help him find a way out for he is in great danger'. It has been suggested that it might have been the *Trinidad* and there is a possibility that she could have made it across the entrance to Dingle Bay to find shelter behind Doulus Head. The night of 15/16 September was rough so, if she had just too much water in her hold, she might have ended her days there.

Fenton's List of Ships includes one that might be the *Trinidad*—'In Desmond … one ship … 300 men'. In 1845 Valencia fishermen found an astrolabe ring with the date 1585 marked on it. Such are the tantalizing scraps of evidence we are sometimes left with.

RÉSUMÉ

The following is a summary of the ships that arrived in Ireland or were off the coast between 11 and 16 September.

Off North Donegal	*Barque of Hamburg* *Castillo Negro* *Gran Grifon* *San Juan de Sicilia* *Trinidad Valencera*	5 ships
Inner Donegal Bay	*Girona* *La Lavia* *Santa Maria de Visón* *La Juliana* And two unnamed ships	6 ships
Tirawley	*Ciervo Volante*	1 ship
Broad Haven	*San Nicolas Prodaneli* *San Pedro el Mayor?*	2 ships
Blacksod Bay	*La Rata Encoronada* *Duquesa Santa Ana* *Nuestra Señora de Begoña*	3 ships
Clew Bay	*El Gran Grin* *Santiago?*	2 ships
Off County Galway	Calderon's *San Salvador*	1 ship
County Galway	*Falcon Blanco Mediano* *Concepcion del Cano* Unnamed ship at Barna	3 ships
Clare Coast	*Zuñiga* *San Marcos* *San Esteban*	3 ships
Shannon Estuary	*Anunciada* *Barque of Danzig* *Santa Maria de la Rosa* *San Juan* of Fernando Horra And 3 pataches	7 ships
Tralee	A patache or zabra	1 ship

Blasket Sound	*San Juan of Portugal*	
	Aramburu's *San Juan Bautista*	
	A patache	3 ships
Valencia Island	*Trinidad* ?	1 ship
		Total 38 ships

Ships lost before 20 September

Off North Donegal	*Barque of Hamburg*	
	Castillo Negro	Leaks, foundered at sea
Kinnagoe Bay	*Trinidad Valencera*	Grounded and sank, leaks
Blacksod Bay	*Rata Encoronada*	Accidental grounding
Clew Bay	*Santiago*?	Unknown
Shannon	*Anunciada*	Scuttled and burned, leaks
Tralee	Unknown	Grounding?
Valencia	*Trinidad*?	Little is known about the fate of the *Trinidad*. It is included here, but might have been lost later, on 20 September
		Total 8 ships

ADDITIONAL SOURCES

At the end of September an official report was prepared by Edward Whyte, secretary to the Council of Connaught, summarizing all the intelligence that had been gathered about the Spanish ships during the month. He gave it a splendid title: 'True declaration of the great losses and overthrow lately suffered by the remnant of the Spanish fleet by shipwreck and otherwise upon the coast of Connaught and Thomond, through the power of God's might and of the prudent care and trouble of the right worshipful Sir Richard Bingham, Knight, governor and chief commissioner of the said province to prevent their landing or the attempting of the King against Her Majesty or the state of the Realm in these parts'.

It is an immensely valuable document and contains a great deal of information not available elsewhere. Without it we would have a much poorer knowledge of September 1588 on the Irish coast. There is, however, a drawback. It implies the kind of unblemished perfection associated with someone who has written his own end-of-term report, and so it should not be accepted uncritically in everything it says. It was signed by Sir Richard Bingham, Thomas Dillon, Anthony Brabazon, Robert Fowle and Nathaniel Smythe. In the calendar it is mentioned briefly on p. 47 as a 'Discourse', but the actual document, which runs to nine pages of closely written Elizabethan secretarial script, is on MIC 223/51 NOS. 237 to 240. It is referred to in the text and the notes as 'Bingham's Report'.

A letter from Geoffrey Fenton, clerk of the Council in Dublin, to Walsyngham on 29 September enclosed a 'note of ships and men of the Spanish fleet perished on the coasts of Ireland'. See CSPI p. 43, which refers to 16 ships. The actual document contains a few vital scraps of intelligence and it is on MIC 223/51 NO. 198, which actually lists 17 ships. It is referred to in the text and notes as 'Fenton's List of Ships'.

NOTES AND REFERENCES

The quote from the crew of the ship at Tralee is in CSPI p. 28 and MIC 223/51 NO. 84.

The quote from Petrus Baptista is on MIC 223/51 NOS 175–176.

The Armada's Sailing Instructions and the examination of Don Luis de Cordoba are calendared in full in CSPI pp 49–51.

The fate of the ships off North Donegal is well described by Colin Martin in his book *Full Fathom Five* pp 189–202, and in CSPI pp 35–36. Colin Martin took part in the exploration of the wreck site and this enabled him to interpret how *La Trinidad Valencera* grounded on a rock on its approach to Kinnagoe Bay. Don Alonso de Luzon's statement is on MIC 223/52 NOS 97–98. Valuable details are supplied by two men who escaped from *La Trinidad Valencera*, Juan de Nova and Francisco do Borja, whose statement is in Hume pp 506–510.

The letter from George Bingham to Richard Bingham that reveals the events in inner Donegal Bay on 15 September is on MIC 223/51 NO. 77.

The ship in Tirawley is in Bingham's Report.

The possible involvement of the *San Nicolas Prodaneli* depends on a report by the survivors of the *San Pedro el Mayor*, which is referred to in Paula Martin's book *Spanish Armada Prisoners* (Exeter, 1988) pp 48–49. This also implies that *San Pedro el Mayor* was in the same area as well, although the date given is not consistent with the movement of other ships.

The grounding of the *Rata* in Blacksod Bay is first referred to in a letter from Bingham to the Lord Deputy dated 18 September: see CSPI p. 29. Further details are in Bingham's Report. The arrival of the *Duquesa Santa Ana* also led to the report of the death of Maurice Fitzgerald, son of James Fitzmaurice Fitzgerald, and his burial at sea.

In Clew Bay, George Wodloke's letter is in CSPI pp 36–37. Comerford's reference to the anchorage of *El Gran Grin* at Clare Island is in Bingham's Report. Fenton's List of Ships has the reference to 'Fynglas'.

At sea off County Galway, the account of Calderon's *San Salvador* coming close to an island on the Irish coast is in Hume p. 449. Calderon is an irritating informant. He is careless with detail and frustratingly inaccurate in places. There is much useful information in his account, but it is devalued by the fact that he continually promotes himself. He tries to convey the impression that he is the Duke's personal confidant. In this extract he cannot resist telling us that 'The Purser ordered her to tack to the northwest'. The reaction of the Spanish seamen to 'orders' from the purser can be imagined. He must have been a pain in the neck to live with. He comes across as an interfering busybody.

The County Galway ships are referred to in Bingham's Report, but unfortunately it is short of substance regarding their specific location. If it were not for the examination of Don Luis de Cordoba in CSPI pp 50–51, we would probably not have been able to identify one of them as the *Falcon Blanco Mediano* in Sir Murrough Na Doe O'Flaherty's Country. The Mayor of Galway was the source of the events involving the ship at Barna, but again it is unsatisfactory not to be told the name of the ship, its exact location or the name of the Captain; it is such a missed opportunity. Niall Fallon's book *The Armada in Ireland* tries hard to extract reliable information from local tradition; see pp 36–42.

On the Clare coast—Boetius Clancy's sighting of the ships near the Aran Islands is in CSPI pp 29–30, which also describes the Irish view of the arrival of the *Zuñiga* in Liscannor Bay. The Spanish version, given by Petrus Baptista, is on MIC 223/51 NOS 175–176. The events here are also referred to in Bingham's Report. Juan de Saavedra's statement was given in Le Havre on 4 October and is in Hume pp 456–457, in which he goes out of his way to tell us that the anchorage at Coolrone was a good one. The fact that de Saavedra was able to seize victuals sufficient for at least 14 days contrasts with the claim in Bingham's Report that Clancy forced them to 'leave their prey behind'.

In the Shannon Estuary—Nicholas Cahan's account of the arrival of the ships at Carrigaholt and Kilrush is in CSPI p. 30 and p. 38, with a fuller version in Bingham's Report. Cahan's discussion with the Spanish crews is on MIC 223/51 NO. 96. The departure of the ships and the burning of the *Anunciada* are in Bingham's Report and in Cahan's letter of 22 September in CSPI p. 38.

Tralee Bay—Events surrounding the arrival of the ship at Fenit are revealed in 'The examination of the Spaniards etc.' in CSPI p. 28 and on MIC 223/51 NO. 84. This is another document that misses the opportunity to provide names of the men and the ship. The reports of the Spanish spy are in Hume p. 454 and p. 463.

Blasket Sound—Most of the details are in Aramburu's diary from Duro, *La Armada Invencible* VOL. II NO. 178. The reference from the report of the soldier from Recalde's *San Juan* is part of a long discourse by Geoffrey Parker in *The Mariner's Mirror*, August 2004, p. 334. There is a suggestion in this report that the successful entry into Blasket Sound might have been accomplished with the help of a Scottish fisherman captured off Orkney. The *Derrotero* is mentioned in Herrera Oria, *Armada Invencible*. A rutter was a collection of notes and sketches compiled by mariners as an aid to navigation before reliable charts were available. Although each was the personal record of the individual navigator, information was generally shared. The first one to be published was in France under the title *Routiers de la Mer*, which was anglicized as 'rutter'. Examinations of the prisoners from the *San Juan of Portugal* are in CSPI p. 39 and p. 40. A full transcription of their statements is in Laughton VOL. II pp 219–228.

Valencia Island—This is regrettably mostly speculation, but the references to the *Trinidad* are in Aramburu's diary. The ship in 'Desmond' is on Fenton's List of Ships.

Chapter 4 ∾

21 SEPTEMBER 1588
THE GREAT GALE

... there blew a most extreme and cruel storm the like whereof hath not been heard a long time ...
(BINGHAM'S REPORT)

... in the morning it began to blow from the west with a most terrible fury, bright and with little rain.
(ARAMBURU IN BLASKET SOUND)

TROPICAL STORMS *WILL* TRAVEL

The season of North Atlantic tropical cyclones runs from about 1 July until the beginning of November. They originate in tropical West Africa. Under intense summer sun the land heats up; evaporation and conduction then transfer heat and moisture into the atmosphere forming thunderstorms. At intervals clumps of thunderstorms join together and begin to drift westwards. Over the ocean evaporation continues to pump more and more moisture into the thunder clouds, building up enormous amounts of heat in the atmosphere. As the cloud masses move west a tropical wave tends to fold them into a comma shape. Above 10°N the curvature of the earth starts to exert a spinning motion on the cloud masses—the Coriolis Effect. The circle closes and a fully-fledged tropical storm is formed, with deep low pressure at its centre, known as the eye.

Under the influence of the northeast trade winds tropical cyclones are usually directed due west at about 15°N. As they approach the northern coast of South America and the Caribbean they continue to absorb energy, becoming increasingly violent. If the internal wind speed exceeds 120 km per hour a tropical cyclone becomes a hurricane. No two tropical cyclones are the same; they seem to have a mind of their own as each chooses in which direction to go and how fast or how slowly it travels. They can come on land anywhere in the Caribbean, Mexico or the coast of North America. When they do they are cut off from the supply of heat and moisture and immediately moderate.

Some cyclones turn northwards into the path of the southwest trade winds, and begin to cross the Atlantic in a northeasterly direction anywhere from 20°–25°N off the coast of Florida or the Carolinas. When a tropical cyclone enters temperate latitudes and can no longer sustain its power from a warm ocean, its winds decrease and its eye disappears. These are said to be 'recurving' tropical cyclones. When they draw cooler air into their western side they can increase in size as they approach the British Isles and Europe; they moderate, but they still retain the capacity to produce threatening weather.

Meteorologists do not like the term 'equinoctial gales', because they rightly point out that gales can happen any time. There is, nevertheless, a seasonal aspect to recurving tropical depressions associated with the hurricane season in the tropics. They are a regular feature of autumn weather on the Irish coast, and tend to occur most often in September. The autumn of 1588 had been remarkably quiet; the depressions of 12/13 and 15/16 September were the only spells of Atlantic weather during the month so far; they had been brief and relatively innocuous. There was nothing to suggest that they were of tropical origin.

Recurving tropical depressions may be fairly regular on the Irish coast, but a genuine hurricane is very rare, a once-in-50-years event. On 16 September 1961 hurricane Debbie hit Ireland and caused enormous damage to woodlands and housing. Eleven people were killed. At the height of its intensity it was bright and sunny. The Irish cricket team had a match against Australia in Belfast that day. Writing about it later the Australian captain, Richie Benaud, described how '… in Belfast we ran into a 90-miles-per-hour gale, which blew down the media centre and everything else'. But it was dry and bright and they played. He recalled that he bowled the quick bowler into the wind and the slow bowler with the wind just to enable the semblance of a cricket match to take place.

Hurricane Debbie has been closely studied and unusual features have been revealed. Based mainly on surface observations, but also using photographs from Tiros III, one of the early weather satellites, its formation has been traced back to Central Africa around 1 September. It moved westwards and on 6 September crossed the African coast near Dakar, by which time it had already acquired the characteristics of an incipient hurricane. A Tiros III photograph on 7 September shows that an eye had formed, even though it had only just begun to absorb moisture from the tropical ocean.

When it moved off the African coast, it did not follow the usual track due westwards to the Caribbean. It turned instead northwest until around the

Azores it moved east, then northeast, heading towards the west coast of Ireland. The eye passed western Ireland on 16 September. In other words it moved more or less directly from West Africa to Ireland, avoiding the regular pattern of recurving tropical cyclones, which spend a long time over the warm ocean absorbing massive amounts of moisture. If there is such a thing, it might be described as a dry hurricane.

HIT BY A HURRICANE

There are one or two features of the Great Gale of 21 September 1588 which resemble Hurricane Debbie. First of all the Duke of Medina Sidonia went through fierce cyclonic conditions on 18 September at 45°N in southwest Biscay. This would be consistent with a weather system approaching the British Isles from the south rather than from the southwest. Then Aramburu in Blasket Sound observed that at the height of the Great Gale it was 'claro y con poco agua', bright and with little rain, similar to the situation on 16 September 1961. The observer who contributed to Bingham's Report knew what to expect from a normal autumn storm, but this was different—'a most extreme and cruel storm the like whereof hath not been heard a long time'.

The evidence points to the Great Gale of 21 September 1588 being a hurricane.

There are only two detailed descriptions of the effect of the Great Gale on the ships. One is Marcos de Aramburu's diary, which covers the course of events in Blasket Sound. These are as close to being contemporaneous notes as it would be possible to be. The other is in the long account given by Francisco de Cuéllar, who was on *La Lavia*, one of the ships wrecked on Streedagh Strand, County Sligo. This was written in Antwerp in October 1589, more than a year later, after a succession of traumatic experiences which amount to a fabulous tale of survival in the face of overwhelming adversity. Apart from being a little shaky on dates, understandably, it is as authentic as anything in history can be expected to be, and his vivid description of what it was like to be on board a ship wrecked in a hurricane is priceless. These two sites are 170 miles apart and they concur on the ferocity and timing of the storm. Although we could wish for more information from the many other locations on the coast, the fact that they are at the southern and northern extremities of the places where the ships were, means it is safe to infer that all Armada ships on the Irish coast were subjected to the same ordeal.

In Blasket Sound, County Kerry

'In the morning it began to blow from the west with a most terrible fury. It was bright and with little rain'. It was, therefore, daylight before the gale really got going.

The seafloor in Blasket Sound is scoured clean by tidal currents and offers very insecure anchorages comprising bare rock and shallow patches of sand, shingle and kelp. Juan Martinez de Recalde and Marcos de Aramburu had been anchored close to each other for four days off the White Strand on Great Blasket Island, but conditions were good, with light or moderate wind, and they experienced no difficulties. All Armada ships had left their best anchors in Calais Roads when the Duke had ordered them to cut their cables to avoid the English fireships. On the first morning after their arrival Recalde and Aramburu had exchanged anchors and cables. 'Juan Martinez gave us two cables and an anchor, since we had only one cable which was in the sea, and I gave him an anchor of 30 quintals, which was useless for us, but of which he had the greatest need'. This may have been just good housekeeping, or perhaps they had become aware that holding in the Sound was precarious.

In the gale on the morning of 21 September anchorages did not hold. First Recalde's *San Juan* dragged down onto the *Bautista*, hit it hard on the stern, shattering the lantern and breaking the stays of the mizzen mast. Recalde regained control of his ship using the anchor he had been given four days earlier and it seems was able to remain roughly in the same area off the White Strand. Aramburu must have had both his anchors in the sea because, unknown to him, the impact of the collision had broken one of his anchors; yet he too seems to have maintained his position near the White Strand.

At midday the *Santa Maria de la Rosa* came into the Sound. Aramburu says it came 'by another entrance somewhat nearer the mainland from the northwest'. This must mean from the north, east of Begenish and west of Clogher Head.

> Coming in she fired a piece as if asking for help, and further on she fired another. All her sails hung in pieces except the fore mainsail. She came to a stop with one anchor, which was all she had, and, with the tide coming in from the southeast, she held steady for a while. At 2 o'clock the tide turned, she began to swing on her anchor and then dragged to within two cable lengths from us, and we dragged with her.

What seems to have happened was that at first the *Santa Maria de la Rosa* was able to come to a stop near the ships of Recalde and Aramburu, but when the tide turned the combined force of gale and tide race dragged both the *Rosa* and the *Bautista* down the Sound together. They dragged about three-quarters of a mile into the narrow southern entrance of the Sound. Recalde seems to have managed to hold his position.

The rocks off Dunmore Head, known as the Lure, continue as an underwater reef across the south of the Sound. A pinnacle of this reef is called 'Stromboli' after a ship which struck it in the nineteenth century. The *Rosa* hit Stromboli and holed her bottom so badly that she immediately filled with water and sank directly behind the reef. It all must have happened in a few minutes for the crew did not even have time to hoist the foresail or launch any of their boats. Aramburu was overcome with shock at all of this. He said 'she went down right away with every man on board, not a soul was saved, a most extraordinary and frightening thing; we were dragged over on top of her in great danger ourselves'. He probably did not go over the top of the reef. The anchor that Recalde had given them held just short of it, even though it had dragged all the way down the Sound. As it came to a stop the ship swung and they recovered the other anchor cable, which had been flapping around uselessly. It came up with only the cross piece and half the shaft; the rest of the shaft and the flukes were still in the anchorage off the White Strand where the *Bautista* had been damaged by Recalde's ship striking it earlier in the day. It was found there 400 years later.

Aramburu records that 'at this moment the ship of Miguel de Aranivar also came in', in other words not long after 2 o'clock. It later transpired this was a patache, but it appears that it was in better condition than any of the great ships. At 4 o'clock another ship arrived which he identified as the *San Juan* of Fernando Horra.

> Her mainmast was gone and, as she came in, her fore mainsail ripped to pieces. She dropped anchor and stopped. With the fierce weather we were not able to hail her or give her any assistance.

At 4 o'clock in the afternoon the Great Gale was still going strong. If she was in hailing distance she must have been close to the *Bautista* in the south of the Sound.

These new arrivals were three of the six ships which had left the Shannon the day before. From the Shannon to the Dingle Peninsula represents a fair day's sailing, especially as they had a good start on an easterly breeze. Unfortunately it turned out to be the northern edge of the deep low pressure system that became the Great Gale. The other three ships from the Shannon were the *Barque of Danzig*, which returned safely to Spain, and two unnamed pataches. The pataches cannot be presumed to have been lost in the Great

Gale: pataches on the whole seemed to tolerate heavy weather at sea reasonably well.

It did not calm down until after dark and it was not until the following morning that Aramburu was able to communicate with the *San Juan* of Fernando Horra. It was soon obvious that without its mainmast its position was hopeless and the crew were transferred to the *Bautista* and the patache of Miguel de Aranivar. Recalde would have liked to salvage the guns and save the ship, but that proved to be impossible. It was scuttled and burned; though where its remains ended up is not known. The sound was thoroughly searched in 1968 and no trace of it was found so she probably drifted south into Dingle Bay before sinking.

Two ships were lost in Blasket Sound, victims of the Great Gale, the *Santa Maria de la Rosa* and the *San Juan* of Fernando Horra. The two remaining great ships, the *San Juan of Portugal*, Recalde's ship, and the *San Juan Bautista*, Aramburu's ship, both survived along with the two pataches.

———

In Streedagh Strand, County Sligo
Like the ships in the Shannon, the three ships that were sheltering in Sligo Bay (or more likely Drumcliff Bay) since 15 September had taken advantage of the east wind on Tuesday 20 September to leave their anchorages. According to George Bingham they 'hoisted up sail and put to sea'. He was garrisoned at Ballymote, about 12 miles south of Sligo town, but he had observers out gathering information all along the coast, and at last he seemed to be on the move himself for he was heading towards Tirawley to investigate the report of a ship there. The next day, Wednesday 21 September, he was on the coast and

> ... perceiving that the wind changed contrary for the three ships that put out of the said bay and blew so strong a gale that they were like to be returned to the same road again, he made all the haste he could back to attend the landing of the men in those ships or wreck of the same ... In the meantime the said ships were cast away on the Carbery coast between Sligo and Bundrowse and the spoil thereof and of the men, the wood kerne and churles of the country took before he returned ... 1,000 men drowned in them and 140 of such as came aland and escaped drowning were executed by him.

The three ships were *La Lavia*, *La Juliana* and the *Santa Maria de Visón*. They would have had several hours of a favourable wind, and must have made considerable progress towards the open sea before they were blown back by the gale.

Francisco de Cuéllar's narrative reveals that nothing in the weather they had experienced until then compared with the destructive force of the Great Gale. He wrote:

> … such a great gale arose on our beam, with a sea running as high as heaven that the cables could not take the strain nor the sails serve us, and we were driven ashore with all three ships on a beach of fine sand with great rocks at each end. Many were drowning within the ships; others threw themselves into the sea only to disappear. Such a thing was never seen for in the space of one hour all three ships were broken in pieces, less than 300 escaped and more than 1,000 were drowned.

He describes many harrowing scenes of men trying to save their coins, gold chains and jewellery only to be weighed down and drowned by them. Seventy men found a boat with a covered deck; they jumped in and closed the hatch hoping to reach land safely. Even a boat this size was tumbled in the surf and eventually cast up on shore with its keel upwards so that the men could not get out. It was not righted until two days later; all were dead except one, but he died at that moment.

Cuéllar's escape was extraordinary. He first tried to use a broken piece of the ship, but it was attached to the hull by chains and he could not remove it. Then he found a hatch door about the size of a table, onto which he was just able to cling. A piece of loose timber crushed his legs, but then:

> There came four great waves one after the other, and without knowing how I got there, nor yet being able to swim, I was cast onto the shore where I arrived too weak to stand, covered in blood and grievously injured.

One of the features associated with hurricane force winds is storm surge. Wind-driven surface waves build up until the water can be several feet above its normal level. If the area is close to the low pressure centre, that can add more height to the surge. Deep water against a high vertical cliff dissipates the surge harmlessly, but on a gradually shelving beach waves break into smaller fragments as the pressure of water from below and behind forces them over the beach and, sometimes, far inland. If the bay is concave with rocks at either end the surge is compressed further.

Streedagh Strand supplies these specifications almost exactly, and Cuéllar's description of how he came ashore unwittingly depicts the classic characteristics of storm surge. The four waves following each other in quick succession cast him onto the shore well clear of the water. 'Without knowing how I got there' adds touching bewilderment to his miraculous deliverance. And he even noticed the rocks at each end of the strand.

It was the tumbling action of these storm surge waves that accounted for the swift destruction of three large ships, and for the fact that the wreckage was mostly deposited above the normal high tideline, although the remains of the ships were later found to be about a quarter of a mile beyond low water.

Cuéllar commented that at about nine o'clock at night the wind dropped and the sea became calmer. That he finished the day alive was marvel enough, but the saga of suffering that he endured over the following months is a most remarkable and inspiring tale of personal fortitude.

Thoughts inevitably turn to the enormous human tragedy that took place at Streedagh Strand on 21 September 1588. The Great Gale caused many more deaths, but these seem most poignant perhaps because of Cuéllar's intimate personal involvement.

During November and December the Lord Deputy undertook a journey into the north and came to view the site of the wrecks:

> As I passed from Sligo to Bundrowse I went to see the bay where some of those ships wrecked and myself had viewed as great a store of timber of ships as would have built five of the greatest ships I ever saw, besides mighty great boats, cables and other cordage and some such masts for bigness and length as in mine own judgment I never saw any two could make the like.

This was after nearly two months during which time the local population had been scavenging the wreckage and George Bingham's soldiers had had their share of pillage as well.

THE OTHER LOCATIONS

The dramatic portrayal of hectic scenes in Blasket Sound and on Streedagh Strand is the best evidence we have of the effect of the Great Gale on the whole of the coast. There are a few other brief authentic references, but in some cases all that can be done is to assume that ships which had been sheltering and became wrecks were also victims of it. That is a fairly safe supposition in the circumstances. Rather than regret the lack of complete coverage for every site, we should perhaps be grateful for the very comprehensive picture that can be put together for this fateful day.

Bingham's Report gives a description of the Great Gale from the Irish perspective:

> … there blew a most extreme and cruel storm the like whereof hath not been heard a long time, which put us in very good hope that many of the ships should be beaten up and cast away upon the rocks as it happyly came out afterwards to our expectation.

This was written about a week after the event, and both he and the Council of Connaught were obviously content to attribute the destruction of many Armada ships to the Great Gale without eyewitness corroboration.

In the Harbour of Calebeg

The two ships that accompanied the *Girona* across Donegal Bay on 15 September were destroyed. The information was late coming out as this was a closed area for government forces and was only occasionally penetrated by spies. Their reports make no attempt to supply dates and apparently compress events that took place over three or four weeks:

> Three of the Spanish ships coming into the Harbour of Killibeggs in McSweeny's Country, one of them was cast away a little without the harbour, another running aground on the shore brake to pieces. The third being a galley and sore bruised with the seas was repaired in the said harbour with some planks of the second ship and the planks of a pinnace which they had of McSweeny.

'Cast away without the harbour' and 'running aground on the shore and brake to pieces' certainly implies that the destructive force of the Great Gale was at work. There is a later report that states: 'Their two ships they burned with powder and great shot because they were driven so far upon the rocks and in dead sand within the same that they were never able to bring them forth again'. The *Girona* was also damaged in the gale, but not beyond repair. It has still not been possible to name these other two ships, nor to identify the places where they were wrecked.

In Tirawley

The information about the ship at Tirawley is in a letter from Edward Whyte, secretary to the Council of Connaught. He was a receiver and distributor of news, not an eyewitness. This is the ship that was presumed to be sheltering in Killala Bay, and if it was taken by the Great Gale it would most likely have been wrecked on the sandy shoals in the east of the Bay, but no trace of it has ever been found:

> There is another great ship cast away in Tirawley, 72 of their men are taken by William Burke of Ardnaree, and a Bishop and a Friar and of the said number there are three noblemen and most of the rest of the men in that ship are either slain or drowned, for as it is written to Sir Richard they were so miserably distressed coming to land as one man named Melaghlin McCabb killed 80 with his gallowglas axe.

In Bingham's Report there is reference to one of the Spanish sailors coming ashore as Don Gransilo de Swaso. This name must have been corrupted beyond recognition, because he has never been identified. The ship itself is presumed to have been the *Ciervo Volante* solely by a process of elimination. This report is frustrating; it could have been more informative with just a little care, because George Bingham did visit the area and prisoners were taken.

In Broad Haven

There is a very brief note in Bingham's Report which simply says that 'there was another great ship with 600 men cast away at the Inver, the furthest point of all Erris'. The Inver is in the narrow channel running south from Broad Haven, but no wreck site has ever been identified. There is the possibility that it could have been the *San Nicolas Prodaneli*. The crew, or at least some of them, were alleged to have marched 12 miles to Elly Bay to join with the Duquesa Santa Ana.

In Blacksod Bay

The *Duquesa Santa Ana* and the *Nuestra Señora de Begoña* both survived the Great Gale. The *Duquesa* was able to sail two days later, on 23 September, though her troubles were far from over. Little is known about the *Begoña* except that she was supposed to be at a place called 'Bealingly'. This has never been identified, though it possibly was in the south of the bay near Inishbiggle. She did get away safely for she met the *Zuñiga* at sea around 27 September and reported to them on the grounding of the *Rata* and the plight of Don Alonso de Leyva. Bingham's Report confuses things here. It says that the *Rata* was 'destroyed at Ballycroy and cast away upon the sands', implying that this was the result of the Great Gale. Of course she had already been grounded beyond recovery on the Tullaghan Bar and had been abandoned by de Leyva. The Great Gale no doubt finished her off properly and Bingham's comment that she had 'broken in pieces' was probably accurate if somewhat irrelevant.

In Clew Bay

The *Gran Grin* had been at anchor for four or five days off Faunglas on the southeastern side of Clare Island, and a number of men from her had been on the island the previous day. Bingham's Report simply states that 'the great ship which was at the Isle of Clare was cast away and sunk with 600 men in her'. She was obviously a victim of the Great Gale. It could have dislodged her from her anchorage or broken her cables. But what happened to her then? She could have ended up anywhere to the east of the island, from just outside the harbour to as far away as the islands of the inner bay. No trace of her has ever been found and the vast expanses of Clew Bay makes searching for her look like an impossible task. Bingham's Report is specific about one thing; it says she was 'sunk'. As we shall see, however, accuracy on the subject of Clare Island is not one of the strengths of Bingham's Report, and it might be a mistake to interpret it too precisely. Fenton's List of Ships says 'In Fynglas Omales Country … one shipp', which seems to imply that it was sunk more or less at the harbour.

Bingham's Report goes on to purvey a spurious tale about the fate of the Spanish left on the island after the *Gran Grin* sank:

> Captain Pedro de Mendoza who came aland with 100 of his men the day before thinking to have taken away certain boats belonging to the islanders and go to other ships which lay at anchor about the coast was put to the sword by Dowdrowe Roe O'Malley and his men saving one Spaniard and an Irishman of the County of Wexford.

Another version mentions 68 men. This story has no credibility at all. The day before the Great Gale the *Gran Grin* was still seaworthy and could have gone wherever Captain Mendoza wanted to go. It was several days before a government official came into the area. He turned out to be George Bingham 'the Younger', that is Sir Richard's cousin, not his brother George who was in County Sligo. Let us suppose that the O'Malleys had already taken the remaining Spanish away to safety in Scotland; they had ample time to do that. But they would have to concoct a story to explain why the survivors were missing. Even then this one is very far-fetched, given the well-known traditional friendship between the O'Malleys and Spain.

Young Bingham quizzed them about alleged treasure taken from the Spanish and the ship, but he reported: 'the contrary did appear, neither would they confess any such thing, nor could it be proved against them'. It is fairly certain that he did not go out to Clare Island, but interviewed them on shore. He accepted their statement that the survivors had been killed. Neither he nor Sir Richard was going to acknowledge even the possibility that 100 Spanish soldiers had been spirited away from under their noses. The simple thing for them to do was to believe the O'Malleys' story, and put it in their reports. So that is what has come down to us in the official records.

But we do not have to believe it! If there was any truth in it then where are the Spanish graves on Clare Island? And can anyone imagine 100 Spanish soldiers tamely submitting without putting up a fight and taking a lot of islanders down with them?

The whole of Bingham's Report gives the impression of being carefully sanitized. Nothing even slightly discreditable is allowed to appear in it. We have already seen that it did not conform to the Spanish version of events in Liscannor Bay, County Clare, which makes it all the easier to dismiss this fanciful story.

In County Galway

Two ships were at anchorage in Íar-Chonnacht. The *Falcon Blanco Mediano* was in the Inishbofin/Ballynakill area, and the *Concepcion del Cano* near Mace Head. Both ships can be presumed to have been victims of the Great Gale, but no wreck sites have been discovered, and no authentic reports emerged from either location. In the absence of other evidence local tradition offers possible solutions.

It is suggested that the *Falcon Blanco Mediano* was wrecked on Freaghillaun Island in the entrance to Ballynakill Harbour, perhaps blown across by the Great Gale from an anchorage in the lee of Inishbofin Island. The *Concepcion* was said to have been wrecked on a rocky islet called appropriately Duirling na Spainneach, just off shore from Mace Head, apparently lured there by lights in the time-honoured tradition of coastal wrecking. It is more likely to have been wrecked in the Great Gale, but we really don't know.

There is opportunity for confusion about ships around the entrance to Galway Bay. Reports of two or even three ships close to the Aran Islands seem to have emerged from both County Galway and County Clare, and one or more of them could have gone in either direction. It seems certain, however, that the *San Marcos* and the *San Esteban* chose the County Clare coast so perhaps the *Concepcion* was indeed lured over to Galway.

In County Clare

The galleass *Zuñiga* was in one of the most dangerous positions on the coast. The crew had described it as being highly vulnerable to westerly winds. Galleasses were shown to be susceptible to heavy weather damage throughout the Armada voyage, especially prone to breaking rudder mountings. The anchorage at Coolrone near Liscannor was firm but exposed. It is more than surprising, therefore, that the *Zuñiga* survived the Great Gale. Her position must have offered just enough protection. Probably the direction of the gale had gradually veered towards the northwest as the day progressed, and the Cliffs of Moher had acted as a kind of windbreak deflecting the worst of the gale over the top of them. The *Zuñiga* seemed to suffer very little damage and two days later was ready to sail.

The *San Marcos* and the *San Esteban* were not so lucky. They were defenceless against the Great Gale, and duly succumbed. The *San Marcos* came to grief on rocks between Mutton Island and Lurga Point, obviously having been dislodged from its anchorage further up the coast. The *San Esteban* was lost in the bay at Doonbeg, probably on the White Strand of Doughmore Bay rather than in Doonbeg Bay itself. It is easy to visualize the *San Esteban* suffering the same fate as the ships on a similarly enclosed shelving beach at Streedagh Strand, County Sligo. The tumbling action of storm surge waves driven by hurricane force winds would have destroyed her more or less instantly. Exact sites for these two ships have never been located and it may be that nothing remains of them.

Boetius Clancy's officious activities have overshadowed the history of the Armada in County Clare, and there was one final stroke to come. Sixty-eight men were said to have survived from the *San Esteban*, which is consistent with wreckage being cast up above the high tide line. They were hanged by Clancy on the hill where the Convent School above Milltown Malbay now stands. A variation to this story is whispered locally to the effect that the Spanish were already dead before they were placed on the gallows.

A GREAT CATASTROPHE

Fourteen Spanish ships were lost in the Great Gale of 21 September 1588. The number of men who died cannot have been fewer than 3,500, about 12 per cent of the force of 30,000 that left Spain. This was the day when the Armada suffered its greatest disaster. It was the pivotal point of the entire voyage.

To place it in perspective, the Armada lost only six ships during the fighting in the English Channel, and most of the men were saved. Eight ships were lost on the Irish coast or at sea during the previous ten days, but these were the result of leaks or accidental grounding, and again most of the men were saved. And of course further tragedy awaited them at the end of October. But 21 September was the crux of the catastrophe.

It has been a cliché of Armada history that ships were driven by gales to destruction on the wild Irish coast more or less willynilly as they arrived. That did not happen. They encountered Ireland because of the weather during the period 21 August to 3 September, the unknown effect of ocean currents and the fallibility of sixteenth-century navigation. They mostly found reasonably safe anchorages and the weather was quiet enough to enable them to acquire some supplies of water and food. The weather during August has tended to be overdramatized. Reports were generally written by soldiers to whom every gale seemed to presage Armageddon. Experienced seamen, however, could handle force 8. It kept them busy and they were uncomfortable, but well-found ships routinely survived them, and there is no record of any Armada ships being lost because of weather before they reached Ireland. The gale on 21 September was different. According to Beaufort, force 12 is a hurricane, which he defined as 'that which no canvas can withstand'. The sails hanging in pieces in Blasket Sound are testimony to the fact that the Great Gale was a hurricane.

To some extent they could claim to have been unlucky. It was a unique event, one of those extreme occurrences of which the headlines of history are composed.

RÉSUMÉ

Ships lost as a result of the Great Gale of 21 September 1588

In Blasket Sound	*Santa Maria de la Rosa*
	San Juan of Fernando Horra
On Streedagh Strand	*La Lavia*
	Juliana
	Santa Maria de Visón
In the Harbour of Calebeg	2 unnamed ships
In Tirawley	*Ciervo Volante*?
In Broad Haven	*San Nicholas Prodaneli*
In Clew Bay	*El Gran Grin*
In Íar-Chonnacht	*Falcon Blanco Mediano*
	Concepcion del Cano
On the coast of County Clare	*San Marcos*
	San Esteban
	Total 14 ships

ADDITIONAL SOURCES

'Storm' by A.B.C. Whipple in the *Time-Life* series pp 84–89 gives the basic physical characteristics of the formation and tracking of North Atlantic tropical cyclones.

The journal *Monthly Weather Review*, February 1963, contains a paper entitled 'An Incipient Hurricane near the West African Coast' by C.O. Erickson, which examines the origin and development of Hurricane Debbie in September 1961.

Further information on Hurricane Debbie was from the Internet, which also supplied the 'Mechanics of Storm Surge'.

NOTES AND REFERENCES

It has to be pointed out that there is a discrepancy between Spanish and Irish sources as to the actual date of the Great Gale. The Spanish references are from Aramburu's diary and indicate that it was on Wednesday 21 September. Some references in the Irish State Papers, including Bingham's Report, give it as Tuesday 20 September. Aramburu's date is preferred for the following reasons. Being from a diary it is part of a continuous sequence of dated contemporary records. Bingham's Report was written about a week after the event by Edward Whyte, probably in Athlone or Galway. Finally, there is one record from an Irish source which conclusively discredits Tuesday 20 September. It is a letter by Nicholas Cahan written in Kilrush, County Clare on Thursday 22 September, in which he states that 'those ships that were here (i.e. on the Shannon) went forth a Tuesday'—CSPI p. 38. This is an eyewitness observation. Nothing could be more certain than that six ships did not go out from the Shannon into the teeth of a ferocious westerly gale. It was a day's sailing to Blasket Sound and that is where three of them appeared next day at the height of the Great Gale, recorded by Aramburu under 21 September.

Apart from the account in Aramburu's diary, further details about the sinking of the *Santa Maria de la Rosa* and the location of the anchors in Blasket Sound are in Colin Martin's book *Full Fathom Five* pp 40–97. This also describes the amazing underwater research expedition of 1968 led by Sydney Wignall, in which Colin Martin took part.

At one stage there were three ships in Blasket Sound all named *San Juan*. To distinguish them Recalde's ship is referred to as *San Juan of Portugal*, Aramburu's as the *San Juan Bautista* or simply the *Bautista*, and the third was the *San Juan* of Fernando Horra.

Streedagh Strand—The confirmation of the ships leaving the Drumcliff Bay anchorage, and the weather conditions in Donegal Bay on 20 and 21 September are in Bingham's Report in a communication from George Bingham. The names of the three ships were not revealed for certain until 1985 when, as a result of an extensive underwater investigation by the Streedagh Strand Armada Group led by Stephen Birch, it became known that they were *La Lavia, Juliana* and *Santa Maria de Visón*. (The *Santa Maria de Visón* is frequently transcribed as *S M de la Vision*. Sixteenth-century documents from Simancas confirm, however, that it is correctly *de Visón*, which seems to mean a mink or other small rodent. Her home port was Ragusa in Croatia. The unusual use of an animal name for Armada ships occurs again in de Leyva's vessel—*La Rata Encoronada*, literally 'the Crowned Rat'.)

An interim report was published in the *International Journal of Nautical Archaeology*, 1999, 28.3, 265–276. Very little of the material discovered has been removed from the wreck sites apart from three large bronze guns plus a small falcon, which are now in the care of the Office of Public Works depot in Dromahair. Ownership of the wrecks was taken over by the Irish Government, which effectively brought further investigation to a halt. Potentially there is a great deal more information still to be brought to light.

Francisco de Cuéllar's narrative was published in Spanish in Duro, *La Armada Invencible* 1884–1885. Since then several translations have appeared. The one most often used in this chapter is by Frances Partridge, which was included in Evelyn Hardy's book *Survivors of the Armada* (London, 1966). The Lord Deputy's visit to Streedagh is in CSPI p. 93.

The wreck of the two ships in Calebeg is in CSPI p. 55, a letter from William Taafe to Secretary Fenton and George Bingham dated 20 October, and also p. 64 'advertisements from Henry Duke'. These were reports of stories related by spies, not eyewitness accounts.

The ship at Tirawley and the one in Broad Haven are in Bingham's Report.

The meeting at sea of the *N.S. de Begoña* and the *Zuñiga* is in Hume p. 458.

For Clew Bay see Bingham's Report and Fenton's List of Ships. Bingham's Report is the sole source of information on the killing of the Spanish on Clare Island, and even there it reads very unconvincingly.

For local traditions surrounding the ships in Íar-Chonnacht see Niall Fallon's book *The Armada in Ireland* pp 36–42.

The *Zuñiga's* departure from Liscannor is in Hume p. 462.

The *San Marcos* and the *San Esteban* are referred to without being named in Nicholas Cahan's letter of 22 September—CSPI p. 38. They were first identified by W. Spotswood Green in *The Geographical Journal*, May 1906, 'The Wrecks of the Spanish Armada on the Coast of Ireland'.

Chapter 5 ❧

22 TO 28 SEPTEMBER AFTERMATH AND DEPARTURE

… as many of the Spanish fleet as escaped shipwreck are gone to sea and clean departed.

(BINGHAM'S REPORT)

ALL THE CHAOS …

Thursday morning 22 September was calm but chaotic, a bit like the morning after an air raid. Fourteen ships were lost in the Great Gale and a further eight had been destroyed before 21 September. There were now very few left. There were four in Blasket Sound—the *San Juan of Portugal*, the *San Juan Bautista* and two pataches (the crippled *San Juan* of Fernando Horra was still afloat, but was about to be abandoned). The *Zuñiga* was still at Liscannor. In Blacksod Bay there were two—the *Duquesa Santa Ana* and the *Nuestra Señora de Begoña*—and the *Girona* was the only surviving ship from at least seven that had been in the inner part of Donegal Bay. We have to presume that the hospital ship *San Pedro el Mayor* was somewhere on the coast at the same time.

The weather during the following seven days was extremely variable. It was in most cases unhelpful for ships wishing to leave Ireland and set sail for Spain. On Thursday 22 and Friday 23 September there was a mixture of calms and fitful breezes of short duration and usually from the southeast. A ridge of high pressure followed the Great Gale, but it began to break down overnight on 23/24 September, when a stronger wind came up from the southeast. On the morning of the 24th a quickly moving front passed over the ships from southwest to northeast giving strong, southeasterly winds and rain for just two hours. As it passed the wind veered to the west and moderated slowly during the rest of the day. On the 25th, 26th and 27th there was a settled period when the wind stayed in the quarter southwest to southeast.

Wednesday 28 September was a rough day; strong southerly winds during daylight hours built up to a full gale and veered gradually to the west and then the northwest. Overnight 28/29 September the wind increased to storm force for a time, strong enough to rip Aramburu's fore mainsail to pieces and hardly less damaging than the Great Gale had been the week before. The next three days, 30 September and 1 and 2 October, winds stayed at northwest and north, cold with squally showers, which did assist ships still able to head south. Getting away from the Irish coast was not going to be an easy task.

———

In Blasket Sound

First priority on the morning of 22 September was to attend to the *San Juan* of Fernando Horra. He launched his chalup and sent a small party over to Recalde and Aramburu to see if they could help him. Aramburu commented that 'it was obvious his situation was hopeless'. All the ships were low on resources both for the relief of the men and for repairs to the vessel. The best thing they could do would be to return to Spain as quickly as possible. The men had to be transferred, and the company of Gonzalo Melendez was taken on board the *Bautista*. The remainder of the soldiers from Don Diego Bazan's company were divided between the two pataches. It is typical of the sense of priority in the Armada that only the companies of soldiers seem to be worth a mention. The sailors from Fernando Horra's ship were probably taken by Recalde as he had been losing men to sickness at a rate of four or five a day,

Recalde's devotion to duty compelled him to try and save the ship. When that proved impossible he sought to recover some of the guns and munitions. But the reality was that the men and the equipment were in such poor condition that virtually nothing could be done.

Aramburu was agitated about his shortage of supplies. It seems Recalde had shared some of his bread and fresh water with him, but now he had extra mouths to feed and he was afraid they would soon be used up in the long voyage ahead. He said, 'I wanted him to set fire to the ship and allow us to sail away'. Recalde hesitated, but eventually Aramburu was able to write, 'he publicly gave me permission to make my way back to Spain'. 'Permission' was important; Aramburu did not want to expose himself to later accusations of abandoning the senior admiral of the Armada. No doubt preparing to leave took some time, because he still spent the night of 22nd/23rd in Blasket Sound.

Aramburu set sail on the morning of 23 September on a light easterly breeze. As we have seen the weather was going to make this a frustrating day with only light fitful breezes or flat calms. He wrote 'as we left harbour we had hardly gone two cable lengths when the wind fell calm and the current began to drive us onto the island'. A cable as an expression of distance was 100 fathoms or 600 feet, so they must have gone no more than 400 yards. The 'island' meant Great Blasket. The whole day was spent dealing with calm conditions made dangerous by tidal currents, and by nightfall he was no further than the rocky islets around Begenish. He put out his only anchor and stopped, hoping for a breath of wind next morning.

Aramburu experienced more than his share of Murphy's Law, however, and an hour after dark the wind began to freshen from the southeast, strong enough to start the ship dragging towards the small islands. That way lay certain disaster and the only option left was to try to sail out of trouble. As the ship swung on its anchor they raised it and, as he said, 'we set sail commending ourselves to the Lord'. The seamen on the *Bautista* did a great job, since it was not just a case of shutting their eyes and hoping, as Aramburu implied. They had to make at least two attempts to find a way out in the dark, with the wind freshening all the time and a sea beginning to run. It was all too much for him and he seemed unable to follow what was going on. According to him their survival was 'thanks to our Lady in whom we placed our trust', but it is time now to give credit to the skill of the Spanish sailors who must have had a busy night.

Once clear of the maze of islands round the north of Great Blasket they had a good wind for heading west, and by dawn on 24 September they reckoned they were eight leagues out to sea, say about 25 miles. If that was right they should have been over the horizon, perhaps just able to see the top of Mount Eagle. Three hours after dawn a weather front passed over them producing two hours of rain and a strong wind from the southeast. As the rain cleared the wind veered westerly and moderated only slowly. They decided to feather their sails and lay to, which looks like a mistake; surely they could have made some headway due south. The strong westerly kept moving them back towards the land. There must have been low cloud and sea mist, because they do not appear to have seen it. At dawn on the morning of 25 September they had flat calm again and were just three leagues from Great Blasket, having made no progress at all in two days. The Irish coast seemed to exercise a magnetic attraction for Aramburu; this was the third time he had been drawn in towards it. There was no mention of Recalde and the two pataches so they can be presumed to have left by then.

The only description we have of the departure of Recalde and the fate of the *San Juan* of Fernando Horra is in a report produced at the beginning of November by Sir Henry Wallop. He said:

A ship of 400 tons that did lie at the Sound of Blaskey within five miles of Dingle Cush after all the men and chief substance was taken out of her, was sunk near that place by John Martinez de Ricalde, Admiral of the Biscay fleet when he departed from there about 22 or 23 September 1588, which ship had floated near the shore and had certain things taken out of her by men of the Dinglecush before she sunk.

A garrison comprising mostly English settlers was at Dingle town, actually about 10 miles away, and they kept a continuous watch over the Spanish activities. Being 'sunk' implies that she was scuttled probably by blowing one or more holes in her with powder and shot, rather than simply set on fire as Aramburu suggested. Wooden hulls were not easy to sink, and, although the ship was doomed, she lasted long enough to drift over towards the shore and for local people to get some plunder from her. Before sinking she must have stayed afloat and drifted south in the strong current into Dingle Bay, because no trace of her has ever been found, even though the whole of the Sound was thoroughly searched by diving teams looking for the *Santa Maria de la Rosa* in 1968.

We do not know how Recalde left the Sound. It appears that it was 23 September, the same day as Aramburu, and he would have faced the same problems posed by calms and tidal currents. But he was a Master Mariner and he would have found a way; possibly using the tidal currents he could have sailed south between Great Blasket and Dunmore Head. He arrived in Spain on 7 October at La Coruña in Galicia, one of very few to reach the prescribed destination. This was a full week before Aramburu came into Santander. But let us not be too hard on Aramburu. He was not an experienced seaman. He was a 'contador', a paymaster, an administrator, an accountant, excruciatingly conscientious doing his best to lead his men home. And we must not omit to thank him for his diary, which makes a priceless contribution to our knowledge of the Armada's Atlantic episode.

Recalde's energy was spent. Three days after his arrival in Spain he died, aged 62.

The galleass *Zuñiga*

The fact that the *Zuñiga* survived the Great Gale is one of the most remarkable incidents of this turbulent week. It does not even appear to have been damaged. There must have been a kind of footprint of quiet air behind the Cliffs of Moher such that the harder it blew the larger the area of safety became. It would make a good subject for an aerodynamicist to explain. We might possibly learn the exact wind direction necessary to create these freak conditions.

The most reliable source of information about the *Zuñiga* is from Juan de Saavedra, the captain of one of the companies of soldiers. He said that the last day they were in Ireland was 22 September, and we can take it therefore that they put to sea on Friday 23 September. This was a day of calms and only an occasional breeze, but the *Zuñiga* being a galleass was able to use its oars to get clear of the coast. This was another stroke of luck for her: what they feared most was a wind from the west or southwest. The only comment he made about damage was to say that they had been able to 'remedy the accident to the rudder and other necessary things'. We know that the accident to the rudder had happened before they arrived in Ireland, so this confirms that they suffered no damage on 21 September. Remarkable!

De Saavedra explains that they were hit by the gale of 28/29 September when they were in latitude 50°N at the entrance to the English Channel, and that they were driven out of their course. Other ships had the same experience. But the following two or three days there were reasonably moderate winds from the northwest, which should have enabled them to resume their voyage to Spain.

Aramburu had suffered the same conditions:

> … such a great gale blew up from NW, with such violent seas and rain that our fore mainsail ripped to pieces; nothing was left of it. We lowered the mainsail, but were not able to take it in, and the ship began to roll badly … we were engulfed by three huge waves, which hit us amidships and we thought we were lost. We attached a boneta to the shrouds of the foremast and commended ourselves to God. With that the ship began to handle reasonably well and we managed that way until the following morning.

On 29 September he was able to sail southwards. They fixed up an old fore mainsail and by nightfall the wind was light. For the next two days they had repairs to carry out and a new topmast had to be fitted, but they maintained southerly headings. On 1 October the Bautista was at 48° 15′N, just south of Ushant.

The question is why could the *Zuñiga* not do the same? She had been driven off course by the gale, but that had lasted only a day and a half and there appears to have been no need to go as far up the Channel as she did. De Saavedra's story was that when they were sighted by French sailors they were told that the governor of the port of Le Havre had given orders for Spanish ships and men to be well treated, as France was at peace with King Philip.

'Being powerless to do otherwise we entered this port'.

There was a Spanish representative in Le Havre. Pedro de Igueldo was purser on the *Santa Ana*, which left the Armada in the Channel before it even got as far as Calais. In port it was attacked and disabled by an English raiding party, and was never able to leave. Igueldo was an officious administrator (another contador) and took over responsibility for the *Zuñiga*, overriding the authority of the existing captains. De Saavedra and Avendaño and most of the soldiers did not take kindly to Igueldo's interference. They were accused of being disorderly and insubordinate, probably with justification. Perhaps they regretted accepting the governor of Le Havre's invitation.

Making the *Zuñiga* seaworthy again was a long, slow business. On 15 April 1589 she left Le Havre but was severely damaged again by another gale. She could be saved only by throwing nearly everything overboard, including twelve guns, ammunition, anchors and chains, and thirty oars (much to the gratification of the convicts). She spent a further week floundering in the Channel, but on 27 April was back in Le Havre once more. Repairs made her ready to sail again on 6 June. This time the problem was that the governor of the port had placed a defensive boom across the entrance, causing it to silt up. It had to be dredged, and even then the *Zuñiga* would have to wait for the next spring tide to provide enough water to clear the entrance. In the middle of July the signs were right and she was all set to go, but at this point she dropped out of the record, and we are not told about her actual departure. It is presumed that she did eventually return to Spain.

—

The *Duquesa Santa Ana*

In Blacksod Bay the stranded *Rata Encoronada* had been reduced to a shattered wreck by the Great Gale on 21 September. If there had ever been any hope that it could be refloated and used again by Don Alonso de Leyva that was now gone. His party was camped ashore around Fahy Castle at Doona near Ballycroy, in danger of being left without means of escape. The 22nd of September was a calm day and there appears to have been a lot of small boat activity around the wreck. Richard Burke and Thomas Burke are mentioned along with James Blake and others, and they took boatloads of plunder out of her.

De Leyva was concerned to save his men, and his hope for them was to join forces with the *Duquesa Santa Ana* anchored 10 miles away at Elly Bay in the northern arm of Blacksod Bay. They still had their own cockboat, but they would need more than that, and we can imagine that de Leyva would have negotiated for the use of local boats. How it was done so quickly is not clear, but by that evening all his party was established at the castle of Tiraun on the Mullet Peninsula overlooking the Atlantic Ocean, only a mile from Elly Bay. Some of the crew of the *Duquesa* were in Elly Castle on the eastern edge of the peninsula. Reports of the numbers involved look to be inflated. According to Bingham's Report there were 600 in de Leyva's party and 800 on the *Duquesa*, which may have included survivors from the ship wrecked at Inver. A more realistic estimate would be about 250 on the *Duquesa* and 400 from the *Rata*, and if the ship at Inver was the *San Nicolas Prodaneli* another 200 or so might have joined the *Duquesa*, making a maximum of 850.

On 23 September Gerald Comerford, one of Bingham's commissioners entitled to claim that he represented the Queen, appeared somewhere in the area with a group of about 50 men. He reported to Bingham in a letter dated 23 September:

> I have stayed within view of the ship that was here at Pollilly by Torrane before I saw both the company of the said ship and the ship that is here joined together and entered into one ship, and this present morning took the sea bag and baggage towards the southwest.

Although this claims to be an eyewitness account, it is not clear where he was when he observed all these activities. It would be easier to accept if Comerford had not used the words 'within view'. Pollilly is Elly Bay. In the same letter he complains about people looting the wreck of the *Rata* and ignoring him when he hailed them. This implies that he was on the shore around Ballycroy. Elly Bay is not visible from there. He could hardly have covered the distance around the land route through Belmullet, and a position on the Doohooma peninsula would have been nearly as difficult. A possible explanation could be that the *Duquesa* left its anchorage in Elly Bay, came round to Doona, and embarked the crew of the *Rata*. If Comerford was somewhere near Ballycroy he might possibly have observed all that. But then it hardly squares with his claim to be 'within view of Pollilly by Torrane'. While there is always reluctance to cast doubt on what should be a highly valuable first-hand account there is a problem to connect it with the difficult terrain in this part of County Mayo. We have, however, no alternative than to go along with it. Letters written even a few hours after the events they describe can be subject to vagaries of memory.

Events seemed to move with remarkable haste. Within 24 hours of the Great Gale de Leyva's whole company was at Tiraun on the Mullet, and the next morning, 23 September, he together with all the men had set sail on the *Duquesa Santa Ana* and headed out of Blacksod Bay towards the southwest.

The presence of Comerford's party may have hurried them up, but de Leyva was a man of action with a great capacity for organization. When he appeared anywhere, things happened.

Comerford had little else to do now. As he said himself all the salvage had already been taken by the local people, much to his disgust. Near the end of his letter to Sir Richard Bingham he almost throws away two very important observations. With the departure of the *Duquesa* he is congratulating himself and says '… this part of the coast is clear and no ship here remaining'. Then as an afterthought he added 'saving one that hath no cockboat at Bealingly and they can put no man ashore'. This was the *Nuestra Señora de Begoña*. It must have left later that day or early the next for the *Begoña* met the *Zuñiga* at sea about the 27th at the mouth of the English Channel and passed on the news of the loss of the *Rata*. We do not know for certain where Bealingly was, although it has been presumed to be near Inishbiggle in the south of the bay. It is a bit of a mystery why de Leyva went to such lengths to transfer everyone to the *Duquesa* if the *Begoña* was available at the same time. The *Begoña*'s crew knew about the *Rata*; surely the *Rata*'s crew also knew about the *Begoña*. She was a substantial ship, an Indian Guard Merchantman of 750 tons, and she made it successfully back to Galicia. At least some of the men from the *Rata* could have been saved.

The other significant comment at the end of Comerford's letter was to say, 'I hope your worship by this time is upon the road near at hand, and if you be it were not amiss that you should make towards Inver in Irris, where there is a ship cast away and all the goods saved'. This has been taken to be the *San Nicolas Prodaneli*, some men from which were now on board the *Duquesa*, so the ship had effectively been abandoned. Bingham was not 'near at hand' and had been conspicuously tardy in coming any further into County Mayo than near Castlebar. Comerford had penetrated deeper into Burke territory than any of the rest of the English garrison, and he had announced his intention to go on as far as Tirawley. The ship at Inver in the south of Broad Haven appears never to have been visited by any garrison troops. Why did Comerford not go to Inver himself, since he was nearer than anybody?

On the evening of 23 September it would have been sobering to reflect that the only Armada ships remaining on the Irish coast were the *Girona* in Donegal Bay and the *San Pedro el Mayor* somewhere in the same area. The rest had come and gone or been destroyed in just thirteen days between 11 and 23 September. The importance of this was understood by Sir Richard Bingham and included in his end of the month report '… as many of the Spanish fleet as escaped shipwreck are gone to sea and clean departed, and no further cause of any doubt of their invasions to be feared at this time'. News of the arrival of the Spanish in Ireland hardly had time to be absorbed by the Privy Council in London before they were gone again. There was more drama still to come, however.

The calms and light breezes on 23 September caused problems for the *Duquesa*. Always aware of the dangers of a lee shore, and finding themselves still within sight of the Mullet, Inishkea, Inishglora and numerous other off-shore islands that night they fired several shots as distress signals. Comerford reported that 'in all men's opinions the ship was sunk in that instant'. There was no one to help them, but it will be remembered that down the coast an hour after dark the wind began to freshen from the southeast, which saved the *Duquesa* and she was at last able to make some sea room. According to one of the men interviewed later it was their intention to head for Spain but, although she was attached to the Andalusian Squadron, the *Duquesa* was a hulk and had all the disadvantages of their inherent inability to sail close to the wind. Over the following four days the wind was at first southerly strong, then westerly strong, and finally there were two days when it settled constantly between southeast and southwest. The outcome was that on 27 September she was sighted again at the entrance to Blacksod Bay having made no progress in any direction. Bingham, probably on Comerford's advice, appreciated de Leyva's predicament and advertised to the Lord Deputy:

> ... by all likelihood he is cast away, for the wind fell contrary immediately after they put to sea and became very stormy and foul weather as not possible he could escape except his ship were most strong and good for he was marvellously pestered with such numbers of men.

At this point de Leyva must have taken the decision to head for Scotland. The weather seemed like an impenetrable barrier, and the problem of an overloaded ship that was leaking badly and was short of supplies left him with little choice. For the rest of that day the southerly wind helped them, and they made good headway round Erris Head and across the entrance to Donegal Bay.

Fate was apparently determined to balk all their best efforts, however, and on 28 September the ferocious weather that had damaged the *Zuñiga* and the *Bautista* reached the Donegal coast. The southerly wind blew up into a full gale, veered to the west and then overnight on 28/29 to northwest and increased to storm force. The *Duquesa* was on a lee shore and it became a question only of where she would be driven onto the land. There are 10 miles of rocky cliffs in southwest Donegal from Slieve League round to Loughros Bay. A ship crashing into any one of them might never be seen again. Whether it was by good seamanship or just good luck the *Duquesa* found itself in Loughros More Bay, the larger entrance to the north of Loughros Point.

An Irishman named James Machary was on the *Duquesa*. He claimed he had been pressed by Spanish soldiers at Lisbon and made to join the Armada by force. His account of the grounding of the *Duquesa* was given before the Lord Deputy during his tour of the north at the end of December, and is the best information we have. He said:

> … they made sail for Spain, in which course, by a contrary wind they were driven back upon McSweeney Na Doe's country to a place called Lougherris, where falling to anchor, there fell a great storm, which break in sunder all their cables and struck them upon ground, whereby Don Alonso and all his company were enforced to go on shore, taking all their goods and armour with them, and there by the ship's side encamped themselves for the space of eight or nine days. Don Alonso before he came to land was hurt in the leg by the capstan of the ship in such sort as he was neither able to go (walk) or ride, neither during the nine days of his encamping, nor upon his remove, but was carried from place to place.

Some further scraps of information are supplied by two men from the *Trinidad Valencera*, Juan de Nova and Francisco Borja, who met a sailor from de Leyva's party in Scotland—(a lucky survivor from the *Girona*). They said that after the anchor cables broke they 'managed to get another cable ashore and make it fast to a rock'. If all this was done in a gale it was great work.

It is quite hard to visualize exactly what happened here. Machary's statement suggests that the *Duquesa* had successfully anchored for a period before the cables broke and that she then grounded during the height of the storm. While she was grounded, perhaps at low tide, some intrepid sailors swam ashore and made another cable fast to a rock. When the tide rose again and the ship refloated, it was held securely and, using the capstan, could even have been kedged into a suitable location where it could be beached safely. Tidal currents no doubt also played a part. This may have been when de Leyva injured his leg. With over eight hundred men on the ship it might be supposed that there was no reason why he should be taking on menial tasks, but in an emergency some leaders like to work in with the men. Most of the time the men want leaders out of the way, but occasionally their help is appreciated. De Leyva was quietly spoken but had a commanding presence and he was popular with his men. Whatever the exact method used, the *Duquesa* seems to have had the good luck to beach where all the crew could land safely, yet at the same time the ship was still protected from destructive wave action. There is no record of anyone losing his life at this stage. The location was Tramore Beach, a huge sandy area just east of the village of Rossbeg on the north shore of Loughros More Bay, and the date was 29 September.

We have to keep reminding ourselves of the size of de Leyva's party and the logistical problems involved in providing basic needs for them. Bingham's perceptive observation that 'he was marvellously pestered with such numbers of men' underlines that they were a burden. According to James Machary he was in a group of ordinary seamen and soldiers 'encamped at the ship's side'. Behind the sandhills about half a mile away is a long narrow lake known as Kiltooris Lough, in which there is a sizeable island. De Leyva organized a second camp on the island for the young noblemen and the senior officers under his charge. This camp was fortified; a gun was transferred from the ship and mounted on the island. The gun, an iron falcon, was still there in 1968 when Robert Sténuit found it while researching the Armada in Donegal. The carriage had rotted away and the gun was well rusted but unbelievably still there after 380 years. The ship itself would have been a source of materials to create shelter and supply food, and they were probably able to exist in passable comfort for a short time. But 850 men in camp around Rossbeg must have looked like a small town.

De Leyva seemed to go from one stroke of ill luck to another in quick succession in Ireland. The one piece of good luck for him was to be shipwrecked in McSweeny Na Doe's country to the north and west of Ardara. This was one of very few places where he could be assured of welcome and assistance. McSweeny Na Doe's actions display a rare quality of human kindness. He personally had nothing to gain in helping the Spanish, nor was he much interested in international politics. They were just people who needed help and he supplied it.

De Leyva's party included an Irish monk called Father James Ne Dowrough and it was through him that de Leyva communicated with McSweeny. According to James Machary they were camped on Tramore Beach for eight or nine days, and at the start it may have taken a few days for them to meet and establish a trusting relationship. The news that another Spanish ship, the *Girona*, was anchored barely 20 miles away must have come as a bombshell, and encouraged de Leyva to believe that his luck had really turned at last. Preparations would have begun at once to take all of his people down to the Harbour of Calebeg. The chieftain of that area was another member of the McSweeny family, McSweeny Banagh, whose castle was at the head of McSwyne's bay. He was young and inexperienced. McSweeny Na Doe appears to have accompanied de Leyva on the trek, and taken on the responsibility of working with him at Calebeg. Correspondence in the State Papers often refers to him rather than to McSweeny Banagh or sometimes to 'the McSweenys'. During the Lord Deputy's journey into the North in November and

December he ordered the Irish chieftains to come to meet him as a gesture of submission. McSweeny Banagh duly submitted and Fitzwilliam described him as 'a young man dutifully affected to the State'. McSweeny Na Doe steadfastly refused to submit at that time, which is hardly surprising considering that he had done all in his power to help the Spanish.

Twenty miles was an awkward distance in those days. The terrain was none too kind either, with a mountain pass to be negotiated. The aim would be to cover it all in one day, which the fit and able could well do. There were bound to be a number of sick and weak individuals for whom it would be a two-day march. The problem of an overnight stop in the open at the beginning of October would have to be endured. De Leyva himself was still unable to walk and had to be carried on a litter. The young noblemen would be having a miserable time. It can be imagined that some of them would have been spoiled 'rich kids' whose vision of the Armada as a path to glory had long been dashed. Yomping over wild Donegal mountainsides was not the experience they had in mind when leaving Spain.

They must have left the Rossbeg area about 8 or 9 October. The first sight of the *Girona* lying at anchor in McSwyne's Bay as the leading group were arriving in Calebeg cannot have failed to lift their spirits. Coming closer they must have been aghast at the numbers of men already camped there, at least as many as they were themselves, being the crews of two ships already destroyed together with the men from the *Girona* including the rowers. And how was the *Girona*? 'Sore bruised with the seas' we are told and probably a bit of a mess. De Leyva's mind would already be working. Plans for her repair and restoration would even now be taking shape. Could they allow themselves to hope?

Apart from small groups mostly in the far north, the Spanish remaining in Ireland were now, in the middle of October, concentrated in one place—the McSwyne's Bay area on the south coast of County Donegal. There were probably about 1,500 men, the crews of six ships, although allowance has to be made for the fact that some would already have set off overland.

NOTES AND REFERENCES

The information about the weather during the week following the Great Gale is based on Aramburu's observations. They are interpreted in the Climatic Research Unit's Paper NO. 6.

Aramburu's diary is the reference for almost all the events in Blasket Sound on 22 and 23 September, the exception being the information relating to the fate of the *San Juan* of Fernando Horra. This is in Sir Henry Wallop's report to Walsyngham of 17 November together with enclosures in CSPI pp 71 and 72 and on MIC 223/52 NO. 55. He was obviously not an eyewitness and there is a certain amount of propaganda in his discourse in that he was apparently trying to discredit the Lord Deputy, but this is all the information we have.

There are three documents in Hume pp 456–462 dealing with the arrival of the *Zuñiga* in Le Havre. Juan de Saavedra's is the one used here. The other two are composite accounts compiled by interviewing unnamed members of the crew in Le Havre. They contain so many mistakes that they are probably best ignored. Igueldo's has the reference to the meeting at sea of the *Zuñiga* and the *N.S. de Begoña*. The events relating to the *Zuñiga* in 1589 are told by Igueldo in Hume pp 534–535 and later on p. 547.

In Blacksod Bay the eyewitness account of the transfer of men from the *Rata* to the *Duquesa* is in Comerford's letter to Bingham dated 23 September, calendared in CSPI pp 41–42 and on MIC 223/51 NO. 173. The confirmation that the *Duquesa* began by heading for Spain is in James Machary's examination in CSPI pp 98–99. The return of the *Duquesa* to the Mullet is in Bingham's Report where he says that they left again almost immediately. Bingham's choice comment about De Leyva being 'marvellously pestered with such numbers of men' is in CSPI pp 48–49.

James Machary's account of the grounding of the *Duquesa* in Loughros More Bay is in CSPI pp 98–99. The report about the attaching of another cable to a rock is in Hume p. 509. Reference to de Leyva's camp in Kiltooris Lough is in Hume p. 510. The finding of the gun is in Robert Sténuit's book *Treasures of the Armada* p. 120.

The quotation about the *Girona* being 'sore bruised with the seas' is in CSPI p. 64.

The Lord Deputy's journey into the North is in CSPI pp 92–98.

Chapter 6 ❧

| THE *GIRONA*

... the said galley departed with as many of the Spaniards as she could carry towards the Out Isles of Scotland ...

THE PERCEPTION OF A SPANISH THREAT

The flow of information from County Donegal was very different from the situation in Blacksod Bay, County Mayo. In Mayo Gerald Comerford had been able to place himself 'within view' of the centre of the action, and provide us with an eyewitness account (albeit one that still left some questions unanswered). In County Donegal there were no English garrison forces in sight. The only Englishmen nearby were George Bingham and Geoffrey Fenton; they were in County Sligo and the nearest they came to the action was when they descended on survivors from the Streedagh wrecks and killed about 140 of them as they lay defenceless on the beach. They were about 50 miles from McSwyne's Bay where the *Girona* and two other ships had been since 15 September, and they stayed there. Sir Richard Bingham remained in Athlone and showed no interest in leaving it. Donegal was in Ulster and his jurisdiction was Connaught. If the Lord Deputy brought a force into the north he would be glad to assist, but he did not have the means to confront what were rumoured to be 2,000 Spanish and several strong Irish communities such as the McSweenys, O'Donnell, O'Boyle, O'Neill, O'Rourke and McClancy. And so they confined themselves to sending so-called spies into the area. George Bingham wrote, 'I do not spare my purse in plying of spies'.

Reports from these 'spies' and their interpretation were a source of much misguided agitation in the English companies. Their subsequent correspondence forms the main part of the record preserved in the Irish State Papers for this period about the end of September and the beginning of October, and it is almost all misleading. It began when news came back that de Leyva and McSweeny Na Doe had marched 20 miles from Rossbeg to Calebeg. This came across as an aggressive manoeuvre. Lack of knowledge of the geography of south Donegal led to it being inferred to mean a march from

Calebeg towards Donegal town. In no time at all it had been blown up to become: 'the Spaniards are eight miles from the Erne' and 'the Spaniards will be in County Sligo within these five days'.

The presence of a large number of Spanish also caused excitement among the Irish population. Sir Brian O'Rourke in County Leitrim was always on the edge of rebellion, and he wrote to the Spanish camp, although there is no indication that they received a letter or responded to one. George Bingham's house in Ballymote was burned down by men from the local septs of Connors, O'Harts and O'Dowds. There was deep insecurity among the English garrisons because they knew they were resented by the Irish, especially in the north. What they feared and what the Irish hoped for was that the Spanish would take part in an uprising against English occupation, what they called a 'combination', in other words a conspiracy. When George Bingham reported the burning of his house he also wrote, 'I am persuaded that they durst not attempt such a matter without great combination'. Another correspondent declared, '... the Irishry are grown very proud and I fear will join with the Spanish'. Rumour feeds on itself and distorts intelligent judgment. But the English were massively outnumbered, and those in the front line were acutely conscious of their basic weakness.

Sir Richard Bingham, writing in Athlone and removed from the contaminating influence of panic and insecurity, could afford the luxury of clear thinking. The crucial factor in all this was the attitude of the Spanish. He gave his opinion to the Lord Deputy: '... of themselves they are marvellous weak and most miserable creatures, and able to do little unless all the North do join them, which is to be doubted greatly that they will'. The Spanish were not fit for any such undertaking. They were not interested in Irish politics, either regarding English occupation or inter-tribal rivalries. They had only one thought: to get home safely as quickly as possible.

There was a lot of psychology at work here, with English fears and Irish hopes distracting most people from the realities. Although this in itself was part of the history of the time, it makes it more difficult to discern what was actually happening. What we want to know from the spies are details of the Spanish camp, news of de Leyva's leg injury, the work on the *Girona* etc. Instead we are left with scraps of information when there should be several comprehensive descriptions. It would be easy to blame the spies for sloppy reporting, but the fault is more likely to be with the members of the English garrison, who were fixated by a non-existent impending rebellion, and who have probably thrown away priceless insights into the Spanish preparations.

If de Leyva had time to consider it he may have wondered where the English garrison forces were. The Spanish camp at Calebeg had been there for at least 25 days before he and McSweeny Ne Doe arrived. He was in camp for a further 16 days, so if the English were going to attack them, they had 41 days in which to do it. Yet there was no sign of them either on land or on sea. There is little enough amusement to be had from these momentous events, but it would surely have allowed de Leyva at least a smile to think that English soldiers were virtually cowering in Sligo Castle, not only afraid to approach within 50 miles of him, but also having worked themselves up into a panic, convinced that the Spanish were coming to get them. In fact de Leyva was expecting to be attacked, 'having been advertised certainly from time to time that the Lord Deputy Fitzwilliam was preparing himself to come against them'. The Lord Deputy's journey into the north would not begin until the middle of November.

––––

IN THE SPANISH CAMP AT THE HARBOUR OF CALEBEG

A letter dated 29 October from John Crofton and others to Sir Richard Bingham looks like the report of some of the spies. They appear to have been merchants with business in Sir Brian O'Rourke's Country. Merchants have always been ideal for combining espionage with commerce; all they have to do is keep their eyes and ears open. They had met 'Dermot McRory McDermot who, being demanded news of the Spanish, declared that there were 3,500 of them, who were fortifying themselves very strongly in McSweeny Ne Doe's town betwixt the castle and the church. All their ships saving one, being broken and past use after they had unladed them, were set on fire and burnt'.

It is interesting that the Harbour of Calebeg is referred to as McSweeny Ne Doe's town. This must be a reflection of the fact that he was giving the orders, although they were actually in McSweeny Banagh's Country. The key information in this report is the position of the Spanish camp—'betwixt the castle and the church'. This places it on the St John's peninsula. McSweeny's castle is at the head of McSwyne's Bay, and about two miles down the peninsula, at Akle Back, is the ruin of a small church. Between them, near a place marked on modern maps as 'Kiln Port', is an area where the hillside has been dug out and levelled into terraces. This looks like the site of the Spanish camp. There would have been plenty of wood and canvas from the wrecked ships to erect shelters over the terraces and would have been a way of accommodating up to 2,000 men. (The figure of 3,500 in the report is obviously an exaggeration.)

A further piece of information from the spies was that the ship that 'was wrecked a little without the harbour' was at a place called Sean's Bullick near St John's Point.

The *Girona* and her two companion ships arrived in McSwyne's Bay on 15 September. One week later the two unnamed ships were wrecked in the Great Gale and the *Girona* was damaged. We do not know if many men were drowned in the shipwrecks, but there could have been about 400 survivors considering that many would already have been in camp ashore. At the Coruña muster the *Girona* had 349 sailors and soldiers plus about 250 convicts as oarsmen, say 600, making a total of roughly 1,000 men in the camp at Calebeg at that time.

The captain of the *Girona* was Fabricio Spinola, a knight of the Order of Malta and a distinguished Italian nobleman. The four galleasses were built in Naples, technically Spanish territory at that time, but many members of their crews were Italian. Spinola was the senior officer and would have been responsible for managing affairs in the camp and on the ship. Unfortunately, despite much coming and going of spies, we know nothing about activities around the ship during the 25 days between 15 September and 10 October when de Leyva's party of approximately 850 arrived from Rossbeg accompanied by McSweeny Ne Doe. If anything serious was being done to repair the *Girona* and make it fit for sea, it should surely have been completed by then. It seems more likely that the *Girona* and the other two wrecks were being used to supply stores to support the camp.

During this period of relative inactivity it is easy to imagine many of the Spanish becoming frustrated and trying to find a way out. There are those who can sit and wait and others who have to be doing something. It seems that an escape route into the north evolved, with Sir Brian O'Rourke in Leitrim acting as conduit for the first stage. Probably another route was used as well through the Barnesmore Gap and Strabane. From the north coast a passage to Scotland could be arranged with the help of both O'Cahan, who had a house on the west bank of the Bann opposite Coleraine, and the Macdonnells of Dunluce. Men from the *Trinidad Valencera* and from the Streedagh wrecks had already been saved this way. It was estimated that more than 500 Spanish survivors passed through north Antrim over this three-month period. The numbers remaining in camp at Calebeg were therefore continually being reduced. The McSweenys not only provided food for the Spanish, but also supplied guides and escorts to help them on their way.

Food for so many people was a major worry. The McSweenys even used up their store cattle and they could not continue for much longer. Sir John O'Doherty of Inishowen complained that 'McSweeny, having subsisted 3,000 Spanish till his country is consumed, directs them now for hate into his country to lie upon it and consume it'. The countryside far and wide was having to contribute to their support. One correspondent reported that 'McSweeny hath made open proclamation to relieve all such Spanish as are straggling up and down the country'. McSweeny Ne Doe deserves unstinted admiration for his humanitarian endeavours at this time.

The arrival of de Leyva and his party made the food situation worse, but everything else changed for the better. It probably took two days or so to get everybody settled into camp and then de Leyva injected a sense of urgency. The process of using ship's stores in the camp was reversed and canvas, cordage and timber went back into the *Girona*. We have a report that says timber planks from one of the wrecked ships and planks from a pinnace of McSweeny's were used to repair the galleass. With so many men available there was no shortage of labour; all that was needed was organization and motivation, which was supplied by de Leyva. Repairs pressed ahead rapidly and within 10 days it became clear that the *Girona* would indeed soon be able to sail.

Decisions now came up for consideration that they had hardly dared to think of before. Where should they go? One report said that 'the Spanish were drawn to the Out Isles by the request of Shane Oge McShane O'Neill who lyeth there hurt … his mother being McLean's daughter'. The McLeans of Mull had long traditions of close contact and many family connections with the population in north and northwest Ulster. Through this connection de Leyva would have learned that the *San Juan de Sicilia* lay at anchor in the bay at Tobermory on the north coast of Mull. He would be encouraged to hope that the excess numbers in his charge could be spread over two ships and that they might eventually both be returned to Spain. Any men they were forced to leave behind in Mull would still have a better chance of rescue in Scotland than in Ireland. Another option that would remain open to them, even while they were still at sea, was to head for Kintyre, home base of the Macdonnells who had already done so much to shepherd survivors to safety. The voyage to Mull would be about 200 miles including a long open sea crossing. Kintyre was shorter by about 50 miles and within sight of land all the way. A lot would depend on how the *Girona* performed.

Another point to be decided that must have taken some pondering was whether or not to take the oarsmen. They were mostly convicts, and not Spanish. In a situation where space was at a premium, it would be tempting to leave them behind in favour of all the young noblemen, soldiers and sailors who would be clamouring for places. We learn that 'George de Venerey of Candie in Greece, a poor wretched creature, was thrust out of the galleass when Don Alonso was received into her'. That seems like one of the rowers. It is highly possible that de Leyva dispensed with both the oars and the rowers. Would soldiers and young aristocrats have been able to take on the task performed by experienced oarsmen? Almost certainly not. The teamwork, physical strength, stamina and technical skill involved would have been beyond them. Oars provided assistance with steering, and although the rudder had been repaired and remounted it was always vulnerable; the extra insurance of oars could be crucial. The galleass could still sail with a moderate breeze but would be dependent on the rudder or the oars for sailing close to the wind. And if the wind became strong it would be in difficulty. It was a gamble in which the stakes could hardly have been higher.

They probably had enough anchors since they would have been able to salvage anchors from the two ships that had been wrecked.

De Leyva and McSweeny appear to have realized early on that they could not carry all of the men at Calebeg and many of them had gradually been dispersed into the escape routes that would take them into Macdonnells' Country in north Antrim. When the time came to start loading the *Girona* there were about 1,300 men ready and waiting to go. It seems to be far too many for a ship like the *Girona* with very limited deck space. But it was for a relatively short voyage, and we can imagine them piling in regardless of any considerations of safety or comfort. Although numbers quoted in contemporary documents are untrustworthy, usually appearing to be inflated, this figure of 1,300 has generally been accepted by historians, and, given that it was composed of the crews of five or possibly six ships, it was possible. It seems that very few were left behind so we can conclude that de Leyva tried to make sure that they were either transferred overland or were allowed to board ship whether there appeared to be room for them or not.

'The Spanish gave McSweeny at their departure 12 butts of sack wine and to one Murrough Oge McMurrough four butts. The McSweenys and their followers have gotten great store of the Spanish calivers and muskets'—small recompense!

A HEROIC LEADER: DE LEYVA

Departure day was 26 October and with all 1,300 on board they set sail and headed west. They had taken on board four local pilots—three Irishmen and one Scot. We do not have continuous weather data for this period so late in the year, but it appears they had a south or southeast wind to help them clear Donegal Bay and Rathlin O'Birne Island. De Leyva would have passed these headlands before in the *Duquesa Santa Ana* and would not need to be reminded to allow plenty of sea room. They were leaving Ireland at last after six weeks of torment. Was their ordeal finally over?

No one could have done more for his men than Don Alonso de Leyva. In Blacksod Bay, County Mayo, he had ensured that they were rescued from the stranded *Rata Encoronada*, even though the ship's boat had been stolen and abandoned on the shore. They had been established in camp at Fahy Castle and then transferred to Tiraun prior to embarking again on the *Duquesa Santa Ana*. When it was wrecked in the storm of 28/29 September on the shores of Loughros More Bay, County Donegal, they were again taken off safely and camped for eight or nine days near Rossbeg. De Leyva was able to establish a relationship with McSweeny Ne Doe that enabled them to secure enough food to survive in an area by no means rich in resources, and despite being injured he withstood the long walk to Calebeg to join with their fellow countrymen. It was his determination that organized the repairs to the *Girona*.

The best leaders are those who think of themselves as servants to the men in their charge. When men know that their commander is devoting his ingenuity and strength of character to their welfare, they respond accordingly. For the right leader they want to do well. Such leaders are rare but de Leyva was one of them.

James Machary, an ordinary Irish seaman who had been pressed into service on the *Duquesa Santa Ana*, was lucky to have been left behind when the *Girona* departed from Calebeg. We do not know how he fell into English hands, but he was later interviewed before the Lord Deputy in the course of which he left a brief description of de Leyva that is pure elegy. (It seems everyone in the sixteenth century was touched by the Muse of Poetry.)

> Don Alonso for his stature was tall and slender,
> of a whitely complexion,
> of a flaxen and smooth hair,
> of behaviour mild and temperate,
> of speech good and deliberate,
> greatly reverenced not only of his own men,
> but generally of all the whole company.

As a tribute, as an epitaph, that can hardly be improved upon. 'Greatly reverenced'—what a perfect choice of words, what a most unusual and inspiring man, the only hero to emerge from the whole sorry enterprise.

––––

THE DASHING OF ALL THEIR HOPES

One of Sorley Boy Macdonnell's men had sighted the *Girona* and passed the news on to Captain Nicholas Merryman, who reported it briefly in a note to the Lord Deputy:

The Spanish ship which arrived in Tirconnell with the McSweenys was on Friday 28th of this present descried over against Dunluce …

That was a bad sign. It implied that the *Girona* was close inshore, which was not a good place to be. Going for the 'Out Isles', she should have been on the open sea. Even heading for Kintyre the pilots would have known that five miles of sea room was hardly enough on this coast. They would not willingly have allowed her to come 'over against Dunluce'. It was clear that even during the daylight hours the *Girona* was in trouble. The rudder had broken again. A wind from the northwest was increasing in strength. She was being forced in towards the shore. The crew were struggling to keep her head close to the wind by tacking continually away from the coast, but they had only the sails to help them and it was a losing battle. Dunluce is only four miles west of the Giant's Causeway, no more than two hours sailing time in good conditions. She was virtually wallowing, using only her topsails. The crew would have deployed her anchors, and a stern anchor might have helped to swing her head round from time to time. It seems clear now that they did not have her oars or they would have been able to turn out to sea.

Long after dark they were still fighting to stave off disaster. They passed the mouth of the Bush River, where a shallow cove at Portballintrae might have offered some shelter, but there can be a lot of surf there. The Giant's Causeway itself does not stick out very far and they probably did not even notice it. The Chimney Tops headland is the prominent feature and they may have felt that when they passed it they might find shelter in the next bay.

But east of the Chimney Tops is a steeply sided, isolated bay shown on modern maps as Port na Spaniagh. It is a trap; anyone caught in it could climb out only with the greatest difficulty. Immediately below the Chimney Tops at the west end of Port na Spaniagh a long, low, narrow finger of rock protrudes into the sea. This is Lacada Point, which sounds Spanish but is in fact Irish, *Leac Fhada,* meaning literally 'Long Stone'.

The *Girona* lost its battle with the tidal currents and gales and was forced in towards the shore. As she slid past the Chimney Tops headland an anchor seems to have snagged the bottom. The *Girona* swung through 180° and crashed against the tip of Lacada Point with the bow facing westwards while the rest of the ship broke off and tumbled into deep water on the east side. Of the crew there were only a few survivors, all of them Italians. One report said there were five, another nine. Possibly they were sailors still on the topmasts, working the topsails, and flung clear when the ship struck.

Lacada Point is indeed long. Any men who were not trapped in the ship were drowned in the surf before they reached the shore. Most died inside the broken hull. In human terms it is one of the most costly shipwrecks in the history of seafaring.

A more bitter tragedy could not have been contrived in the most twisted imagination. How could the fates have dared to demand the death of every Spanish person on board and in a setting which, on that dark October night, must have looked like one of the entrances to hell?

De Leyva deserved success if ever any man did. One more day and they could have been in Kintyre. Even now the poignancy is heart-rending.

NOTES AND REFERENCES

The quotation in the heading is in 'Advertisements from Mr. Henry Duke' in which he reports news from one of his spies. It is calendared in full in CSPI pp 64–65.

George Bingham's note about 'plying of spies' is in his letter to Sir Richard Bingham calendared as Oct. 10 XIX in CSPI p. 55. The original on MIC 223/52 NO. 67 gives details about the burning of his house in Ballymote by the Connors, O'Harts and O'Dowds and purveys the rumour about the Spanish being in Sligo in five days.

The speculation of the Spanish marching towards Sligo and being near Lough Erne is in Fenton and George Bingham's letter to Sir Richard Bingham in CSPI Oct. 10 IV p. 53 and on MIC 223/52 NO. 65.

The reference to the 'Irishry being grown very proud' is in CSPI Oct. 10 XX p. 55.

Sir Richard Bingham's opinion of the weakness of the Spanish survivors is in his letter to the Lord Deputy dated 20 October on MIC 223/52 NO. 52. At that time he was in Athlone but promised to leave for Sligo on Tuesday 25 October. There is no indication that he actually did. Even then he would still have been 50 miles from them. The presence of Geoffrey Fenton in Sligo at this time is a little mysterious. He was secretary to the Council in Dublin, the Lord Deputy's executive. Had he been sent to Sligo to check up on what the Binghams were doing, and explain to the Lord Deputy why there was so much shadowboxing going on and very little action? He was ordered to return to his post in Dublin.

De Leyva's natural expectation of some kind of show of aggression from the Lord Deputy is mentioned in James Machary's account in CSPI pp 98–99.

John Crofton and others gave the position of the Spanish camp at Calebeg in CSPI Oct. 39 III p. 64 and on MIC 223/52.

Details of the career of Fabricio Spinola, Master of the *Girona*, are in Robert Sténuit's book *Treasures of the Armada* pp 207–211.

Reference to McSweeny Ne Doe being in the camp at Calebeg at the same time as McSweeny Banagh is in Foxe to Walsyngham 24 October, CSPI p. 59 in which he uses the phrase 'both the McSweenys'.

Clues to the escape routes into the north are scattered throughout the sources. The one through Sir Brian O'Rourke's Country is in Francisco de Cuéllar's narrative. He was actually shipped to Scotland from Lough Foyle in April 1589. A letter from William Taafe to Fenton and George Bingham reporting that Spanish were camped at Forreside More within six miles of Strabane is in CSPI Oct. 10 XVIII p. 55. The route through the Macdonnells of Dunluce is in the Lord Deputy's letter to the Privy Council dated 22 October which is on MIC 223/52 NO. 45.

Sir John O'Doherty's gripe about having to help feed the Spanish survivors is in CSPI Oct, 39 IV p. 64.

Repairs to the *Girona* are in Henry Duke's account in CSPI 39 VI p. 64, which also has the reference to the Out Isles on p. 65. These are reports from one of the so-called spies and are not as detailed or as authentic as we would like.

The ejection from the *Girona* of George de Venerey of Greece is in CSPI Dec. 25 II p. 99. It may be stretching things a bit far to presume that he was an oarsman, but the fact that he was from Greece and 'a poor wretched creature' suggests that he was more likely to have been a convict or slave than a serving soldier.

The dispensing of butts of wine to McSweeny and others is also in Henry Duke's account, CSPI p. 64.

James Machary's marvellous tribute to de Leyva is in CSPI p. 99.

The sighting of the *Girona* 'over against Dunluce' is on MIC 223/52 NO. 195. The abstract in the Calendar (p. 68) unbelievably leaves this out.

The position of the *Girona* on Lacada Point was brilliantly revealed by Robert Sténuit's underwater archaeology, which is described in his *Treasures of the Armada* pp 164–195.

With the exception of County Galway the quantity and quality of information about the Armada in the public record in the rest of Ireland is amazingly good. By contrast, that coming out of County Donegal is disappointing. Much of what is available is distorted by inaccurate reporting and/or obtuse interpretation by members of the English garrison. The lack of a genuine eyewitness account is crucial. There are some good basic signposts such as the time of the arrival of de Leyva's party in the Harbour of Calebeg and the date the *Girona* sailed. But details of the activities there are frustratingly sparse.

The detailed description of how the *Girona* met its end was interpreted by Robert Sténuit, based on the position in which objects were found, such as an anchor, guns, ingots, cannon balls and the many pieces of personal wealth and jewellery. See his book *Treasures of the Armada* p. 163 *et seq.*

Chapter 7 ∾

| LOOSE ENDS

The *Gran Grifon*, the *San Juan de Sicilia* and the *San Pedro el Mayor*

… the ship was unseaworthy and was driven ashore and wrecked at a place called Hope.

(PRISONERS FROM THE *SAN PEDRO EL MAYOR*)

Although they were eventually wrecked elsewhere these three ships are entitled to be included in the history of the Armada in Ireland, because two of them, the *Gran Grifon* and the *San Juan de Sicilia*, were in Irish waters for a time, and the *San Pedro el Mayor* was definitely in an Irish port for an extended period. The *Gran Grifon* and the *San Juan de Sicilia* were part of the group of five ships off northwest Donegal around 10 September. Before the *Barque of Hamburg* sank some of her crew were taken on board the *Gran Grifon*; the remainder were on *La Trinidad Valencera* when she entered Kinnagoe Bay on the Inishowen peninsula on 14 September. The *San Juan de Sicilia* was also one of this group although we do not know the details of how or when she ended up in Tobermory Bay on the Isle of Mull. The *San Pedro el Mayor* has always been presumed to have spent time in Ireland, because of her late arrival in Devonshire, but this is now confirmed by a recently discovered document in Spanish sources.

The *Gran Grifon*

We have already seen that the *Gran Grifon* tried to ride out the second half of September at sea. Although in a sinking condition most of the time, she stayed afloat until, arriving at Fair Isle, she anchored off Swartz Geo in the southeast of the island on the evening of 27 September, intending to beach there next day. During the night she was carried south by the current and was grounded instead in Stroms Hellier, a short, narrow inlet with steep sides at the southern entrance to the Geo. It will be remembered that the next day and following night another severe gale affected all the remaining ships and was responsible for the loss of the *Duquesa Santa Ana* in Loughros More Bay, County Donegal. The crew of the *Gran Grifon* were therefore lucky to make good their escape when they did. If they had been caught at sea their ship could hardly have survived. It was actually well sheltered in Stroms Hellier, and as the masts and yards leaned against the side of the cliff the men were able to climb to the top of the rigging and out to safety.

It was, however, a case of good luck mixed with bad. They were lucky to survive the shipwreck, but Fair Isle was isolated and impoverished. The Spanish found a population of just 17 families living a life barely above subsistence level. Their food consisted mainly of fish, supplemented by dairy products from their few cattle. The only grain cultivated was barley from which they made small loaves. Three hundred Spanish seamen more than doubled the numbers on the island and there would not be the resources to sustain them all for very long. Although they were generous about paying for what they took, competition for the limited supplies available led to conflict. The islanders began hiding their food and their stock of cattle and sheep, and there were rumours that, when the opportunity presented, they threw some weakened mariners over the cliffs. In the seven weeks up to 14 November about fifty men had died, mostly from starvation. Many were already weakened by the privations of the voyage and sickness was common.

About the end of October some seamen borrowed a boat and set out to make contact with Shetland. They returned with a Shetland islander who had a boat large enough to transport the remaining Spanish survivors to Quendale in the south of Shetland Main Island. Here with good food and comfortable shelter they were able to recover their strength. In early December they were shipped to the Scottish mainland and arrived at Anstruther near Saint Andrews. From there they were taken overland to Edinburgh, where they joined up with about 400 of the survivors from Ireland. They were in Edinburgh for more than six months. They were not prisoners but were treated as non-combatants of a friendly foreign power, seeking sanctuary and passage home.

It was the end of July 1589 before passage to Flanders could be arranged for them in four chartered Scottish ships. In view of what happened to other Armada seamen they came off surprisingly well in the end.

The *San Juan de Sicilia*

Since about 14 September the *San Juan de Sicilia* had lain at anchor in Tobermory Bay on the Isle of Mull in the Inner Hebrides. Reference has already been made to the possibility that Don Alonso de Leyva's first intention when leaving Donegal Bay was to join forces with her. Together they might have been able to bring all the remaining Spanish in Ireland and Scotland back to Spain. As we know he and the 1,300 men under his charge died on board the *Girona* at the Giant's Causeway on the night of 28/29 October. It seems destiny had decreed that all de Leyva's plans were doomed to failure, because the *San Juan de Sicilia* was destroyed in an explosion at its anchorage in Tobermory Bay exactly one week later, on 5 November.

Tales surrounding the fate of the *San Juan de Sicilia* belong in the realms of mythology and readers can take their pick of at least three versions. And they should also be aware of the obligatory ingredient of sunken treasure, as the tradition would not be complete without 30 million gold ducats waiting to be discovered in the bottom of the bay!

First you have to visualize a sixteenth-century edition of the character of James Bond. Then can you believe that one of Francis Walsyngham's spies was able to journey through England and Scotland to the west coast? There he had to get a ship to take him out to Mull, accompanied by enough explosives to sink a large galleon. After that it would be a simple matter to place the charges and carry out the deed. Walsyngham is credited with being the founding father of organized espionage. He was good, but not that good! There is no evidence that they even knew about the *San Juan de Sicilia* in London and they would have had difficulty finding Tobermory on a map. Perhaps Walsyngham started this rumour himself to add mystique to his already shady reputation! This is the most appealing, but least likely, of the three versions.

The second version evolved internally on the island. It concerned the clan chief of the Macleans of Mull at that time, Donald Maclean. He began by treating the Spanish well, supplying them with food, water and shelter. In return he expected to receive payment, and he also negotiated for the services of 100 soldiers to help him in a dispute with a neighbouring clan. From time to time he entertained the Spanish nobility at his home, Duart Castle. The ship was around for a long time; by the beginning of November it had been there seven weeks. The bill for food was mounting up and he still had not been paid. As every day passed rumours increased the amount of treasure on board and he was not seeing any of it.

Then it seems seamen were clearing the decks, storing water and food, testing the rigging and giving a good impression of preparing to leave. Donald Maclean could stand it no longer. If he could delay the departure he would have a better chance of getting his hands on some of those gold ducats and jewels. He is supposed to have sailed out to the ship with a small party of his men, set the explosives and made good his escape before they actually blew up. As we have seen before, a wooden ship does not sink easily and the *San Juan de Sicilia* did not go straight to the bottom. The explosion caused a fire and that eventually destroyed her.

This is a good story especially as it involves only the islanders. It is, however, a test of our gullibility to believe that several hundred armed Spanish soldiers would stand by and allow all this to happen. One hopes Donald Maclean did in the end get his share of the gold ducats.

The third version has some claim to credibility because it emanates from the Irish State Papers for January 1589, just two months after the event. Lord Deputy Fitzwilliam, in a letter to the Privy Council dated 10 January, confirms that in response to a request from them, he is sending 'a ship to the Isle of Mull in Maclean's country for the destroying or taking of a great ship lying on the west of Scotland'. Writing to Burghley and Walsyngham on 11 January, he reported that he had despatched a pinnace over to the Out Isles as requested. The pinnace returned with the story that, yes there had been a galleon at Tobermory, but that it had already been destroyed. The circumstances apparently were that a Frenchman, who was a prisoner on board having been accused of embezzling treasure and jewels, managed to set fire to a barrel of gunpowder hoping to make good his escape in the subsequent confusion. A slight variation to this account is that the powder was ignited by one of Maclean's clan angered at being held on board as a pledge. Walsyngham would hardly have been asking for information if one of his spies had already caused the explosion.

A later report appeared in the State Papers for February from Captain Charles Eggerton of the garrison based at Carrickfergus Castle on the shore of Belfast Lough. He was probably captain of the pinnace. It adds a few extra details. He said, 'it was a galleon of Venice of 1,200 tons and had been burnt in Maclean's Country. Seven hundred men had been burned to death including five of Maclean's pledges. A captain and 100 men were ashore at the time and survived'.

Whether the part about the Frenchman is correct or not, the rest of this story has a convincing amount of detail about it, which is probably the best information available. It emphasizes that in those days access to the Out Isles was easier by boat from the north of Ireland than overland through England and Scotland. As is so often the case the numbers of men seem to be grossly exaggerated. In the Lisbon muster the *San Juan de Sicilia* was listed as having 342 soldiers and mariners; if 100 of them survived then the number killed in the explosion and fire cannot have been more than about 250.

The *San Pedro el Mayor*

On 7 November the *San Pedro el Mayor* materialized as if from nowhere and entered Hope Cove near Salcombe, County Devon. It is listed in both the Lisbon and Coruña musters and appears in later lists of ships missing, but throughout the whole of the voyage there is no mention of it in the State Papers. For some reason it remained completely anonymous in the fighting in the Channel, at Calais, in the escape from Gravelines and in the subsequent trip around Scotland and Ireland. In fact for a long time we were reliant on a statement dated 15 June 1590 for proof that it was on the voyage at all. This statement was given by a group of Spanish prisoners from the ship who had just been released and returned to Nantes in Brittany. It is mostly concerned with negotiations for the release of 12 or 15 others who were still in custody, but it contains the following sentence: 'After they had sailed round the islands of England, Scotland and Ireland, they were pursued by continual tempests; they were in want of food, and the ship was unseaworthy, and on 6 November '88 was driven ashore and wrecked at a place called Hope …' (We can be fairly sure that the date was actually 7 November as given in contemporary English sources.)

It is the very late date of this shipwreck that has stimulated so much studied conjecture. Assuming that it was with the rest of the Armada during the north about voyage, there is a period of six or seven weeks between mid-September and the beginning of November when it was missing, and these missing weeks demand to be explained. There was a credible presumption that the *San Pedro el Mayor* must have spent some time in Ireland, but no record of it appears in the Irish State Papers.

Quite recently, however, a document has been uncovered in the Spanish Archivo General de Simancas which confirms that she did indeed enter an Irish port and stay for several weeks. Three prisoners had escaped from captivity in Kingsbridge, County Devon, and made their way back to Spain as early as February 1589. They are named as Pedro Robledo, Francisco de la Desma and Pedro de Samillan, and they appear to have been medical staff who had some freedom of movement. Their statement is dated 18 February 1589, just three months after the shipwreck. Reports by soldiers can be frustratingly inaccurate, but medical staff it seems are worse. They are confusing on dates and use place names that are not recognizable so we still do not know where the *San Pedro el Mayor* was in Ireland.

They say they landed on 28 September at a place called 'Ross' or 'Rus'. They found there the wreck of the *San Nicolas Prodaneli* from which about sixty men had survived and of these nine were prisoners in a nearby town, which they named as 'Calivia'. They made contact with about sixty English soldiers and started negotiations for the release of the prisoners. The English refused to accept money and killed three of the negotiating team.

The barony in northwest County Mayo was called 'Erris'. It was sometimes written as 'Irrus' and was probably pronounced the same way, so that could be the 'Rus' referred to. 'Ross' was, however, a common name and there is nothing conclusive about it. Finding the wreck of the *San Nicolas Prodaneli* could possibly be the ship at Inver, in the south of Broad Haven. The 60 English soldiers that they met might also have been Gerald Comerford's party, which visited Blacksod Bay briefly and then headed eastwards to Tirawley and Killala Bay. But they had witnessed the departure of the *Duquesa Santa Ana* on 23 September and the *San Pedro el Mayor* was not supposed to have arrived until 28 September. The town 'Calivia' does not so far suggest any identifiable place, and the date 28 September seems far too late for her arrival in Ireland. None of the other ships recorded in Ireland arrived later than 16 September, and it seems likely that their recollection of the date was faulty. There is a possibility that she might have been somewhere else in Ireland for a time before moving to Broad Haven, but their statement does not mention it.

It is hardly possible to construct a plausible sequence of events from this quality of evidence, but the feeling is that we are being guided towards the Broad Haven area as the most likely harbour for the *San Pedro* in Ireland. There were very few places where the presence of a Spanish ship could go undetected for several weeks, but Broad Haven was one of them. Comerford's party were in the area, but did not go there, and his suggestion that Sir Richard Bingham should check it out was never taken up. And Comerford does not report meeting any Spanish on land.

The statement says that they left Ireland on 21 October. The anchor was fouled and could not be lifted, and they had to cut the cable in order to get away. This left them without an anchor, and as they came into Hope Cove on 7 November all they could do was try to find a suitable place to ground her.

The *San Pedro el Mayor in County Devon*

Sir John Gilberte and George Carey had been appointed Deputy Lieutenants of County Devon to serve on land during the emergency. They had a notable role to play in the Armada summer of 1588. The English fleet had assembled in Plymouth before the battles in the Channel and had to be supplied with victuals, men and munitions. In the first days of the fighting during the first week of August, the flagship of the Biscay Squadron, the *Nuestra Señora del Rosario*, had been captured by Sir Francis Drake and was taken into Dartmouth. This was an enormous prize with wealthy Spanish noblemen on board carrying great ransom value, including Don Pedro de Valdés, Admiral of the squadron and second only to Juan Martinez de Recalde in the hierarchy of Spanish Admirals. The ship itself was hugely valuable in terms of the treasure chest, the armaments and the lavish appointments in the luxury cabins. Saving all this 'to Her Majesty's use' was a task that fell largely on the Deputy Lieutenants. Some brass guns from the *Rosario* had been taken into the *Roebuck*, under the command of Captain Jacob Whiddon, for use during the fighting.

As late as 15 November George Cary was in Plymouth trying to persuade Jacob Whiddon to release these brass guns into his care, when the news came through that a Spanish ship had been 'cast up at a place called Hope near Salcombe'. The *San Pedro el Mayor* had been in Hope since 7 November. Although only 16 miles from Plymouth, Hope Cove is in a remote area, which explains why it took more than a week for the news to reach Cary. His concern that 'great pilfering and spoils were made by the country people' was entirely justified. He set off for Salcombe at once. In his letter to the Privy Council he made a show of 'restoring and rehaving' what was left. Needless to say there was very little. Being a hospital ship it was expected that 'pothecary stuff' might be recovered, but apparently it was all water-damaged.

Cary did find out about the vessel itself and reported that 'the ship is a hulk and called *St Peter the Great*, one of those two ships appointed for the hospital for the whole navy. She is not to be recovered as she lieth on a rock, and is full of water to her upper decks. There are now remaining of her crew about a hundred and forty or thereabouts'.

Despite the fact that George Cary was within view of the wreck for several days its exact location was never recorded. Hope Cove is not large, but after many years of searching, the wreck site has not yet been discovered. It is slightly complicated by the huge rock, known as Shippen Rock, that divides the cove in two. To the south the cove is called Inner Hope; to the north it is Outer Hope. A small number of scattered artefacts have been found over the years, but none of them indicated the location of an Armada ship. The recently revealed statement by Pedro Robledo does give a scrap of information that may provide a clue. He says that when they arrived 'English boats came out to help them ashore'. At one time it was thought that the wreck was in the intertidal area and that the crew had been able to walk to safety. There is now the possibility that the ship grounded on a rock a little further out, which would comply with Cary's statement that she was 'full of water to her upper decks'.

After about two weeks it was 'through tempestuous weather broken in pieces and scattered on the seashore', but there should still be ballast stones and ship's timbers on the bottom at the site of the original wreck. We can only wish good luck to Devonshire divers who are still searching.

The estate behind the cove was owned by Sir William Courteney and the responsibility for looking after the survivors fell first of all to him. He had obviously provided food and shelter for them for more than a week before George Cary arrived. It is certain also that he would have had more than his share of any valuables from the wreck and placed them out of the reach of any prying Deputy Lord Lieutenant.

Cary set about dividing up the men. He said he 'severed the captains and chiefest of them to the number of 10 persons'. He left eight with Sir William Courteney and took two himself, the pothecary and a sergeant. The rest, in other words about 120, he put in safekeeping and provided 1½ pence a day each for their sustenance. There were, he said, 'no men of account in the ship—soldiers and such as have risen by service and bestowed all their wealth in this action'. Cary also points out to the Council that, in addition, he is bearing the cost of subsisting more prisoners in Bridewell; they are ordinary seamen from the *Rosario*. A list is enclosed naming 18 men from the *San Pedro* who should be able to offer ransom, though the amounts are small, the highest being 80 ducats.

There are two things going on here. On the face of it Cary is granting very humane treatment to Spanish prisoners at some personal cost to himself. But there is a prospect of later profit and it seems the Privy Council ended up making an allowance of 4 pence a day for each prisoner, so although there were no high stakes Cary probably did all right out of it. Courteney had been in charge of all the crew for a time, but Cary had descended on him and taken over more than a hundred of them. A year later on, 24 November 1589, the Queen granted an order releasing all the prisoners but was persuaded to allow Sir William Courteney to retain a small number—12 or 15, from whom he could expect to derive a ransom. But it was well known that they were poor men so the amount would not be large. Courteney was furious and felt he had been cheated out of the profit that was due to him. He refused to release his prisoners, demanding 5,000 ducats for them, though he knew full well they could not afford to pay it. A year later he still had them and the price demanded had gone up to 12,000 ducats; a year after that it was 25,000 ducats. The ransom paid for Admiral Don Pedro de Valdés was 1,500 ducats! Courteney had gone crazy.

The outcome of it all was that in Devonshire the crew of the *San Pedro el Mayor* were well looked after and eventually returned home safely. Those held by Sir William Courteney did not have a great time, but at least they were still alive three years later.

NOTES AND REFERENCES

The quotation in the heading is from the statement given by the prisoners from the *San Pedro el Mayor* after their release, and is in Hume p. 583.

The details surrounding the adventures of the crew of the *Gran Grifon* in Fair Isle and the Scottish mainland are well described by Colin Martin in his book *Full Fathom Five* pp 145–155.

The various theories about the fate of the *San Juan de Sicilia* in Tobermory are by their nature not well authenticated. The one about Walsyngham's spies is particularly dubious in view of the request by the Privy Council for Lord Deputy Fitzwilliam to send to the Out Isles for information, which they would hardly have done if one of their agents had carried out the attack. The currency of Walsyngham's espionage was information. 'Knowledge is never too dear' was his maxim. He gathered it through a wide network of spies and double-agents, intercepted correspondence, penetrated codes and ciphers, and always kept secrets secret. He seldom initiated action, and then, as in the Babington plot, through agents provocateurs—but never sabotage. His activities are brilliantly revealed by Stephen Budiansky in his book *Her Majesty's Spymaster*. The story about the involvement of Donald Maclean, laird of the Macleans of Mull, is on the Internet travel guide to Mull. The references from the Irish State Papers are in CSPI pp 97, 108 and 121.

The arrival of the *San Pedro el Mayor* and the subsequent treatment of prisoners from the ship are in Laughton VOL. II pp 289–291. Sir John Gilberte and George Cary's connection with prisoners from the *Rosario* is in Laughton VOL. I pp 326–327. The very detailed, carefully dated account of the release of prisoners and Sir William Courteney's maniacal demands are in a statement from one of the prisoners, Gonzalo Gonzales, an English translation of which is in Laughton VOL. II Appendix F pp 371–375 and in Hume pp 583–584. Part of the statement of Pedro Robledo etc. is quoted in Paula Martin's book *Spanish Armada Prisoners*. Its original source is the Archivo General de Simancas, Guerra Antigua, document no. 245/188.

Chapter 8 ∾

THE TREATMENT OF SPANISH PRISONERS

… not justified by military necessity, unlawfully, wantonly …
(THE FOURTH GENEVA CONVENTION)

'NO SAFEKEEPING FOR THEM'

Orders from the Lord Deputy, William Fitzwilliam, and Sir Richard Bingham, governor of Connaught, led to survivors from the Spanish Armada ships being killed. Fitzwilliam, writing from Dublin, decreed that it was the duty of everyone 'to apprehend and execute all Spaniards found of what quality soever'. Sir Richard Bingham's proclamation was more long-winded but it had the same effect:

> It was thought good by the governor and council for as much as many of the Spaniards which escaped shipwreck were kept by divers gentlemen and others, the inhabitants of this province, and used with more favour than they thought meet, to set forth a proclamation, upon pain of death, that all such persons as kept any Spaniards should bring them in and deliver them to the provost martial, justices of the peace, sheriffs or other head officers, or that any man should detain any of them above four hours after the publication of the said proclamation, should be holden and reputed as treason against Her Majesty, which was sent abroad and published in every place.

Fitzwilliam's decree required the killing of prisoners by private citizens. Bingham's proclamation meant that anyone who sheltered survivors was guilty of treason and could themselves be executed, but that the intention was for prisoners to be killed by appointed officials rather than by private citizens. There are many examples of the order being carried out.

In Tralee, County Kerry

Twenty-four survivors who struggled ashore from the small boat in Barrow Harbour surrendered to Lady Denny. It is assumed that they were taken to the garrison in Tralee where they were cursorily examined and killed. Three of them had offered ransoms for their lives. Two were servants of the Duke of Medina Sidonia and two were little boys—technically non-combatants. The reason given in the report for killing them was 'because there was no safe-keeping for them'. But the killers did not really need a reason since they were covered by the Lord Deputy's decree. In any case 'no safe-keeping' can be used as justification only if the prisoners posed a potential threat, which these did not since they had surrendered their weapons and some were non-combatants.

At Dingle, County Kerry

Eight men were sent ashore in Blasket Sound from Recalde's *San Juan of Portugal* 'to reconnoitre' and did not return. They were captured by members of a local militia led by James Truant. Four were examined in Dingle and all were killed. Only one man survived the sinking of the *Santa Maria de la Rosa*. He was kept for a time and gave three statements, but in the end he too was killed.

On the coast of County Clare

Two ships were wrecked on the Clare coast, the *San Marcos* at Lurga Point just off shore from Quilty, and the *San Esteban* in the bay at Doonbeg. Local reports refer to 68 survivors who were supposed to have been hanged. Bingham's Report says 'the 300 which escaped and came aland were taken prisoners and put to the sword according to instructions …'

The situation in County Clare takes some explaining. Although the local Irish family, the O'Brians, were in charge, English law and social organization had been established. Turlough O'Brian was a knight and a member of the Irish parliament in Dublin. Boetius Clancy was county sheriff. There were no English garrisons in the area. The killing of these prisoners was carried out, therefore, by Irish officials, probably by Boetius Clancy who seemed to take his sheriff's job very seriously. The killings would almost certainly not have taken place if it were not for the Lord Deputy's decree and Bingham's proclamation. One prisoner, a member of the crew of the *Zuñiga*, survived; he was Petrus Baptista, the 'scrivener' who was captured in Liscannor Bay. In order to be examined he had to be taken before someone who could speak Latin and that fortunately was '… the Reverend in God, Daniel, Bishop of Kildare'. The examination was extensive and must have taken several days. The Bishop must have been impressed with Baptista, because he retained him in his service, and Baptista was still there several years later. Whether this was just a lucky escape or the Bishop's way of saving Baptista's life is not known, but we can certainly be glad for him.

At Tirawley, County Mayo

George Bingham, Sir Richard's brother, was based in Ballymote, County Sligo, with a small garrison of English soldiers. He received intelligence about a ship being wrecked in Tirawley, probably in Killala Bay, which said that 72 men had been taken prisoner by William Burke of Ardnaree, including a Bishop, a Friar and three noblemen. It was from this ship that Melaghlin McCabb had killed 80 of the rest with his gallowglass axe as they came on shore. William Burke must have scrambled to stop him and at least save some of the crew, whom he took to his house. A gallowglass was a professional soldier, usually of Scottish origin, in the service of Irish families. George Bingham arrived and claimed to have 'put to the sword 100 saving two or three of the chiefest whom he reserved alone'. He named one as Don 'Gransila de Swaso' and it must have been at this time that he also saved five or six Dutch boys. Both George and Sir Richard Bingham again seemed to overestimate numbers.

At Streedagh Strand, County Sligo

George Bingham went straight from Tirawley to Streedagh. News reached him that the three ships which had been in Sligo Bay 'were cast away on the Carbery coast between Sligo and Bundrowse and 1,000 men drowned in them'. It took him about two days to get there and he found '140 of such as came aland and escaped drowning', and he killed them. As we know, about 250 escaped from the ships so 110 were strong enough to head off inland, where they were guided to Sir Brian O'Rourke's Country. One of these was Francisco de Cuéllar.

The 140 still on the beach when George Bingham arrived were the ones who were so weak and injured that they could not walk to safety. Bingham made no attempt to cover up what he had done to them; in fact he reported it as if it was something to be proud of.

Greatly to the annoyance of the Binghams, the prisoners in Sir Brian O'Rourke's Country 'were by him gladly received and newly apparelled and relieved. The said Sir Brian being earnestly written unto to send them to the Governor hath utterly refused so to do'. Some of these would have been from the Streedagh wrecks and others survivors of the ships in Calebeg.

O'Rourke opened an escape route into the north, which took the Spanish through Leitrim and Fermanagh to the north coast. Further help was then provided by O'Cahan and Sorley Boy Macdonnell and in all about 500 Spanish survivors were conveyed to safety in Scotland. Cuéllar did not reach

Flanders until a year later, September 1589, and he actually left through Lough Foyle, where the Catholic Bishop of Derry, Redmond O'Gallagher, was able to help a small number as well.

———

SIR RICHARD BINGHAM IN GALWAY

The 'discourse' of events in Connaught, prepared by Edward Whyte and signed by Sir Richard Bingham and others, contains several references to the killing of prisoners. This is the document that, for convenience, has been called 'Bingham's Report'. It is the source of most of the information on prisoners in counties Clare, Mayo and Sligo, based on reports from commissioners in those areas.

Bingham himself was involved directly in the killings that took place in Galway City. He had made Athlone his headquarters and had just begun to take his forces into the field on 24 September. His initial intention was to head for Blacksod Bay where Don Alonso de Leyva and about 1,400 Spanish survivors were reported to be 'fortifying'. Next day, however, he learned that they were all 'shipped and gone to sea', and so he turned back and set out for Galway City, where he arrived on Saturday 1 October. He had sent orders into Íar-Chonnacht, to Sir Murrough Na Doe O'Flaherty and Tadgh Na Buile O'Flaherty, that all Spanish survivors were to be brought into the city. Some were already there in the custody of the townsmen, and some had been captured by the provost martial. The O'Flahertys brought in about 130, including the most important prisoner taken in Ireland, Don Luis de Cordoba. Bingham conducted his examination himself.

On Bingham's orders all the prisoners had been killed except for 40, regarded as the 'best'. Bingham killed 30 of these and saved just 10, including of course de Cordoba. While he was there a further 14 were brought in 'as well Spaniards as Portingals whom he likewise commanded to be executed'. His own estimate of the number of prisoners killed at this point in Connaught and Thomond was 1,100.

> And having made a clear despatch of the Spaniards both within the town and in the country, he bestowed all the rest of this day in giving thanks and praises to Almighty God for Her Majesty's most happy success in that action and our deliverance from such dangerous enemies.

Bingham's Report is hard to take at the best of times. Admittedly it contains much valuable information, but the incessant self-congratulation is difficult to swallow. And this hypocritical, pseudo piety is beyond endurance. The man was a mass murderer!

By whose authority?

Not only was all this killing completely unnecessary, but there was no clear authority for it either. The Privy Council wrote to Fitzwilliam on 28 September giving their Lordships directions for the handling of prisoners:

> Whereas of occasion aforesaid it must needs fall out that divers Spanish prisoners are taken, their Lordships' pleasure is that great care be had of their safe custodie and keeping in some convenient place that hereafter they may be forthcoming, where their Lordship shall require them at his handes. Their Lordships' pleasure is to send the names and condicions of such Spanish prisoners as are or shall be taken together with their examinations.

There is no mention here of execution, and it certainly does not convey any authority for the kind of decree issued by Fitzwilliam. He could hardly show that he had taken 'great care of their safe custodie that hereafter they may be forthcoming' when, in fact, the Spanish prisoners in Ireland were all dead.

Fitzwilliam was exhibiting signs of unease. He was now exposed to accusations that he had exceeded his authority, and he began to try to cover his tracks. On 10 October in a letter to Burghley he asks him 'to intervene with the Queen on his behalf if any seek to move her against him for clearing the country of Spaniards'. Then on 22 October in a letter to the Privy Council he expresses 'the intention of offering mercy to such as shall submit'. This was too late; by that time over 1,000 of them were already dead. It was an empty promise anyway for he continued with the needless killing. Again on 6 November in a letter to Walsyngham he 'desires to know what he shall do with the Spaniards who may come to his hand and who would gladly be prisoners'. He seems to be implying here that until now he has not left Dublin and that all the killing so far has been at the hands of that fellow Bingham. Someone had scared Fitzwilliam and there are grounds for believing that it may have been the Queen.

It did not change his conduct, however, and as late as November he was himself directly responsible for gratuitous killing. It comes to light in a letter from Sir Richard Bingham to the Queen written from Athlone on 12 December. He reported that his brother George had retained 'Don Graveillo de Swasso and some five or six Dutch boys and young men'. Bingham said he had spared them 'as coming after the fury and heat of justice was past'. But Fitzwilliam, at the beginning of his journey into the north, 'in his passing along caused both these two Spaniards which my brother had to be executed, and the Dutch men and boys who had been spared by me reserving none …'

This is nothing short of whistle blowing. He felt he had carried all the guilt until now, but he was going to make sure Fitzwilliam bore his share. The policy of killing prisoners was being recognized by the perpetrators as indefensible, and they were trying to find positions that might enable them to evade the Queen's displeasure. They cannot evade the judgment of history.

——

SPANISH IN IRISH HANDS

Questions are often asked about the conduct of the native Irish in dealing with Spanish survivors. The answer has to be that it was very mixed, depending mainly on where they were. We have seen that in County Clare English administration was established, and Irish officials complied with the Lord Deputy's decree. At least 68 prisoners were killed. In County Galway the O'Flahertys held about 130 men from two ships and they were compelled to surrender them to Sir Richard Bingham. He had virtually all of them killed, the only exception being Don Luis de Cordoba. The story of the killing of 100 Spanish survivors on Clare Island by Dowdragh Roe O'Malley can be dismissed as fiction. And the killing of 80 Spanish by the gallowglass Melaghlin M'Cabb was also dubious; even if it did happen it was almost certainly not with the approval of William Burke, his chieftain, who made prisoners of 72 others.

On the coast of County Sligo survivors from the Streedagh wrecks had a terrifying experience at the hands of the Irish, which is best described by Francisco de Cuéllar. He said, 'these people were the first to rob us and strip to the skin all those who came ashore alive'. But he also acknowledged that '… these savages showed us favour, because they knew we had come against the heretics and were their great enemies. If they had not guarded us as well as they did themselves none of us would still be alive. We had to be grateful to them for this'. With one other exception the Sligo coast seems to have been the only place where the Spanish were robbed of their clothes. There is at least one case of a naked young Spaniard dying of exposure. It is a paradox that can hardly be understood by modern readers. The native Irish risked their own lives by helping the Spanish, yet at the same time regarded it as their right to rob them of everything they possessed. Perhaps a provision in Brehon Law, by which they were entitled to take everything washed ashore on their land, has something to do with it. Anyway, of the 250 or so who survived the shipwrecks just over a hundred were robbed and left destitute by the Irish, while about

140 were murdered by George Bingham and his soldiers.

Two Irish chieftains from north Leitrim were instrumental in rescuing men not only from the Streedagh wrecks but also from the ships at Calebeg. Sir Brian O'Rourke, according to Bingham, 'gladly received those coming to his country, and newly apparelled and relieved them, and being earnestly written unto to send them to the Governor hath utterly refused so to do'. He became a conduit by which the escaped Spanish could be taken into the north and on to safety in Scotland. Tadhg Oge MacClancy of Rossclogher (sometimes written as McGlannough) sheltered Cuéllar and nine other survivors for more than two months. In the process they openly defied the Lord Deputy for which both he and O'Rourke eventually paid with their lives. Fitzwilliam was a vindictive and unforgiving tyrant.

In County Donegal McSweeny Na Doe was a shining light. He spared neither himself nor his neighbours in providing food and shelter for shipwrecked survivors, whose numbers seemed to increase geometrically on him as the weeks passed. Sir John O'Doherty complained that 'McSweeny having subsisted 3,000 Spanish till his country was consumed directs them now for hate into his country to lie upon it and consume it'. McSweeny quickly established a close working relationship with Don Alonso de Leyva and helped him to secure materials with which to repair the *Girona*. He refused to be intimidated by threats from the English garrison, who skulked below the Erne and dreaded to come into Ulster. When the Lord Deputy made his journey into the north and commanded that the Ulster chiefs come to meet him as a gesture of submission, McSweeny Na Doe steadfastly refused.

In the north most of the Spanish who escaped to Scotland were routed through the Macdonnells of Antrim. O'Cahan at Castleroe shipped some in the early days, but he was intimidated by the Lord Deputy and declined to give help to Cuéllar when he needed it. Sorley Boy Macdonnell and his son James controlled most of the boat traffic between Kintyre and Dunluce or Ballycastle. They were a vital link in the escape route for more than 500 Spanish survivors who returned to safety through Scotland. Sorley Boy was impervious to threats from Fitzwilliam, having already suffered the ultimate tragedy at the hands of English troops. Just thirteen years earlier, in July 1575, the Earl of Essex was waging a campaign against the Scots in Ulster. The Macdonnells had moved their families out of the fighting to what they thought was the safety of Rathlin Island. Essex withdrew to Newry as a decoy, but his deputy, John Norris, assembled an invasion force at Carrickfergus and sailed for Rathlin with a small flotilla. On 22 July they committed one of the worst atrocities in the history of English/Irish relations. The women and children on the island were all killed. Sorley Boy watched the massacre from Fair Head and was said to have 'run mad for sorrow, tearing and tormenting himself and crying that he had lost all he ever had'. Essex's motivation was to impress Elizabeth—what a futile waste! There was nothing more the Lord Deputy could do to Sorley Boy now. The latter had no difficulty in ignoring Fitzwilliam's threats, and he continued to help the Spanish refugees.

As events unfolded during October and November the passage to safety for the Spanish was through Ulster. In the very early stages, however, probably about 20 September or before, survivors from *La Trinidad Valencera* had the misfortune to encounter a garrison of soldiers from Castle Burt in the southern part of the Inishowen peninsula. They carried the Queen's ensigns but were mostly, if not all, Irish mercenaries under the command of Richard and Henry Hovenden, who were 'English born in Ireland'. Sir John O'Doherty had been helping the Spanish, but when the Hovendens took over they tricked them into laying down their arms on the assurance of safe passage to Dublin. The Spanish were then stripped of all their clothes and attacked. Many escaped, however, and were guided into the north Antrim safe routes to Scotland through O'Cahan of Castleroe and the Macdonnells of Dunluce. Probably not more than a hundred to one hundred and fifty were killed out of about 400 who survived the shipwreck. These killings are something of an anomaly. It is difficult to classify them as being at the hands of the Irish, although there was no English administration in Ulster at this time and only isolated groups of English soldiers at scattered locations throughout the province. The killings were actually carried out by Irish mercenaries under orders from the Hovendens. The Hovendens claimed to represent the Queen but were greatly distrusted by the Lord Deputy, and there is a strong suspicion that they acted solely for personal gain.

There was no concerted policy among the Irish on how to receive the Spanish survivors. By their own standards they did not treat them badly, although in County Sligo robbing them of all they possessed and leaving them destitute can hardly be regarded as welcoming. The Irish were not involved in killing them, with the exception of those in County Clare where English rule prevailed, and the peculiar situation on the Inishowen where the Hovendens seemed to engage in a bit of private enterprise. There are outstanding examples of where the native Irish chiefs risked all to help the Spanish. O'Rourke, MacClancy, McSweeny Na Doe and the Macdonnells deserve to be recognized for their humanitarian endeavours.

SPANISH PRISONERS IN ENGLAND

We have already seen that survivors of the *San Pedro el Mayor* were given proper treatment as prisoners of war. They were housed, clothed and fed; it was no picnic for them, but they had the basic necessities.

The same applied to the nearly 400 men from the *Nuestra Señora del Rosario*. On 1 August, the first day of the fighting off Plymouth, the *Rosario* had been damaged in collisions with two other ships. It fell out of formation and was virtually abandoned by the rest of the Armada. Francis Drake, ever the opportunist, saw his chance and pounced on the stricken *Rosario*, taking it as his prize. Drake had to rejoin the rest of the fleet so it was left to the *Roebuck*, captained by Jacob Whiddon, to escort the prize into Dartmouth.

In Dartmouth the care of the prisoners fell to the same Sir John Gilberte and George Cary who were later to attend to the *San Pedro el Mayor*. The men were split up into groups. About 40 officers were retained by Drake on the *Revenge*, and 30 sailors were left on board the *Rosario* to help bring it into harbour. The remainder were divided up on land; 226 were placed in the Exeter prison known as Bridewell, and 160 were accommodated around Dartmouth for a time but were such a burden on the local community that they were soon returned to the ship and looked after there. Cary pleaded with the Privy Council for help in paying for all this and was granted 4 pence a day each 'for their relief'.

Gilberte and Cary had a dispute which, in the context of everything else that was going on, offers some light relief. Gilberte lived near Dartmouth close to where the *Rosario* was moored and it seemed natural that he should be responsible for the prisoners on board. Cary lived at Cockington, a suburb of Torquay, so he was 16 miles from his prisoners in Bridewell. Gilberte was able to put prisoners from the ship to work in his garden and this upset Cary. 'He is too wise for me to have their daily labour and yet the allowance from Her Majesty of 4 pence per day. I have no grounds to level nor work to set them to so far from my house so the match is not equal'.

All this is a far cry from the beach at Streedagh Strand, littered with bodies, and George Bingham picking his way through them killing those who were not already dead, or the Lord Deputy murdering five Dutch boys as a mere gesture.

In the correspondence relating to prisoners in England, reference to 'execution' appears only once. A clerk of the Privy Council, Anthony Ashley, was sent down to Hope to supervise the salvage of the *San Pedro el Mayor*. In his report he 'thought convenient that they should cause the Spanish born to be executed'. An immediate reply from the Privy Council ordered that the execution of the Spanish be 'deferred'. It seems likely that the leadership on this came from the Queen. She did not like executions. She particularly did not like the execution of Mary Queen of Scots. And who was governor of Fotheringhay Castle at that time but William Fitzwilliam now, in 1588, Lord

Deputy of Ireland? He was already in bad odour with the Queen and he feared her. When he asked Burghley for help whenever his conscience (or whatever it was) began to prick him, he betrayed his basic insecurity. A year later, on 24 November 1589, an order was issued to release the Spanish prisoners; it came from the Queen. As early as 2 October 1588 she had accepted the principle of ransom for ordinary prisoners of war.

The treatment of Spanish prisoners in England would stand up quite well to any twentieth or twenty-first century court of enquiry. There is no good reason why they should not have had similar treatment by the English garrison in Ireland.

––––

GETTING AWAY WITH WAR CRIMES

Warfare had long been outside of the control of a formal set of rules. Its conduct varied between outright savagery and a kind of gentlemen's game where the combatants showed respect for each other and could shake hands at the end of the day.

When Don Pedro de Valdés had to surrender the *Rosario*, he did so on the deck of the *Revenge* and formally handed his sword to Drake. He was then Drake's prisoner and was placed by him in a safe house in Esher in Surrey. There he was free to wander the countryside and ride with the local hunt. There were no formal rules, but even in the sixteenth century there were unwritten ones.

In the twentieth century an attempt was made to define 'The Laws and Customs of War' in what became known as the Geneva Conventions, to which all leading countries subscribed. From them emerged the concept of war crimes, which were specified at length in Article 147 of the Fourth Geneva Convention. The relevant words for our study of the situation in Ireland in 1588 are: 'a war crime includes wilful killing not justified by military necessity, and carried out unlawfully and wantonly'.

Even today it is very difficult to bring anyone charged with a war crime before an international court. Making a formal charge of war crimes against someone from the past is probably a fruitless exercise. But history can condemn acts that fall within the definition of war crimes. Until now Bingham and Fitzwilliam have 'got away with it'. Their conduct has been passed over as if it was just one of those things that happened in war in those days—regrettable, but there is nothing we can do about it now, so there is no point in dwelling on it.

But there is. We can highlight their crimes and pass judgment on them.

Their barbaric acts fall clearly within the definition set down in Article 147 of the Geneva Convention. 'Wilful killing'—yes. 'Not justified by military necessity'—of course not; the Spaniards all wanted to be prisoners and posed no military threat. 'Unlawfully'—absolutely; the instructions from the Privy Council conferred no permission to kill prisoners. 'Wantonly'—the murder of five Dutch boys in November long after the drama was passed is wanton enough.

What the twentieth century has done is to give us the legal terminology with which to condemn them. Bingham and Fitzwilliam were war criminals.

NOTES AND REFERENCES

Fitzwilliam's decree is printed in Colin Martin and Geoffrey Parker *The Spanish Armada* (London, 1988) p. 235. This is the most scholarly general history of the Armada to date. It is from the Calendar of Carew Manuscripts 1588 pp 490–491.

Sir Richard Bingham's proclamation is in Bingham's Report.

The killing of prisoners in Tralee is in CSPI p. 28 and MIC 223/51 NO. 84.

The men from Recalde's *San Juan* and the survivor from the *Santa Maria de la Rosa* are in James Truant's letter to Sir Edward Denny of 11/21 September on MIC 223/51.

The killing of prisoners on the Clare coast is in Bingham's Report. Petrus Baptista's account is on MIC 223/51 NOS. 175–176.

Events around County Mayo and County Sligo, including both Tirawley and Streedagh Strand and the correspondence with Sir Brian O'Rourke, are in Bingham's Report.

Bingham's Report ends with the killings in Galway together with a summary of the shipwrecks and an estimate of the total numbers killed.

The directions from the Privy Council to the Lord Deputy for the 'safe custodie and keeping' of prisoners are in Acts of the Privy Council of England VOL. XVI under the date 18(28) September 1588.

Fitzwilliam's signs of panic are in CSPI pp 48, 53 and 65.

Bingham's whistle blowing letter to the Queen is in CSPI pp 76–77.

The treatment of Spanish prisoners in England is based mainly on the correspondence of Sir John Gilberte and George Cary in Laughton VOL. II. The subject is dealt with more expansively in *Spanish Armada Prisoners* by Paula Martin (Exeter, 1988), a beautiful book, very professionally prepared. It deals only with prisoners in England; Ireland is not mentioned.

McSweeny Na Doe's refusal to meet Fitzwilliam is in CSPI p. 94.

Sir Brian O'Rourke's defiance is in Bingham's Report.

The Essex/Norris atrocity on Rathlin is in George Hill *The Macdonnells of Antrim* (Belfast, 1873), reprinted 1978, pp 183–186.

I am indebted to my niece Louise Burton, a law student at Queen's University Belfast, for help with the question of war crimes. She directed my attention to an essay 'What is a War Crime?' in which Article 147 of the Fourth Geneva Convention is quoted at length.

Bingham's honest assessment of the ability of the Spanish survivors to pose a threat is on MIC 223/52 document NOS. 52 and 53. It is referred to in CSPI pp 53 and 54, NO. 10 v, but for the full text the microfilm copy is essential.

The Lord Deputy's report to the Privy Council on his journey into the north is transcribed in full in CSPI pp 92–98.

When the word 'execution' appears in original documents relating to this chapter I have chosen to transcribe it as 'killing'. The dictionary definition of 'execution' is 'the carrying out of a sentence of death'. It implies a lawful verdict after a fair trial, and is not appropriate to apply to Spanish prisoners of war. It is a euphemism, used in this case to soften the reality of the unlawful killing that occurred. The purport of this chapter is to lay bare the unacceptable conduct of the English representatives in Ireland, and it is important to use the correct terminology to describe it. England has much to be proud of in the Armada campaign, but the killing of prisoners by the English garrison forces in Ireland is a stain on her reputation and to some extent serves to subdue immoderate celebration.

Chapter 9

OFFICIAL REACTION IN DUBLIN AND LONDON

... the Spanish forces are so much weakened whereby there is no great doubt had here of any hurt that may grow thereby.

(SIR JOHN POPHAM)

THE INCIDENTAL BENEFITS OF MASTERLY INACTIVITY

It was the beginning of September before confirmation reached London that the Armada had sailed through the Fair Isle Channel and out into the Atlantic. The fishing boat from Southampton reported on 1 September, and the two pinnaces left to follow the Armada returned on 2 September to certify that they had left it 'to the westwards of the Islands of Orkney'. On the other side of the English Channel reports came through that the Duke of Parma had marched his army away from the coast and had unloaded the food and munitions from his barges. This should have allowed the Queen and Privy Council to relax in the knowledge that any threat of Spanish invasion had now passed.

Their equanimity was to be short-lived, however, and the unforeseen threat of Spanish forces from the Armada in a virtually undefended Ireland was to become a reality. No contingency plans had even been contemplated for such an eventuality.

Intelligence began to reach London that during the third week in September Spanish ships had started to appear on the west coast of Ireland. Thomas Norreys, Vice-President of Munster, reported to Walsyngham on 18 September that a small Spanish ship had arrived near Tralee, County Kerry. With the same correspondence a letter from Dingle was enclosed advertizing the arrival of three ships in Blasket Sound. The following day further news about the ship at Tralee was sent, together with an examination of the prisoners from it, in which they declared that they 'fell with the coast of Ireland not knowing where they were but resolved to return for Spain'. So the first information the Privy Council had of Armada ships in Ireland strongly suggested that their arrival was accidental and on a small scale, not part of an invasion.

Lord Deputy Fitzwilliam wrote the same day to Burghley giving the same information and enclosing a letter from George Bingham to Sir Richard Bingham, advising of nine Armada ships in Donegal Bay. (He wrongly added the six ships seen at Aringlas on 14 September to the three off the Carbery coast on the 15th, but of course they were part of the same group.) Donegal Bay is 160 miles north of County Kerry so these two groups were obviously not connected with each other, but the question was how many more were there on the rest of the coast?

Fitzwilliam did not at that stage think the Spanish were a threat in themselves, but he was concerned that their presence would awaken the potential for insurrection, never far from the surface in sections of the Irish people.

RUMOUR AND COUNTER-RUMOUR

By 20 September rumours began to pour in. The Mayor of Waterford reported eleven ships in the Shannon (there were in fact seven, four of which had been seen the previous day off Loop Head) and 140 ships on the rest of the coast! This was an altogether different proposition and Fitzwilliam immediately wrote to the Privy Council in London asking for 6,000 men together with munitions and supplies as apparently there were only '750 foot in bands in the whole realm'. It was at this time too that he issued his proclamation 'to apprehend and execute all Spanish found of what quality soever'.

Also on 20 September Sir Richard Bingham reported to the Lord Deputy on the situation in Connaught. He wrote of 'strange ships', but was not sure whether they were 'of the dispersed fleet which are fled from the overthrow in the Narrow Seas or new forces come directly from Spain'. His uncertainty was understandable—a full seven weeks had elapsed since the Armada entered the English Channel. There was a report of Richard Burke, the Devil's Hook, taking a dozen skiffs into the islands, but Bingham did not know at that time it was to plunder the wreck of the *Rata Encoronada* in Blacksod Bay. From the coast of County Clare, Boetius Clancy advised of two ships at the Islands of Aran and one at Liscannor. Along with the ships in the Shannon and six more in Donegal Bay, Bingham, as President of the province of Connaught, now had fairly reliable information on at least 17 Spanish ships at seven different locations within his jurisdiction. He was at Athlone with fewer than 200 men so it is hardly any wonder that he was bemused by the magnitude of the responsibility that could potentially confront him, and was not slow to transfer it to the Lord Deputy—'I beseech you to signify to me your pleasure'.

So on 20 September there seemed to be plenty for both Bingham and Fitzwilliam to worry about.

On the same day, however, Sir John Popham writing from Cork to Lord Burghley placed an altogether more sanguine interpretation on these same events. He acknowledged that many in the Irish community were 'dangerously affected towards the Spaniards', but stressed that they had no power to do anything about it. He recognized that, even at the end of the sixteenth century, Gaelic Irish society still retained its ancient cellular structure. There was no political mechanism by which the Gaelic Lords could act as a cohesive unit and turn their rebellious instincts into effective action. And as for the Spanish, he had already concluded that 'their forces are so much weakened whereby there is no great doubt had here of any hurt that may grow thereby'. Sir John Popham was Attorney General of England; since July he had been on a visit to Ireland along with Lord Chief Justice Sir Edmond Anderson. His opinion carried considerable authority and it had a profound effect on the Privy Council, for in the crucial period that followed no move was made to send reinforcements to Ireland.

The only positive intent seems to have come from Queen Elizabeth herself. On 24 September she asked Sir Richard Grenville 'to put in readiness some forces to be sent to Ireland as further occasion shall be given us. We require you that upon the coasts of Devon and Cornwall make stay of all shipping meet to transport soldiers to Waterford'.

We have the unfair advantage of knowing that the next day, 21 September, more than half the Spanish ships were destroyed in the Great Gale, and by 23 September all the remainder were departed with the exception of the *Girona* and fewer than one thousand men still in Donegal Bay. Any threat, if it ever existed, lasted for such a short time that the system for distributing information could not keep pace with it. The Privy Council in London did not in any case have the means to respond quickly to a crisis in Ireland, and on Sir John Popham's advice were already inclined to do nothing. By the beginning of October it appeared that the immediate emergency was passed and their relative inactivity had been justified. It became a case of managing the situation with the forces they had.

In Ireland, however, October was an uncomfortable month for the Dublin government; 800 men on the *Duquesa Santa Ana* suddenly returned to Ireland, landed on the coast of County Donegal, marched 20 miles and joined with those camped around the *Girona* at Calebeg. Sir Richard Bingham, writing in Athlone, expressed the opinion that the Spanish could do nothing—'for no question it is but of themselves they are marvellous weak and most miserable creatures, able to do little unless all the North do join with them'. The trouble was that there was nothing but the unreliable reports of spies and rumours coming out of Donegal. None of the English garrison in Sligo would venture into Ulster. And rumours soon fed their fears about a conspiracy or 'combination' between would-be Irish rebels and the Spanish. Local Irish groups around Sligo also believed them and the Conors, O'Harts and O'Dowds burned George Bingham's encampment at Ballymote, in the process declaring their allegiance to the Pope and King Philip.

Much to the Lord Deputy's irritation, Geoffrey Fenton, Secretary to the Council in Dublin, was actually in Sligo, and he seems to have been at least partly responsible for distorting the news from Donegal. The fact that de Leyva's party marched 20 miles from Rossbeg to Calebeg was reported by him on 17 October as a march from Calebeg to Lough Erne and a threat to be in Sligo in five days. Then on 19 October his imagination conjured up a full-scale rebellion with O'Rourke, McGlannough, Maguire and the Burkes of Mayo all combined with the Spanish.

Whether he believed all this or not, Lord Deputy Fitzwilliam had to take it seriously. On 22 October he wrote to the Privy Council enclosing over twenty copies of the correspondence from the north. For the second time he asked for reinforcements: 'that there may be presently sent hither 2,000 sufficient and well appointed men and so many more after as speedily as your Lordships shall deem this dangerous time and services to require'.

———

AN IMAGINED INVASION AND A LAME RESPONSE

The Privy Council could move only at a majestic pace and it was not until 8 November that they replied saying that they 'had given orders for sending over 2,000 soldiers under the command of Sir Thomas Perrot'. Again the speed of events overtook the faltering news service, and before any of this could happen, the Spanish in Calebeg had departed on the *Girona* and been shipwrecked at Giant's Causeway. On 7 November the Lord Deputy reported this to Walsyngham and openly acknowledged that the danger had finally passed. The reinforcements were never sent. Until this point he had done literally nothing against the Spanish survivors, but now he promised that he 'will be God's soldier for the despatching of those "ragges" which yet remain', and on 18 November he began his journey into the north. He met no Spanish forces, but he did kill a few prisoners. He claimed that, by ordering the northern chieftains to come in and make token submissions to him, he had settled any potential for rebellion. Maybe he had.

The English garrison in Ireland were hardly more than spectators to the disaster that befell the Armada. At only a very few locations did they make direct contact and never in an orthodox battle situation. On the west and north coasts there was virtually no significant English military presence. Sir Richard Bingham spent a long time in his base at Athlone. He set off into Mayo but before he could encounter any Spanish he turned back and headed for Galway, where he was instrumental in the massacre of prisoners. Otherwise, apart from George Bingham's small contingent around Sligo, any bands were mostly composed of a kind of home-guard drawn from settlers and led by civil officials commissioned for emergency service. Gerald Comerford, an attorney, took about fifty men into northwest Mayo, where, in theory, he could have been up against at least four hundred Spanish soldiers under Don Alonso de Leyva at Ballycroy, with another six hundred or so from the *Duquesa Santa Ana* not far away in Elly Bay. It was laughable really. On the few occasions when they met, the Spanish surrendered, handed over their weapons and expected to be treated as prisoners of war. Nowhere did they offer resistance.

The impact of Armada ships in Ireland on the English authorities in Dublin and London was physically negligible. Psychologically it worried them a bit. It was a momentous event, but it was over so quickly that in practice there was not enough time to do very much. The English in Ireland were lucky. They were never called upon to fight against vastly superior numbers of Spanish soldiers, whose only thoughts were to return to Spain. In the end they just seemed to melt away. As indeed the whole mighty Armada melted away from the coast of England while still an immense threat, and with invasion not even attempted. If the Spanish had been in Ireland for six months or more it might have been a different story.

NOTES AND SOURCES

The report of the return of the pinnaces to London is in Edward Wynter's letter to Walsyngham dated 3 September in Laughton VOL. II p. 150, which also refers to the Duke of Parma's withdrawal from the coast of France. According to Drake (Laughton VOL. II p. 99) one of the pinnaces was the *Advice* captained by 'Young' Edward Norreys, and the other was in fact a caravel belonging to him.

There are several letters breaking the news of the arrival of the Armada in Ireland; they are to be found more or less together in CSPI pp 26, 27, 28 and 29. Of course this was followed up with further information about other locations, but these are the ones that set the tone of the reaction in Dublin and London.

George Bingham's letter to Sir Richard Bingham is on microfilm on MIC 223/51 document NO. 77.

Sir John Popham's influential letter to Burghley from Cork is calendared in full in CSPI pp 31–32 and in Laughton VOL. II p. 218. His visit to Ireland is referred to in Laughton VOL. I p. 291.

Queen Elizabeth's request to Sir Richard Grenville is in CSPI p. 37.

The ships on the Shannon reported by the Mayor of Waterford are in CSPI p. 36.

The situation in Donegal Bay during October is in CSPI pp 53, 54 and 55, where they are calendared in notes and extracts. The full texts are on microfilm on MIC 223/52 document nos 52–67.

Confirmation that the Spanish survivors had departed from Calebeg to the Out Isles of Scotland and their subsequent shipwreck is in CSPI pp 63, 64 and 65.

The Privy Council's decision to order 2,000 soldiers to Ireland is in CSPI p. 69.

The Lord Deputy's letter to Walsyngham that showed he was convinced the danger was passed is in CSPI p. 68.

Confirmation that the Lord Deputy's journey into the north had begun is in his letter to Burghley written in Athlone on CSPI p. 74.

PART III

The Discovery of the Armada in the Twentieth Century

Chapter 10 ✍

A SALUTE TO THE DIVERS

I've found it, Marc.

(ROBERT STÉNUIT)

REDISCOVERING THE HISTORY

For three hundred years the history of the Spanish Armada in Ireland was buried in the archives. It existed only in mythology and local tradition, and it remained closed to historians and the general public alike. But in 1885 the Calendar of State Papers for 1587–1592 was published. Many old documents were transcribed in full and others summarized. Historians awoke to the possibility of discovering what really happened in the autumn of 1588.

In 1906 William Spotswood Green, Chief Inspector of Irish Fisheries, combined his personal experience of the Irish coast with the newly published State Papers and produced a paper entitled 'The Wrecks of the Spanish Armada on the Coast of Ireland'. This was delivered as a lecture to the Royal Geographical Society in London in February 1906 and was published in *The Geographical Journal* in May of that year. For sixty years it remained the standard work on Armada wrecks in Ireland. A few of his sites were identified accurately, but most locations were only approximate, largely because sixteenth-century knowledge of places on the Irish coast was extremely vague. Further investigation was needed if the true history of the Armada in Ireland was to be revealed.

After the Second World War, what began as underwater sport swimming, using the recently invented scuba equipment, opened up the opportunity for the investigation of historic shipwrecks without the need for expensive and elaborate diving equipment. By the 1960s two men in particular had become absorbed by the challenge of trying to find Spanish Armada wrecks. They were Robert Sténuit, a Belgian diver working as a professional in the North Sea oil industry, and Sydney Wignall who had some experience of organizing the exploration of an ancient shipwreck in the Mediterranean. The place to find Armada wrecks had to be Ireland, and both men independently began to research the documentary evidence to try to pin down likely sites.

Finding Armada ships in Ireland four hundred years after they were lost is really the second half of the story. The divers advanced historical knowledge in a way that no one else could have done. Not only did they produce wonderful physical evidence, they also burrowed into the archives and became scholars in their own right.

The work of the divers inspired further research and in 1978 the Climatic Research Unit contributed the first accurate daily weather situations for the summer and autumn of 1588. This was followed in 2003 by the *Journal for Maritime Research*, which highlighted the limitations of sixteenth-century navigation and explained how so many Armada ships came in contact with Ireland.

It is the combination of all these elements, assembled over the past hundred years, that has enabled us to reconstruct what happened to the Spanish Armada on the Irish coast in the autumn of 1588.

Robert Sténuit—The *Girona*

Sténuit was only in his late teens in 1952 when he became captivated by the dream of finding treasure under the sea. 'Spanish gold' was there waiting to be discovered, and looking for it was as legitimate a romantic adventure as any other youthful ideal. He got down to the practicalities of learning to become a deep-sea diver and combined it with a genuine passion for historical research.

Successive failures to find gold soon dispelled the early ambitions, but he went on to become a professional diver. His historical research also developed to the extent that he became more interested in the history than in the prospect of treasure. He thought of himself as an underwater archaeologist, although at that time the subject had not been formally developed as an academic discipline.

Of all the potential Armada shipwrecks in Ireland the *Girona* stood out for him as the most fascinating. From the late 1950s its tragic fate stirred his imagination. The concentration on board one ship of the flower of Spanish nobility—what a find that would be, enough to satisfy all those youthful romantic ideals, and yet at the same time fulfil his ambition to advance the frontiers of historical knowledge.

Time passed slowly for him. As a professional diver he was involved in the setting up of the North Sea oil industry and moved to London as head of one of the underwater engineering companies. *Girona* research became a spare time interest confined to the British Museum Library Reading Room and the Public Record Office. Original State Papers gave only a few sparse references to the location of the *Girona*, none of them eyewitness accounts. It seemed that only two places on the Antrim coast were known by name to the English garrison—Dunluce Castle and the so-called Rock of Bunboyes, which was in fact the Bushfoot near Portballintrae. When these names were used to report the wreck they were nothing more than approximate. Deliberate deception has been suspected, but sloppy reporting is more likely. The area was controlled by the Macdonnells of Kintyre; it was not exactly closed to English forces, but they were not frequent visitors.

The mystery had been compounded by an obtuse determination on the part of nineteenth- and twentieth-century historians to follow each other in misinterpreting the evidence. Even Spotswood Green, who had surveyed the entire coast and knew there was a place called Port na Spaniagh, concluded that the *Girona* was 'off the mouth of the Bush River near Portballintrae'. The result was that the wreck site remained undiscovered until Sténuit decided to do the obvious thing and look in Port na Spaniagh.

In June 1967 Robert Sténuit and his friend Marc Jasinski visited County Antrim for the first time, intending to make a few reconnaissance dives in the area of Port na Spaniagh. They booked into a guesthouse in Portballintrae. The weather was foul when they arrived and they were unable to launch their inflatable zodiac. All they could do was drive round to the Giant's Causeway and head out on foot along the cliff-top path. Sténuit was bowled over by the setting, made even more menacing in gale force winds. He later wrote, 'It's too much. A film set. Nature has overdone it.' To him it called out for tragedy. They wondered if anything could be left of the *Girona* after four hundred years of such conditions.

At last on 27 June the weather improved. They were able to launch the zodiac and headed for Port na Spaniagh. Sténuit dived around two submerged reefs at first, a likely place for the *Girona* to suffer fatal damage, but he found nothing. Then he moved in close to the east face of Lacada Point and immediately came upon a large lead ingot stamped with five Jerusalem crosses—the first Spanish Armada artefact to be discovered in modern times. 'I've found it, Marc', he said as he surfaced close to the zodiac. But Marc already knew from the elation on his friend's face.

Sténuit had found the *Girona*! It was not the fabled chest of gold, but to him it was more precious than that; it was the promise of fulfilment of his life-long quest.

There was more to come. A deep crevice seemed to surround Lacada Point as if the sea had been trying to undermine it. This acted as a collecting point for loose items from the ship. They found a large bronze cannon, a demi-saker, then a smaller breach-loading gun also bronze, and more lead ingots, cannon balls and a coin.

Of the *Girona* itself there was nothing left, not even a pile of ballast stones, and no ship's timber. Proof of the wreck would rest on an assembly of artefacts, but what an assembly that would turn out to be.

On 1 July it was a calm day for once and they were able to carry out a second dive. More articles were found—coins, a gold ring and fragments of a gold chain. But they were completely unprepared for the commitment demanded by their discovery. A team of divers would be needed, along with loads of equipment. They would need funding and their legal position would have to be protected. Under salvage law as it existed then, the finder of a wreck only had sole title to be considered 'salvor in possession' if he was working on it uninterruptedly and had marked it with a buoy. It would be the following year before Sténuit could set this up. In July 1967 all he could do was place the finds at the back of an underwater cave and try to keep everything secret. If another diver came along and found them he would take precedence. It was a worry.

Lapis lazuli and other treasures

In April 1968 Sténuit returned to Portballintrae along with Marc Jasinski and four French divers. Work began on the site on 28 April. Sténuit was determined to follow the precepts of archaeology as far as conditions would allow. In the Mediterranean, where the techniques of underwater archaeology evolved, the sites were stable and rope grids could be laid out to assist in recording the locations of all the finds. In Port na Spaniagh nothing was stable and the grids were quickly swept away. In order to draw up a chart, a set of fixed points had to be established from which bearing and distance measurements could be taken. As the excavation progressed the chart soon filled up with location symbols; gold and silver coins became regular finds.

The work was slow and arduous in the extreme, and exhaustion was constant, but Sténuit hardly noticed because he was working on an Armada ship and his dream was coming true. His exhilaration can be imagined and was richly deserved.

He realized from the start that the *Girona* would not have been carrying a treasure chest of official Spanish funds. They did exist, but only on board the flagship and vice-flagship of the respective squadrons. What was unique about the *Girona* was the concentration on one ship of the personal wealth of the many young adventurers who had attached themselves to de Leyva. It was never going to add up to a vast fortune, but they gradually uncovered a marvellous assembly of small items—rings and other jewellery carried as sentimental tokens of families and sweethearts left behind in Spain. These emerged as the real treasure of the *Girona*.

Sténuit delighted in researching as many of these small pieces as he could. A gold ring, bent and with the setting empty, was inscribed 'Madame de

Champagney 1524'; it puzzled him for a while until he realized that it must have been a departing gift from the lady to her grandson. No details could be discovered about the ring, shaped as a hand clasping a heart and inscribed 'No tengo mas que dar te'—'I have no more to give you'—but it speaks for itself. In his book *Treasures of the Armada* Sténuit describes in great detail the course of the work of excavation and the daily uncovering of new delights. There were so many, but two are worth special mention: the little golden salamander set with rubies that became the signature of the *Girona* exhibition, and 11 lapis lazuli cameo engravings of the Caesars set in gold and pearl; there would originally have been 12. The excitement at finding such beautiful things in a place like Port na Spaniagh can hardly be imagined.

During the early part of May 1968 Sténuit was so absorbed in the underwater archaeology that he was perhaps a little naïve and slow to realize the fact that their activities were not going unnoticed. Returning to their base in Portballintrae each evening they could not conceal the bags and boxes that accompanied them. Northern Ireland is a village; the grass whispers and news spreads. Sténuit made the mistake of being secretive. When questioned by journalists he tried to bluff them. He had in fact complied with the legal requirements. The representative of the Receiver of Wreck in Coleraine had been informed of the discovery and been supplied with a regular inventory of their finds. He had anchored a buoy over the site in Spaniard's Cove declaring that he was 'salvor in possession'. But all this should have been made public, and particularly the local police should have been informed. It was a legally protected site but nobody knew that.

The Belfast branch of the British Sub Aqua Club got to hear about it and naturally they were interested. Some of their members planned to visit Port na Spaniagh on Sunday 26 May. The previous Friday 24 May Sténuit had asked his Belfast solicitor to write to the club chairman informing him of the legal position and also extending an invitation to his members to view the site solely as observers. This was all too slow. On the Sunday twelve club members arrived at Portballintrae, kitted up and headed for Port na Spaniagh.

The Battle of Port na Spaniagh

Sténuit's party got there first and mounted guard on the active part of the site. The 'battle' was more of an angry confrontation than a violent exchange, but it was unpleasant just the same. Club members accused them of being 'only foreigners'. Sténuit was attacked by four divers; one of them tried to pull his flippers off. The French divers made it clear that if they had to defend the site physically they would do it. The invaders had a meeting and decided to withdraw. Sténuit explained the legal position to them and stated that he had written to the club chairman. Later they apologized, but of course at that time the solicitor had not yet sent the letter. In order to get the legal situation publicly acknowledged Sténuit had to spend the next four days in the Belfast Law Courts before Mr Justice Robert Lowry later Lord Chief Justice of Northern Ireland, who eventually on 31 May declared that 'Mr Sténuit is indeed the exclusive salvor in possession'.

To some extent Sténuit and his team were out of their depth. This was the most significant historic shipwreck in which scuba divers had become involved up to that time. They were inexperienced in the subtleties of salvage law, and their legal representatives were hardly better off. The principle of 'salvor in possession' rested on a decision reached as recently as 1924. It was not backed by statutory legislation nor was there a record of much case law on it. But it was all they had to protect a sensitive historic site from a free-for-all by treasure hunters. And they were innocents abroad when it came to the demands of public relations and the media. If Sténuit had it to do again, no doubt it would be done differently, and he would have learned that if a secret cannot be kept it is better to reveal it early.

By the beginning of June 1968, however, the problems had been overcome and the methodical excavation of the *Girona* could continue unimpeded. 1968 was the best summer on record in Ireland and work was carried on right through to September. Every day seemed to produce some new treasure. A gold, eight-pointed Cross of Malta started Sténuit off on an investigation of the orders of Knighthood and the various holders known to be on the Armada. He found that Fabricio Spinola, captain of the *Girona*, was the owner. The pleasure and satisfaction Sténuit derived from the discovery of these small objects can be sensed even today. It has to be remembered that very little material from the Armada had been found until then. These were the first to be recovered under archaeological conditions.

They returned in 1969 to try to complete the excavation. It has been possible here to mention just one or two highlights, which hardly convey the extent of their success. It should be appreciated, however, that the inventory lists handed to the Receiver of Wreck had expanded to over 12,000 items.

In an incredible demonstration of goodwill, Sténuit designated that they should all be displayed together in the Ulster Museum in Belfast. This entailed complex negotiations by the museum staff, long and expensive work on curation, and generous financial support by the Northern Ireland government as well as private subscribers. The *Girona* rooms were opened in June 1972. They are a unique display, which should not be missed by anyone interested in Armada history. This was the first time that an entire assembly from an underwater excavation was purchased by a single institution and preserved for the nation.

As an almost fairytale postscript, a local diver, Wes Forsythe, was granted

Clew Bay, Co. Mayo. This shot shows the drumlin islands of the inner bay, and it was in the northeast corner of the bay that the *Santiago* was lost 'about the islands at Burrishoole'. (© *Michael Diggin Photography*)

The O'Malley castle on Clare Island, Co. Mayo. The Spanish galleon *El Gran Grin* of the Biscay squadron was anchored for six days near here in the shelter of the southeast of the island. The crew were supplied with fresh water and food by Dowdra Roe O'Malley and the islanders, but the ship was a victim of the gale of 21 September and a number of men on board were lost. (© *Michael Diggin Photography*)

Aran Islands, Inishmore, Co. Galway. Two Armada ships were seen on the seaward side of the islands on the night of 15 September 1588. They later moved down onto the Clare coast, but were lost in the gale of 21 September. (© *Imagefile*)

The galleon *San Marcos* had been off the Aran Islands, but moved down to the Clare coast to find safe anchorage. It was hit by the gale of 21 September and lost on a rocky island between Lurga Point and Mutton Island, though traces of the wreck have never been found.

The Cliffs of Moher. Their dangers are obvious here, but Armada ships managed to avoid them. They played a part in the survival of the *Zuñiga* in Liscannor Bay by deflecting the gale of 21 September 1588. (© *Michael Diggin Photography*)

Loop Head, Co. Clare. Four Armada ships were reported off here, but they eventually ended up in the Shannon off Scattery Island. (Not wrecks, they later sailed.) (© *Michael Diggin Photography*)

Scattery Island, Lower Shannon, Co. Clare. Seven Armada ships sheltered in Scattery Roads for several days. One of them, the *Anunciada*, was abandoned and scuttled. The other six left the Shannon on Tuesday 20 September. (© *Michael Diggin Photography*)

The old castle on Fenit Island, at the entrance to Barrow Harbour, Co. Kerry. A small Spanish ship was lost near here and 24 survivors were taken into custody by Lady Denny. They were later killed, presumably by garrison troops in Tralee. This was the first record of Spanish survivors being killed. (© *Michael Diggin Photography*)

Blasket Sound, Co. Kerry. This illustrates Dunmore Head, the Lure, Great Blasket Island and the Sound on a beautiful day. The *Santa Maria de la Rosa* was, however, sunk during the gale of 21 September 1588 between the Lure and Great Blasket, with all hands. (© *Michael Diggin Photography*)

Swivel gun, bronze and iron, from *La Trinidad Valencera*. (*Courtesy of the National Museum of Northern Ireland*)

Pestle and mortar, bronze, from *La Trinidad Valencera*. (*Courtesy of the National Museum of Northern Ireland*)

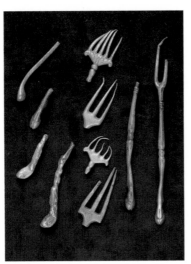

Selection of silver forks from the *Girona*. (*Courtesy of the National Museum of Northern Ireland*)

Hollow gold buttons from the *Girona.*
(*Courtesy of the National Museum
of Northern Ireland*)

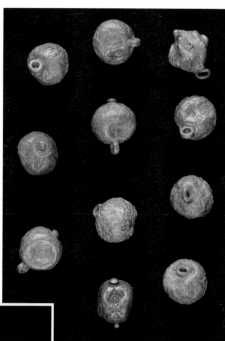

Agnus Dei reliquary from the
Girona. (*Courtesy of the National
Museum of Northern Ireland*)

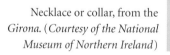

Necklace or collar, from the
Girona. (*Courtesy of the National
Museum of Northern Ireland*)

Salamander. (*Courtesy of the National Museum of Northern Ireland*)

a licence to visit the site in 1997, and he found the twelfth lapis lazuli cameo. With the help of the National Art Collections Fund, it has now joined the others in the Ulster Museum's *Girona* collection.

We owe Robert Sténuit an enormous debt. By finding the *Girona* and recovering so many artefacts from it he enormously enriched the cultural heritage of Ireland. Above all he removed the *Girona* from the realms of speculation and mythology and gave it the reality that springs only from material objects.

―――

Sydney Wignall—*The Santa Maria de la Rosa*

Sydney Wignall was a determined adventurer. Whatever project he embarked upon he gave it his total commitment. In the 1950s he had already experienced a hair-raising escapade during an expedition to survey a high altitude, unmapped area of the Himalayas. He was taken prisoner by the Chinese who had just marched into Tibet, and he was given the full treatment of communist 'persuasion' to confess to spying. By a miracle he escaped with his life and returned to India. He realized that his energies would have to find fulfilment in a different activity, and he turned to scuba diving.

After a successful dive in the Mediterranean he became interested in the wrecks of the Spanish Armada in Ireland, which promised to offer a suitably demanding challenge. In 1963 he visited Ireland and carried out a reconnaissance of potential sites. Following Spotswood Green he looked for the *Girona* at the Bushfoot and naturally found nothing. He eventually decided that the *Santa Maria de la Rosa* in Blasket Sound, County Kerry, would become the target of his Armada ambitions.

Wignall did not have private funds and he had to spend the next five years trying to raise the money to finance a full season of diving. Blasket Sound is a huge area, covering about four square miles, and he would need a large team of divers. He had an interest in underwater photography, which helped to bring in some money. But he always seemed to relish the task of organizing and controlling a large-scale expedition. He was fortunate too in that he seemed to be able to enlist the help of recognized experts such as John Grattan of the Royal Navy's Middle East Clearance Diving Team and Joe Casey of the St Helens diving group. Desmond Brannigan, a Dublin-based marine consultant and historian, carried out a survey of Blasket Sound. His report stressed the difficulties involved in searching such a large area with a hazardous tide race even in calm conditions.

Wignall was conscious also that the legal position regarding historic shipwrecks was not clear-cut, and he tried to acquire for his expedition some kind of legal protection. He asked the Irish government for a salvage licence, but at that time the government was inclined not to get involved and took the view that ownership of the wreck lay with the government of Spain. This was probably not legally correct, but Wignall negotiated an agreement with the Spanish by which he was granted a sole salvage licence. Wignall was also aware of the legal principle of 'salvor in possession', which in 1969 he would be compelled to use to defend the wreck site from intruders. The offhand position taken by the Irish government was a mistake that would take almost twenty years to correct.

It would be 1968 before he could start his operation, and it was therefore a worry when in 1967 his friend Joe Casey and the St Helens diving group came to Blasket Sound and began to search for the wreck. When working south from off Young Island one of the divers thought he saw a mound of stones with three guns sitting on top of it. The weather was very bad at the time with sea mist blotting out any view that would have given them a navigational fix on their position. They never re-located it and all they could say was that it was in the northwest of the Sound, probably off Beginish. This was to become a bit of a red herring and a real nuisance. It did not tie in with the eyewitness account of the sinking of the *Santa Maria de la Rosa* in Aramburu's diary, but it would eventually have to be investigated.

In February 1968 Wignall began to organize his expedition for the coming season. He would need the services of a large team of amateur divers. In an article he wrote for the magazine of the British Sub-Aqua Club, he described the project, pulling no punches as to the hardships involved or the strict regime he intended to run, but he still had applications from 116 would-be volunteers. He accepted forty-three of them, although they would not all be used at the same time. The first group of eleven assembled at Dingle on 13 April. One of them was Colin Martin who was to make a huge contribution to the course of the whole operation during both 1968 and 1969.

The search
Because Blasket Sound was so big, the search had to be ordered systematically. Diving conditions were also a problem with a three-knot tidal current running most of the time. This was where John Grattan's experience proved vital. He arranged a method of covering the area in blocks, which was essential to ensure that none of it was left out or that time was not wasted going over the same place several times. Six or more divers had to swim in parallel, joined by lengths of twine and controlled by someone in a surface boat. It was known as the swim-line system.

Diving began on 17 April and was concentrated on the northwest part of the Sound off Young and Beginish Islands where the St Helens divers had seen 'something'. They spent two weeks on this and it was eventually confirmed as a false alarm when all they could find was some modern piping.

Systematic searching then extended into the rest of the Sound and on 9 May an anchor was found off the White Strand on Great Blasket Island. It had lost a fluke and the ring was broken. Two days later another anchor was found about 200 yards north of the first one. This was also broken and was only the bottom part of an anchor—the flukes and half the shaft. Colin Martin was familiar with the documentary evidence and immediately realized that it all reflected Aramburu's account of events on 21 September 1588. Recalde's *San Juan* had come off its anchorage (hence the broken ring) and struck Aramburu's ship on the stern. Later that afternoon when Aramburu recovered his loose anchor cable it came up with only the cross piece and half the shaft, leaving the lower half to be found by Wignall's team off the White Strand on 11 May 1968.

Searching the whole of Blasket Sound using the swim-line system was a long and laborious process. At the end of it they had found no sign of a historic shipwreck. This was disappointing. But in the southern part of the Sound they came across three more anchors. One of them had a massive 17-foot shaft and was still hooked to the reef in the middle of the southern entrance to the Sound. This was almost certainly the *Santa Maria de la Rosa*'s sheet anchor. On the afternoon of 21 September 1588 when the *Rosa* had dragged down the Sound along with Aramburu and Recalde her anchor did not hold until it struck the reef. Then when the ship started to sink the anchor was probably cut free. The vivid description of the *Rosa*'s sinking in Aramburu's diary was coming to life before their eyes. 'At 2 o'clock the tide turned and she began to swing on her anchor. She dragged to within two cable lengths from us and we dragged with her. We could see she was going to sink any minute. They tried to hoist the foresail but she went down right away with every man on board—a most extraordinary and frightening thing'. This could only mean that the *Rosa* had struck the reef between Great Blasket Island and Dunmore Head and had sunk immediately to the south of it. They must be getting close at last.

Part of the reef was a high pinnacle of rock named on modern charts as 'Stromboli' after an English gunboat which struck it in the nineteenth century. This looked as if it might have been the instrument of the *Rosa*'s sudden destruction. Although it has 25 feet of water over it today, H.M.S. *Stromboli* was responsible for removing 8 feet from the top of it and so in 1588 there would have been only 17 feet. Bearing in mind that the Great Gale was at its height and there would have been deep troughs, it seems more than possible that the *Rosa* could have crashed into the Stromboli reef, catastrophically holing its hull. No other interpretation explains the speed of its sinking. The place to look for it would therefore have to be immediately to the south or southeast of Stromboli.

The reef falls quickly to the seabed, which then shelves away to a depth of more than 120 feet. This marked the safe limit for divers to operate, and the permitted time at the bottom without decompression facilities was only 14 minutes. Additional problems the divers had to face were the three-knot tidal current, which meant that they could enter the site only at slack water, and poor visibility at that depth even when the sun was overhead at midday. A disciplined routine was essential if accidents were to be avoided.

They resumed their swim-line search technique and, in a much smaller area than Blasket Sound, managed to cover the sector in just over a week. But still nothing!

What everyone was looking for were guns. At the Lisbon muster the *Rosa* was listed as having 26 guns on board. The bronze guns in particular should have survived. And, as vice-flagship of the Guipuzcoan Squadron, she was recorded as carrying 50,000 ducats of Spanish capital. They could expect the rest of the ship to have been devoured by the passage of time and the furious tidal current, but the guns should be there, perhaps sitting on a pile of ballast stones or stuck in nearby sand and shingle. And the treasure chest, if it existed, was a reasonable expectation as well. They did find two piles of stones. One was close to the reef and contained mixed sizes of stones scattered over a wide area; it looked like the natural scree at the base of the reef. The other pile was about 200 yards off to the southeast of Stromboli. It was long and low and consisted of fairly evenly matched, medium-sized boulders. There appeared to be nothing unusual about it, and there were no guns or other artefacts that would connect it to a shipwreck. The three divers who found it—Jack Sumner, Chris Oldfield and Joe McCormick—noted it on the chart but continued the search.

Disappointment was turning to desperation. They had to decide what to do next. As they met to discuss the situation it emerged that during the search of the Sound two of the less experienced volunteers had not been swimming deeply enough and areas could have been missed. They would have to go over it again. Searching the whole Sound a second time occupied three more gruelling weeks; in a way it kept them busy when there might have been thoughts of giving up. But again nothing!

Wignall was driven by a stubborn determination to carry on, and none of the rest wanted to quit at this stage. It was decided to go over the area south of Stromboli again. At the end of June he had to leave the group to attend to personal business in Malta. He left Colin Martin in charge since Colin had come to the fore as the outstanding member of the team both for his thorough knowledge of Armada history and his meticulous expertise as an archaeologist.

On 4 July 1968 the mounds of stones were re-located. The scattered pile of irregular stones was identified again as an underwater avalanche and was not important. It was Squadron Leader Mike Edwards who found the other stones just as the search was ending for the day. He picked up a lava-like concretion and broke it open with his knife. The outer shell fell away in a cloud of black oxide, revealing an iron cannon ball underneath. So this was the *Santa Maria de la Rosa* after all. It was in exactly the place it ought to have been, about 200 yards southeast of Stromboli, but it was scarcely recognizable. It took a fresh pair of eyes to see something different in a pile of stones that most of the divers had swum over more than once. And there were no guns!

Next morning they all dived on the site and, before the day was out, had found more cannon shot, musket balls, lead ingots and, at the edge of the mound, the ends of oak beams, implying that part of the ship's timber had been preserved under the ballast. News had to be sent to Wignall in Malta. It must have come as an enormous relief to him after all he had put into the project. Colin Martin did not seem to register the expected elation at finding the wreck. He seemed quietly to reflect upon the tragedy that engulfed more than 300 people there on that September afternoon nearly four hundred years earlier.

The survey

With Colin Martin in charge there would be no impatient digging into the site. The rest of the 1968 season was taken up in surveying and mapping the area so that when excavation started the following year all the finds could be accurately recorded.

As Sténuit found in Port na Spaniagh, a grid of weighted lines was quickly swept away. They had to set up four permanent markers from which bearing and distance measurements could be taken. Chris Oldfield and Jack Sumner built two 15-foot square metal grid frames painted with black and white scale markings. Only then did they begin the very careful mapping of the site. This was important because, owing to poor visibility at that depth, they never had an overall view of it.

The picture that emerged was surprisingly undramatic. The mound of ballast stones was about 100 feet long, described as tadpole shaped, about 40 feet broad at the head tapering to less than 20 feet at the tail, which was angled off by about 50 degrees. The head was pointed more or less due north and was located on the bottom just 50 feet from the southern edge of the reef, and exactly 220 yards southeast of the pinnacle of Stromboli. It might have seemed undramatic, but this was where Colin Martin's brilliant interpretive ability came into play. Through his knowledge of sixteenth-century shipping he was aware that ballast stones were not evenly distributed. They were used to counterbalance the extra weight of large sterncastles, and so were concentrated mainly in the forward part of the ship. The distribution of the ballast stones indicated that what they had here was only the bottom of the front end of the *Rosa*. The way the mound tailed off at an angle suggested that the stern section had broken away during the sinking, allowing ballast stones to spill out. The stern was nowhere to be seen.

There seemed to be no doubt that this was the *Santa Maria de la Rosa*, but there was no absolute proof as yet, and there was more than a little uneasiness about the prospect of having only part of the ship to work with. There were no spectacular guns and no iron-bound treasure chest immediately visible. Explanations would have to wait until the excavation stage of the operation, which could not begin until the following year.

The excavation—1969

Administration and financial support were Sydney Wignall's specialty and he had succeeded in providing enough funds for another season of diving in Blasket Sound. They would not need a large team that year, and their group was based around a small core of experienced divers—Colin Martin, Chris Oldfield, Jack Sumner, 'Smudge' Smith and Karl Bialowas, with of course Wignall himself.

They met at Dingle on 2 April 1969 and planned the coming operation. Their first task was to carry out a metal detector survey of the site and surrounding area using the metal grids they had built the previous year. This survey took nearly two weeks and yielded only sparse, scattered contacts, none of them a large object. This was again disappointing and they began to wonder if it was the *Santa Maria de la Rosa* after all. They knew that another ship, the *San Juan* of Fernando Horra, might have been lost in Blasket Sound at roughly the same time and that Recalde had removed her guns before abandoning it in the Sound. It was a possibility: there had been no sign of her during the two searches of the Sound.

When the excavation got under way they started to find iron roundshot and among other items a small pewter plate, which when cleaned revealed the name 'Matute' inscribed round its rim. Wignall had all his research documents with him at Dingle and on going through them the name 'Matute' popped up. Captain Francisco Ruiz Matute was commander of the soldiers on board the *Santa Maria de la Rosa*—final confirmation of the identity of the wreck.

Nearly everything seemed to be bound together in lumps of concretion, which had to be broken open before any preserved artefacts could be revealed.

In this way they accumulated several small items such as fragments of metal, wood, rope and leather. Chris Oldfield made the gruesome discovery of human remains under some ballast stones at the southern end of the pile, included in which was a small concreted disc. When this was opened it was found to be two coins, one gold and the other silver. The gold coin was minted in Seville, the silver one was from Mexico City, obviously this poor man's savings. They were the only 'treasure' found on the *Rosa*.

The Grey Dove *Affair*

The 1969 season was interrupted in the middle of May by what became known as the 'Grey Dove Affair'. A group of Liverpool businessmen had acquired an ex-World War II German E boat christened the *Grey Dove*. They made a poor job of keeping secret their plans to descend on the wreck of the *Santa Maria de la Rosa*, where they hoped to discover 50,000 gold ducats, worth at that time about £1,000,000. They appeared to be an affluent and powerful consortium, who had already invested a considerable sum on the project to gatecrash the excavation. Some of them had applied to join the 1968 diving team but had been turned down.

Sydney Wignall was the right man to take on the challenge of the *Grey Dove* consortium. He was resourceful and determined and knew that the place to fight them was in the Irish law courts, not the waters of Blasket Sound. He duly secured a restraining order preventing them from interfering with the wreck.

That should have been enough to deter any normal group of people, but the *Grey Dove* consortium pressed on regardless. On 26 May they were quoted in the *Daily Telegraph*: 'We are carrying on with our salvage operations'. On 28 May they sent a telegram to Éamon de Valera, the Irish President, promising that in return for permission to dive on the wreck they would conduct their operations 'with extreme care and respect for items of archaeological value'. But next day one of them spoiled it all by giving a radio interview stating: 'All this talk of archaeology is poppycock. People don't spend this sort of money on archaeology, and as far as I am concerned this is a straightforward business venture and we will recover all items of value as quickly as possible'. The interview was tape-recorded. One wonders what kind of business they were in that they expected to use force to get what they wanted. It was crazy, but they were dangerous.

Wignall's salvage boat had just been refitted, but on its way from Dublin to Dingle it experienced a number of mechanical problems. Wignall was convinced that it had been sabotaged. The police were informed but no culprits were arrested.

They were back in court again on 5 June. The consortium had engaged a counsel on this occasion, and they had cooked up a new plea, claiming that they were in fact co-adventurers with Wignall, because they had been involved in the 1968 season. This was easily disproved. Mr Justice O'Keefe was not deceived by their contorted arguments and extended the injunction effectively for the rest of the 1969 year. Their counsel withdrew from the case on 31 July. It appeared that the consortium was running up some unpaid bills.

Wignall won the legal battles hands down. He was unquestionably the 'salvor in possession'. But one suspects that if the *Grey Dove* consortium had got as far as Blasket Sound there would have been a physical battle that would not have been so easy.

It would be nice to know when the consortium learned the fact that no treasure was ever going to be found on the section of the ship that had survived. If they had succeeded in digging into it with a bucket dredger they would still have come up with nothing. All their machinations and expense were futile, which gives the good guys some cause for satisfaction. There is in fact considerable doubt as to whether the *Santa Maria de la Rosa* had a treasure chest on board. It is true that treasure chests were generally allocated to the flagship and vice-flagship of each squadron, and that the *Rosa* is listed in both the Lisbon and La Coruña musters as vice-flagship of the Guipuzcoan squadron under Miguel de Oquendo. During the account of the fighting off Plymouth, however, the explosion on the *San Salvador* was reported in Medina Sidonia's diary as being on 'Oquendo's vice-flagship'. And the following day when the *San Salvador* had to be abandoned it was recorded that 'orders were given to tranship his Majesty's treasure'. It would seem, therefore, that the *San Salvador* had replaced the *Rosa* as vice-flagship of the Guipuzcoan squadron. This may have been because the *Rosa* had lost her mainmast in the storm off Galicia and, though she eventually did sail with the Armada, her participation must have been doubtful until the last minute.

Excavation and interpretation

Back in Blasket Sound Colin Martin was continuing with the serious work of excavation. This produced two contrasting results. Firstly, recovery of artefacts was proving to be frustratingly unproductive. Even the surrounding shingle yielded very little. In the area of the galley fire they found some charcoal and brushwood, and some storage casks had the bones of sheep, cattle and chickens. Also of interest was an iron-bound, wooden cap of the type used on mastheads to guide flag ropes, but they could have hoped for more in the way of personal possessions, weapons and ship's stores.

It was in the investigation of the ship's structure, however, that the real 'treasure' of the *Santa Maria de la Rosa* was to be discovered. Colin Martin's painstaking examination of every piece of wood, his inspired interpretation of what he found, and the deductions he was later able to draw from them, really had a touch of genius about it.

In order to examine what remained of the ship's timber, ballast stones had to be removed, which was done by exposing a trench through them. Immediately he observed that the stones were not just piled into the hold in a haphazard way; they were built into place like a dry stone wall. Not only did this method keep the ballast stable when the ship was bouncing around in heavy weather, but also the crew were then able to dismantle and replace the stones systematically when looking for and repairing leaks.

The part of the ship that Colin Martin examined first was the keelson, which was attached to the top of the keel by clamping down the ribs and forming a solid framework. He measured the way it was made and found that it was composed of jointed lengths, each 10 inches broad and 8 inches deep. His knowledge of sixteenth-century shipbuilding alerted him to the fact that these measurements were disproportionately slender for the overall size of the ship. As vice-flagship of the Guipuzcoan Squadron it was naturally assumed that the *Santa Maria de la Rosa* was a Spanish galleon, built to withstand the rigors of Atlantic voyages. It now appeared, however, that her dimensions were at least similar to Mediterranean cargo vessels. They derived their strength from a kind of eggshell construction of the hull, which was adequate for their normal trade especially when fully loaded, but they were vulnerable to heavy weather and seriously weakened if the integrity of the structure was violated by gunfire or other external damage. Initial interpretation pointed to the *Rosa* being one of the ships compulsorily requisitioned like those of the Levant squadron.

As the excavation continued, 35 feet from the bow they uncovered a complex wooden framework which was soon deduced to be the step-box for the mainmast. Neither the step itself nor the mast had survived. Surveying and excavating this small section took six weeks. The meticulous care taken in recording the precise details of the remains of this complicated structure would be amply repaid. There was some very rough workmanship surrounding the box, which was not typical of the rest of the ship. Then they remembered that the *Rosa* had lost her first mainmast during the voyage from Lisbon to La Coruña. The replacement had probably been fitted by the crew rather than by specialist shipwrights, and that could account for the jerrybuilt appearance. Its weakness may have contributed to the *Rosa*'s final traumatic disaster.

Based entirely on his examination of the mainmast step-box, an area no more than five feet square, Colin Martin was able to reconstruct the probable course of events as the *Santa Maria de la Rosa* sank on that gale-lashed afternoon of 21 September 1588. As her sheet anchor caught on the reef the ship swung so that it hit Stromboli broadside about amidships on the starboard beam. She was holed from keel to waterline and quickly filled with water. Drifting in the current she began to sink stern first. The breaking open of her hull had undermined her structural integrity and contributed to her immediate disintegration. As she hit the bottom the mainmast was ripped out, damaging the keelson. She broke in two, the stern section separating just aft of the mainmast and taking with it the decks and superstructure of the forward section. Ballast stones spilled out from the stern section, leaving it light enough to drift further south into Dingle Bay before settling on the bottom. Only the bottom of the hull and ballast stones of the forward part of the ship were left to be found by Sydney Wignall's divers nearly four hundred years later. The rest of the ship, together with presumably the guns and treasure chest (if there had been one) is, therefore, somewhere in deep water beyond the reach of scuba divers.

After the excavation was complete, Colin Martin was not yet finished. He wanted confirmation that the *Santa Maria de la Rosa* was indeed of Mediterranean origin and had to research the problem himself. He discovered that one of the main differences between Atlantic galleons and Mediterranean cargo vessels was the formula for positioning the mainmast. On Atlantic galleons it was exactly on the mid point of the keel. On Mediterranean ships it was well forward of amidships on a point three-fifths of the distance from stern to bow. He knew the tonnage of the *Rosa* and the distance from bow to mainmast, and he calculated that the tonnage could be accommodated only in a ship built to the same specification as large Mediterranean cargo carriers.

Further research in the Spanish archive in Simancas, however, revealed that the *Rosa* was indeed a Spanish ship, built in San Sebastian in 1586–87 by Martin de Villefranca, a merchant involved in the Labrador whaling trade. Before she could be brought into service she was requisitioned and given a prominent role in the Armada as vice-flagship of the Guipuzcoan squadron. It is therefore a startling revelation to find that not all of the vessels employed in the Armada as warships were galleons. The *Rosa* had the dimensions and structure of a merchant ship, and although she had been built to withstand the stresses of the North Atlantic and would have been a good sea-going vessel, she would have been a poor warship, since gunfire from armed merchant ships often inflicted as much damage on themselves as incoming enemy action.

A treasury of information

It would have been all too easy to dismiss the remains of the *Santa Maria de la Rosa* as being hopelessly inadequate to reveal very much about the ship and its sinking. Colin Martin's superb work on it demonstrated maritime archaeology at its best. Guns and bullion, if they had been found, would now reside in museums, but he produced a treasury of information we all can share. And he gave us an absorbing tale of detection and deduction based on seemingly insignificant scraps of evidence. We can only gasp in admiration.

The City of Derry Sub-Aqua Club—*La Trinidad Valencera*

Members of the Club had been diving in Kinnagoe Bay on the Inishowen Peninsula for more than two years. They knew about *La Trinidad Valencera* of course. It was well documented in the Irish State Papers, but many searches had produced no result. The location of the ship in the State Papers is given as near 'a creek named Glanganvey'. The Glenagivny River enters the bay towards its eastern end, and it was generally believed that the ship was somewhere off shore there. The description of the way she was wrecked also conveys the impression that she had grounded on a shelving beach and that the wreck should be fairly close to the shore. Robert Sténuit had taken time out from his work on the *Girona* to spend several weeks looking for it, but without success. He even declared that it was not there.

On Saturday 20 February 1971 when the club met in Kinnagoe Bay it was merely for a training session. Only about half of the members were qualified to 'Club Diver Standard' and these training meetings, under their training officer Charles Perkinson, were serious lessons designed to bring the others up to club diver level. The car park is at the western end of the bay and they decided for convenience to do their training in the sea off here. There was, therefore, no thought of searching for the *Trinidad Valencera* as they felt they were in the wrong place. Nevertheless, it was always at the back of their minds.

Opposite the car park a rocky promontory crosses the beach and enters the sea, where it continues as an underwater reef. The divers split up into small groups to carry out their respective training routines in this area. Two of the experienced divers, Archie Jack and Paddy Stewart, followed the low reef about 30 feet down and traced it out to where it seemed to disappear some 300 yards from the shore. They were just about to turn back when they noticed that it re-appeared as a higher mound of rock about thirty yards further on. They had not been out as far as that before and so they decided to have a look. As they approached they could see something lying on top of the rock—a 10-foot long bronze gun!

Panic stations! They had found *La Trinidad Valencera*. It was much further out than had been expected, which explains why, despite extensive searching, it had not been found previously. Instead of grounding on the shelving beach, it had struck a mound of rock much further from the shore.

Paddy Stewart immediately surfaced and shouted to other divers on the surface: 'We've found a cannon', and just as quickly disappeared again. Three divers had heard the shout and they swam over to where they thought Paddy Stewart had been. When they dived they could not see him: visibility was only about five yards on the bottom. But they did see a gun sticking up out of the sand—a monster three-ton bronze cannon, highly ornamented with a coat of arms and two lifting dolphins. Where was Paddy? Well he was nearby attending to his gun. There were in fact two guns at that stage; the first on top of the rock was a culverin, the second in the sand was a huge 7¼-inch siege gun. Two more would be found before the end of March, and a fifth later.

For a short time they were almost incoherent with excitement. They scrabbled about looking for a buoy or anything colourful to mark the location, but could find nothing, which shows how unexpected the discovery was. There were 13 members of the club present that day. To compose themselves and decide what to do they adjourned to Keaveney's Hotel in Moville.

They may have been amateur divers, but they were professionals in their other careers and well understood the implications of what they had found. They had the example of the *Girona* operation not very far away in County Antrim, and were aware of the work on the *Santa Maria de la Rosa*. They especially knew the importance of protecting the site from intruders and establishing the right of the club to be recognized as 'salvors in possession'. Unfortunately this meant keeping the find secret from other members of the club until the legal formalities could be observed.

Two of the divers, Father Michael Keaveney and Dr Jim Whelan, went to Dublin the following week to inform the Spanish Embassy, but the Embassy showed no interest in the discovery. Regrettably the Irish government was not interested at that time either. It was an anxious week, but actually in retrospect they did move with commendable speed, because the next Saturday, 27 February, they assembled at Kinnagoe Bay along with their solicitor, Paddy O'Doherty, and the representative of the Receiver of Wreck from Letterkenny, Paul O'Rourke. The wreck site was buoyed off with a club marker and they were confirmed as 'salvors in possession'. It was only then that the rest of the club members were told, administrative arrangements were made and preliminary operations planned. On 4 March their press officer, Stan Donaghy, released the news to the media. Right from the start they stressed that it would be treated as an archaeological site. In any case it was common knowledge that, apart from the guns, no treasure was likely to be found because the crew had had two days to remove all valuables from the ship before it broke up and sank.

One of the club members, Eamon Molloy, was a surveyor by profession, and during March he carried out the first survey and mapped the visible parts of the site. A pontoon was moored over the wreck.

Father Michael Keaveney as club treasurer arranged a bank loan to cover initial expenditure, but eventually the BBC was to become a major source of funding for the project. The *Chronicle* programme wanted to film the raising of the first of the guns, which was to be at Easter. They asked Colin Martin to do the filming for them and he was delighted to be involved in the venture. Once on the site his enthusiasm for the whole operation, but especially for the guns, led him to become committed to the future exploration of the wreck. The club was grateful for his help as no one had more experience in dealing with Armada artefacts. He arranged for a metal detector survey to be carried out by himself and Jeremy Green of Oxford University, who had also surveyed the *Santa Maria de la Rosa* in Blasket Sound. This survey was highly productive and indicated that there was a large amount of material buried in the surrounding sand and silt. All of this was extremely promising, as artefacts buried this way were likely to be relatively well preserved.

At Easter 1971 four guns were raised and taken round to Moville, where they were placed in a tank of water which would protect them from exposure to the atmosphere until they could be properly conserved. Legal and logistical complications presented a difficulty. No suitable conservation facilities were available in the Irish Republic at that time, but none of the artefacts could legally be taken into Northern Ireland for treatment until a year had elapsed. A provisional export licence was issued by the Irish Customs and Excise, authorizing the Receiver of Wreck in Letterkenny to transfer material from *La Trinidad Valencera* to the Ulster Museum for conservation. Later a laboratory was established at Magee College in Londonderry, which was much closer to the site, and was operated as a kind of holding area.

Colin Martin was particularly stimulated by the guns. These were the only surviving Spanish guns from the Armada and he subjected them to scrupulous examination and research. (It was thought that the guns on the *Girona* were of Italian origin.) Two of them were 7¼-inch bronze cannon of startling beauty, elaborately decorated with the full escutcheon of King Philip II and dated 1556, the first year of his reign. The gun founder had inscribed his name on the base ring—Remigy de Halut. Colin Martin traced this name and found that he was Master of the Royal Gunfoundry at Malines near Antwerp. They were identified first as full cannon, but measurements showed them to be 'curtows'—curtailed by about a quarter in length and weight, presumably to make them easier to handle.

Also found were six large-spoked guncarriage wheels, implying that the 7¼-inch cannon were mounted on fieldgun carriages, not truck mounted as would be normal for use on board ship. This led to speculation that they might have been carried in the hold for later use in the land campaign, rather than on deck for ship-to-ship fighting. Colin Martin researched the history of Spanish gunnery techniques in great detail and discovered that there were records of fieldgun carriages being used on board ships. Apparently they tried to keep the massive recoil under some semblance of control by lashing them. If they did try to use these guns on deck, the probability is that they would not have been very effective owing to the complicated gun-drills that would have been involved. There is also some evidence that both truck mountings and field carriages could be carried so that the guns could be used on board ship and later transferred to land use.

The 1971 season was largely exploratory, and when a plan of the site had been completed by adding the metal detector contacts it revealed that they were concentrated in two groups lying apart from each other. This indicated that the ship had broken in two after riding up on the mound of rock, which confirmed the eyewitness account of events on the morning of 16 September 1588.

The Club members carried out a careful excavation operation during 1972 and 1973 under Colin Martin's supervision. Using a compressed airlift supplied by the BBC, they worked their way through the huge amounts of sand and silt and uncovered a tremendously rich collection of artefacts. Apart from the military equipment such as weapons and armour, there were pottery and pewter goblets, plates, bowls and cutlery. The promise of well-preserved organic material was amply fulfilled in the shape of woollen and other textile pieces, leather boots and shoes and rope sandals and a considerable amount of wood such as ship's pulley blocks, shot gauges, barrel staves, bellows, musket and arquebus stocks, wheel axles and wagon yokes. It all amounted to an amazing assortment of the everyday implements of life on board a sixteenth-century warship.

Progress was remarkably smooth. There were no cowboy gatecrashers. All the members pulled together and played their part with great enthusiasm. They knew the importance of the task they had embarked upon and were determined to carry it through.

It had been the wish of the Irish Prime Minister (Taoiseach), Charles Haughey, that the finds should be preserved as a unit and eventually displayed at a suitable location in Derry. This was brought about in 1981 as part of an agreement between the Irish government and the Ulster Museum. The Irish authorities were conscious that the Ulster Museum was already bearing the considerable expense and responsibility of conservation. The question of payment of salvage rights to the City of Derry Sub-Aqua Club also still remained to be settled. It was decided to sell the artefacts to the Ulster

Museum for a nominal sum on condition that the Ulster Museum further paid the salvor's award and agreed to place the artefacts on long-term loan in a suitable Derry venue. Under this agreement outright ownership of all *La Trinidad Valencera* material resides with the Ulster Museum, which has the right to call upon it for special displays and additional research. Their remarkable success can now be seen in the superb display of guns and artefacts in the Tower Museum in Derry.

This chapter is meant to be a tribute to the divers and none deserve it more than the amateur members of the City of Derry Sub-Aqua Club. The way they handled themselves in a most challenging situation and the results they achieved are worthy of the highest praise.

———

The Streedagh Strand Armada Group—*La Lavia, La Juliana and the Santa Maria de Visón*

The most famous of all of Ireland's Armada wrecks are the three ships wrecked on Streedagh Strand, County Sligo, on 21 September 1588. The documentary evidence could hardly be more conclusive. In Spanish sources Captain Francisco de Cuéllar, one of the few survivors, wrote a graphic description of the shipwreck and his miraculous escape. This has been translated several times and widely used in nearly all twentieth-century histories of the Armada. In Irish sources George Bingham reported being on the spot within two days and how he 'courageously' killed any remaining survivors. Ten weeks later Lord Deputy Fitzwilliam visited it during his journey into the north, when wreckage was still to be seen along the shore. The wrecks were also marked on an early map dated 1612. Yet the individual wreck sites had never been found.

There was plenty of precedent from the 1960s and 1970s about the processes involved in setting up an expedition to look for Armada wrecks in Ireland, and in the early 1980s plans were being made to search for the Streedagh wrecks. Research and the initiative to embark on this ambitious project came from Stephen Birch, an experienced diver then working as a scallop fisherman on the island of Scalpay in Scotland. Like the earlier diving groups he was primarily interested in the history that could potentially be revealed if the sites could be discovered, but he was also well versed in the archaeological principles that had evolved particularly at Blasket Sound and Kinnagoe Bay. He could not claim to be a qualified maritime archaeologist, but very few people could. It would later emerge that there were none in Ireland at that time. He was supported by Alan King and Harry Chapman, also experienced divers with business interests in preparing divers for the North Sea oil industry. They provided the initial investment in electronic equipment, vehicles, boats and cameras, and recruited a team of eight other volunteer divers. They were aware of the legal implications of their task and the importance that the principle of 'salvor in possession' had played in previous expeditions. They felt that if they followed the example set by their predecessors they would not be far wrong.

1985: State involvement

On 26 April 1985 they were ready to begin operations. Their solicitors wrote to the Office of Public Works informing them of their intention to look for the Streedagh wrecks. Mr Dunleavy, for the Office of Public Works, replied on the same day to the effect that no licence was required at that time to search using magnetometers, echo sounders and metal detectors. If the wrecks were discovered, however, he asked that they be reported to his office in accordance with the National Monuments Acts. In a final paragraph he gave the divers advance warning that 'our normal procedure would be to protect the site by preservation order, and for further work a licence would be required'. It would appear that their solicitors did not pass on to the divers the contents of this paragraph.

On 30 April the actual survey began and, almost at once, part of a large gun-carriage wheel was found 'at about three cables (i.e. 600 yards) from the shore line at the northern end of the bay'. Diving was prevented by bad weather for the following few days, but on 7 May they revisited the site, and some 20 yards to seaward of the wheel found a complex of articulated ship structure overlaid with iron and stone shot, three anchors and three bronze guns. Nearby a 35-foot-long ship's rudder was also revealed.

They immediately informed Colin Martin, by then director of the Institute of Maritime Studies at St Andrews University, and invited him to inspect the site in order to confirm its identification as an Armada wreck. They also informed Mr Dunleavy at the Office of Public Works, Mr Kevin Carruthers of the Maritime Institute of Ireland in Dún Laoghaire and officials in the National Museum. It was arranged that representatives from these bodies should visit the site on 16 May. Colin Martin confirmed the identification. The officials were openly excited by what they saw and realized that a major maritime archaeological discovery had been made.

The measurements of the guns enabled the wreck to be identified as *La Juliana*. In the meantime the sites of the other two ships had been located. About half a mile southwest of *La Juliana* they found the *Santa Maria de Visón*, and 600 yards southwest of that a quite large group of magnetic contacts indicated *La Lavia*.

Colin Martin recommended that the guns should be lifted right away for security reasons and so that conservation could start without delay. Mr Dunleavy agreed, 'with some reluctance' it was said. The guns were lifted and transferred directly to the Office of Public Works depot in Dromahair Castle under police escort. The Receiver of Wreck in Sligo was also informed. The guns have remained at Dromahair ever since.

Up to this point the indications for the project were extremely positive. The divers and the officials from the Irish authorities seemed to share the same enthusiasm, and the presence of Colin Martin guaranteed that everything would be done under the supervision of the most highly qualified maritime archaeologist in Britain or Ireland. The divers now felt that they had complied with the legal obligations, which previous experience had shown should entitle them to be regarded as salvors in possession.

Then on 27 May the Commissioners of Public Works made a preservation order preventing further work on the site. This had already been indicated as normal procedure by Mr Dunleavy in his letter to their solicitors of 26 April, but it obviously came as a shock to the divers. It was greeted with some irritation and they later claimed that it had been done without consultation and without their knowledge, which was a bit unfair to the Office of Public Works. It was, nevertheless, frustrating that progress should be stalled barely three weeks into the project and only eleven days after the positive reaction of representatives from the National Museum and the Maritime Institute of Ireland.

On 6 June a meeting was arranged at the Office of Public Works, attended by the divers' London solicitors. As a conciliation exercise this was a failure. The London lawyers were later described as being 'confrontational' and they seem not to have helped to advance their case very well. They were forthright in asserting the group's rights as salvors in possession and contested the validity of the preservation order.

Further dives took place in August and September 1985 at which representatives of the agencies of the State were present as observers. The volatile nature of the site was apparent, as there had been significant changes since May. Another small gun, an esmeril, had been exposed in a very vulnerable position not far from the shore. The divers asked for it to be placed with the other guns in Dromahair Castle. After a bit of official dithering, somewhat irrationally, permission was refused. This gun later disappeared, possibly re-covered with sand, but perhaps pilfered. Relations between the parties appear to have become strained.

The various agencies of the State were then co-ordinated by the formation of an inter-departmental committee under the auspices of the Taoiseach's office. This committee seemed to adopt a more conciliatory approach and were willing to discuss ways towards an amicable settlement. They made clear at a meeting on 27 November 1985 that their main concern was the cost of excavation and the apparently open-ended commitment of resources to conservation. The different agencies of the State were all dependent on funding allocations which were already tight in relation to land-based projects. The National Museum had in addition the problem that many of its archaeological treasures had to be confined to storage because of lack of display space. The more important the Streedagh finds appeared to become, the greater the problems they created. Hesitation at allowing the project to proceed is understandable in the circumstances.

1986: Confrontation and legal wrangling

In March 1986 the Streedagh group's London solicitors again responded to the inter-departmental committee in what they regarded as confrontational terms. They still held to the argument that, because the group were salvors in possession, they had the right to carry on with the project. Even under existing law, however, they still required a licence from the Office of Public Works for a pre-disturbance survey, and this did not seem to be the best way of getting one.

In June 1986 the group wished to view the site again to assess any changes that might have taken place over the winter months, and they were allowed to do so under the supervision of Mr Kevin Carruthers of the Maritime Institute. Inspection revealed that all the artefacts that had been exposed the previous year were now covered up and there was nothing to be seen. This was probably a reflection of the processes that had been going on for the previous four hundred years. It was ostensibly volatile, but what had survived until now was in no immediate danger, provided it was covered with sand for most of the time.

During the course of the visit Mr Carruthers handed the group a letter from the inter-departmental committee to the effect that, according to their legal advice, the Irish State was the owner of the wrecks. This was met with some displeasure. It prompted the group to begin litigation in the Admiralty Court to try to sustain their claim as salvors in possession.

The hearing did not take place until July 1987. The preservation order was challenged and, as it was known to be of dubious legality, the State did not defend the case. The judge then issued an injunction preventing the divers being interfered with when they visited the site for inspection purposes.

The question of salvor in possession was overtaken by other events. In April the Irish Parliament passed the National Monuments (Amendment) Act 1987. This had the effect of claiming ownership for the State of all historic artefacts including ancient shipwrecks within its territorial waters. It firmly removed the Streedagh wrecks from the realm of salvage law and the Admiralty Court, and ended the divers' rights as salvors in possession. This was perfectly reasonable and a similar law, though less sweeping in its effect, had been enacted in Britain—The Protection of Wrecks Act 1973. For too long the law had failed to distinguish between the commercial salvage of modern shipwrecks and the archaeological significance of wrecks more than a hundred years old now abandoned by their original owners. The Streedagh wrecks clearly belonged to the Irish State.

The debate in the Irish Parliament had been accompanied by a fair amount of emotive language. There was considerable anger about Ireland's cultural treasures being appropriated and sold abroad. This may have happened with some items found on land, but it definitely did not apply to the Streedagh divers. The group's conduct in relation to the handling of finds had been impeccable, as was later acknowledged by the judge, and their intention was for any discoveries to be preserved as a unit and displayed in Ireland. They wanted to contribute to Ireland's cultural heritage in the same way that had been successfully accomplished in the cases of the *Girona*, the *Santa Maria de la Rosa* and *La Trinidad Valencera*. Nevertheless, when speeches were made in the Senate arousing passions about 'foreigners plundering Ireland's cultural heritage', it seemed quite unjustly to stick to the Streedagh divers in popular perception. They were all English or Scottish, except for one Irish volunteer, and were easily branded as foreigners. But they had the support of the people of the village of Grange who were intensely interested in the project and could anticipate that a successful excavation of the Streedagh wrecks would benefit their community. They promoted the De Cuéllar Trail, which traces de Cuéllar's journey from Streedagh through Ulster to his eventual safe departure from Lough Foyle, County Derry, to Scotland. Their enthusiastic support for the divers has not wavered.

In August 1987, while still under the protection of the court injunction, the divers visited the site again and found other artefacts not seen before, including a gun-carriage in good condition and nearby a small falcon swivel gun partly made of bronze. On their own initiative they lifted this gun and delivered it themselves to the Office of Public Works depot in Dromahair under the supervision of the Receiver of Wreck in Sligo. Official permission was not sought and the judge felt that was justified, having regard to what he described as 'the unreasonable response of the Office of Public Works to a similar request to save an esmeril' the previous year.

The terms of the new National Monuments (Amendment) Act 1987 were now in operation, however, and it was realized that, in order for further work to continue, a licence would have to be sought from the Commissioners of Public Works. On 11 September 1987, therefore, the solicitors of the Streedagh diving group prepared an application. In the process they went into a lengthy preamble, reviewing the course of events leading up to the present situation. They claimed that in July 1987 the divers had carried out a 'full survey of the site using sophisticated electronic equipment', and they then went on to apply for a licence to 'excavate'. The solicitors obviously hoped to clear the hurdle of a pre-disturbance survey and go straight into a full exploration procedure. Colin Martin would later testify that a proper survey would take four to five months and would include a study of the marine environment affecting the wrecks. If and when such a survey was complete, then would be the time to talk about excavation.

The door was open, therefore, for the Commissioners of Public Works to refuse a licence, which they did on 11 December 1987. They were able to submit as a reason for the refusal that 'conservation and other resources available to the State at present would not be adequate to deal with the amount and range of archaeological material that is likely to be recovered'. This was undoubtedly true. If, however, the application had been for a full pre-disturbance survey it could hardly have been refused. In any case, it would have been necessary and, if Colin Martin was to be the supervising archaeologist, would have been insisted upon. The way the application was presented was a tactical mistake. Not for the first time it appeared that the group's legal advisers were inexperienced in this field of law and insensitive to the niceties of dealing with Irish officials.

Lack of resources was to become an unanswerable obstacle to any future hopes of excavation. It was clear that the agencies of the State did not want this operation to continue and they now had a reliable way of stopping it. The Streedagh diving group were therefore not to be able to realize their plans for a major contribution to the history of the Armada in Ireland. This was a disappointment to them and to everyone whose primary interest is history.

The 'do-nothing' approach wins out

It was not, however, the end of protracted court proceedings. Lawyers for the Streedagh diving group sought to challenge the effect of the National Monuments (Amendment) Act 1987, in that it extinguished their rights as salvors in possession. In July 1994 they began judicial review proceedings in the High Court in Dublin, with a subsequent appeal being heard in the Supreme Court in June 1995. Predictably this failed. The State had the constitutional right to enact such legislation and there was nothing the divers could do about it.

There was an element of manoeuvring to establish entitlement to damages and finder's reward, but this remained unresolved because the amounts would depend on the estimated value of the site, and this could not be calculated in the absence of a full pre-disturbance survey, which had still not been carried out.

The Court showed a good deal of sympathy for the divers, whom it recognized as 'honourable, responsible and competent'. Colin Martin gave lengthy evidence during which he recognized the authority of the State to determine the progress of the work on the site, but pleaded that the State in turn should find a way to accommodate the involvement of 'law-abiding, well-motivated people whose aim was academic and scholarly research, not commercial salvage'. The Commissioners of Public Works were criticized by the judge, Mr Justice Barr, as 'having failed in their duty to the State and the people of Ireland' in not having a detailed survey and investigation of the site carried out.

It seemed that there might have been tactical reasons why the agencies of the State did not want such a survey, and it is easy to be impatient with them. The doctrine of 'do-nothing' does not have much appeal. But there are no villains here. The divers wanted to realize the enormous potential of the wrecks, but the Commissioners of Public Works could see that they would be overwhelmed by the commitment involved. Their advice was that the archaeological material would come to no harm if it was left in place for a while longer. Historians are the losers and Ireland's cultural heritage at Streedagh remains covered in sand. There is an obvious contrast between the quality and extent of historical knowledge made available by those ships that have been excavated by divers and those that have not, and the suspension of work on the Streedagh wrecks has left a gap in Irish history that should some day be filled.

REAL SHIPS, REAL PEOPLE, REAL PLACES BROUGHT TO LIGHT

The heroic days of the 1960s and 1970s are gone. Thank goodness for those divers who found and explored the *Girona*, *Santa Maria de la Rosa* and *La Trinidad Valencera*. Without them the history of the Armada in Ireland would have remained relatively obscured by mythology and local tradition. It is a matter of great regret that the Streedagh diving group were not allowed to produce similar historic results. The potential was there for them, and it is truly sad to see this ambitious project degenerate into rather undignified legal wrangling.

Maritime Archaeology has changed. The high cost of excavation and curation, and the fact that State agencies have now assumed paramount responsibility in this area, mean that old-style excavations are unlikely to be repeated. We must get used to a new vocabulary, which includes such phrases as 'in situ preservation', 'non-invasive survey', 'long-term resource management' and 'minimal site disturbance'. The tools of the trade now amount to echo-sounding equipment, side-scan sonar, sub-bottom profiling equipment and magnetometers, while suction hoses are frowned upon. This new archaeology has the backing of most national governments (though up to 2007 not the United Kingdom) and the endorsement of the 2001 UNESCO Convention for the Protection of Underwater Cultural Heritage.

It is here to stay, at what cost to the history of the Spanish Armada in Ireland remains to be seen.

When the divers embarked on their different projects their motivation was purely the excitement of discovery. They had no idea that it could stimulate a powerful reaction from people not previously interested in history. In July 1985 Bob Ballard and his team were similarly innocent of the chain reaction that would follow the finding of the *Titanic* on the floor of the Atlantic. One of them said, 'we did not realize we were giving the *Titanic* back to the world'. They ignited the imagination of millions of people who felt they could now share in one of the most dramatic events of the twentieth century. The outcome was truly amazing. Books, TV films, a blockbuster movie and deep-sea tourism sprouted. Groups of visitors now come to Belfast nearly every day to see the Harland and Wolff design office and the slipway where the *Titanic* was built. The site no longer builds ships, but it is the centre of a new civic development with the universally alluring title 'Titanic Quarter'.

The divers of the 1960s and 1970s did the same for the Spanish Armada in Ireland, perhaps on a smaller scale but with the same effect: they made it tangible for a wide audience. From that time onwards the Armada was not just a collection of dusty State Papers, accessible only to historians. It became real, with real ships, real people and real places—in Ireland very special real places, which everyone can visit and share the experience.

NOTES AND REFERENCES

The authority for most of the sections in this chapter is from the divers themselves who have written books about their adventures. It required only a modicum of objective interpretation to select those sections of their accounts that are relevant to the history of the Armada in Ireland as a whole.

Robert Sténuit—The *Girona*
Sténuit's book *Treasures of the Armada* was published in 1972. Like so many authors writing about the Armada he feels it necessary to try to cram in the whole story. But when he gets down to his personal involvement this is stirring stuff. Bear in mind that this is a translation from the original French.

Sydney Wignall—The *Santa Maria de la Rosa*
Wignall's own book *In Search of Spanish Treasure* was not published until 1982. He was more interested in diving than writing. The details of the work on the *Santa Maria de la Rosa* are superbly told in Colin Martin's book *Full Fathom Five* (1975) pp 23–135. Wignall was the author of the appendix recounting 'The *Grey Dove* Affair'. The reference to a treasure chest on the *San Salvador* is in Hume pp 396–397. Research into the origins of the *Rosa* is further described in 'Ships of the Spanish Armada' by Colin Martin, a chapter in the book *God's Obvious Design*, edited by Gallagher and Cruickshank (1990).

The City of Derry Sub-Aqua Club—*La Trinidad Valencera*
Again Colin Martin's book *Full Fathom Five* has a section describing the exploration of the *Trinidad Valencera*, pp 189–224. In 2003 one of the club members, Jack Scoltock, published a book entitled *We've Found a Cannon* in which he has collected the memories of some of the divers who found the wreck. Also included are a large number of contemporary photographs.

The Streedagh Strand Armada Group—*La Lavia*, *La Juliana* and the *Santa Maria de Visón*
This part of the history is inadequately reported. In 1999 an account was published in the *International Journal of Nautical Archaeology* (28.3), by the divers Stephen Birch and D.M. McElvogue. Again this wastes a lot of space summarizing the Armada voyage. Information about the debates in the Irish Parliament was from the Internet. The Irish Law Reports VOL. 3 pp 413–482 includes Mr Justice Barr's extended and detailed review of the course of events from April 1985 through to the decision of the Supreme Court in June 1995, and is the most fruitful source of information about the whole Streedagh saga.

| A SITE GUIDE

A by-product of researching the history of the Spanish Armada in Ireland has been the necessity to make many visits over many years to the Irish north and west coasts. This has invariably been a source of great pleasure. Most of the sites are dramatically beautiful in their own right, but their association with the stirring events of that momentous autumn over four hundred years ago adds savour to the adventure.

The majority of the sites are reasonably accessible. A few involve a boat trip to one of the off-shore islands, but they are generally well served by modern ferries. Sometimes the distances to be covered can be surprisingly long; for example the narrow, though perfectly adequate, road system in northwest County Mayo around Blacksod Bay and Broad Haven is tortuous in the extreme. It takes time and one should not be in a hurry.

It hardly needs to be said that the Irish people are warm, welcoming and helpful. Accommodation is of a high standard and is available everywhere, both hotels and bed and breakfasts. Farmhouses can be worth a visit, if there are any close by. Irish Tourist Offices in most areas offer a booking service. Don't expect good weather every day; it is part of the experience that weather almost always comes out of the Atlantic, so be prepared to dress accordingly. But you can hope to miss a destructive gale like the 21 September 1588.

On-site information is generally not present so do your homework and be your own guide. Where information is available it can sometimes lag behind the most recent research and needs to be read with caution.

It is virtually guaranteed that a tour of Armada sites on the Irish coast will live long in the memory. Logistically it is not difficult and, for everyone interested in Armada history, it is a compelling adventure.

Site 1: Port na Spaniagh, County Antrim—The *Girona*
This is part of the geological phenomenon on the north coast of County Antrim known as the Giant's Causeway. It stretches for about two miles from

the Causeway visitors' centre east to Benbane Head. This part of the coast is now owned by the National Trust, so facilities are good and paths are well maintained. A bus service takes visitors down to the Causeway itself, which is what the crowds come to see.

To view Port na Spaniagh you have to walk the cliff-top path, which starts just outside the back of the visitors' centre. It is steep for the first quarter of a mile, but reasonably flat thereafter. Although not more than a mile, it follows the twists and turns of the coast, which adds a bit to it. The walk takes a little under half an hour. You can soon look down on the Causeway, which is usually crowded with visitors in summer.

The Chimney Tops are a landmark that is always in view, and the path brings you out right on top of them. The next bay to the east is Port na Spaniagh. Just under the Chimney Tops are Spaniard's Cove and Lacada Point. This is where the *Girona* was wrecked. The view from the path here is partly obscured, because the cliffs are so steep they create an overhang. It is a dangerous place, so do not be tempted to creep near to the edge. To get a clear view walk round Port na Spaniagh until you can look back and see the western side of the bay. Lacada Point is the low, flat finger of rock sticking out from the bottom of the cliffs. It hardly looks like the rest of the rock formations and must have been formed by the first of the lava flows some 70 million years ago.

You will see that the bay is completely enclosed by a semicircle of vertical cliffs 400 feet high. Even if someone managed to struggle ashore here there would still be no escape. A worse place to be shipwrecked cannot be imagined. It is a test to envisage the scene on the morning of 29 October 1588 with the bay covered in wreckage and bodies.

The five (or nine) who survived must have been rescued by boat. The Macdonnells had seen the *Girona* in difficulty as it passed Dunluce the day before and would have come out looking for it. Their boats would have salvaged all they could take away and saved the poor survivors.

The GPS reference for the cliff above Lacada Point is N55° 14.746', W06° 30.036' and the altitude is 410 feet.

Dunluce Castle is still there four miles west of the Causeway and can be visited. The elaborate additions to the Castle were said to have been paid for by the wealth the Macdonnells salvaged from the *Girona* wreck. Portballintrae is no longer a sleepy village, having been overrun with weekender development, but the little harbour is unchanged from the time when Robert Sténuit and his team launched their zodiacs there every day before heading round to Port na Spaniagh. The next bay to the east is the mouth of the Bush River, known as the Bushfoot, and the big black 'Rock of Bunboyes' still stands just off shore. Although it figures prominently in the early literature, it is now known to have had no connection with the Armada.

Site 2: Kinnagoe Bay, County Donegal—*La Trinidad Valencera*

Kinnagoe Bay is in a remote corner of the Inishowen Peninsula. You have to search for it and some maps are not very helpful.

In the Republic of Ireland road signs are in kilometres except for some old signs still showing miles. The town of Moville is about 30 km north of the City of Derry on the west side of Lough Foyle. If you are approaching from the north coast of County Antrim and using the car ferry from Magilligan to Greencastle, drive south 5 km to Moville. In the middle of Moville take the road heading northwest signed for Carndonagh number R238. About 6 km along this road a right turn is marked with a whole collection of roadsigns, one of which is a brown sign to Kinnagoe Bay 6 km. Turn right, follow this road for 1 km, and take another right turn, also marked with a brown sign, to Kinnagoe Bay 5 km. This road bends almost immediately to the left at a large church, and from there it takes you straight to Kinnagoe Bay. It gets narrow and steep as it descends to a very good car park at sea level. The bay has a magnificent beach and nearly always has several visitors and even campers.

The car park overlooks the rocky promontory that extends underwater for about 300 yards where *La Trinidad Valencera* was found. This is a considerable distance from the beach and it can be appreciated that the crew needed the assistance of Sir John O'Doherty's boats to get everyone ashore. The beach is certainly big enough to hold the 400 or so soldiers and mariners who would have had two uncomfortable days camped there in the open. The surrounding grassy cliffs are high and steep, but there was obviously a route out, which they all took as they marched to O'Doherty's castle at Illagh just north of Derry. There is very little left of it, but Castle Burt, where the Hovendens were camped, is still a significant building overlooking Lough Swilly off the N13 about 12 km west of Derry.

The GPS reference for the car park at the Kinnagoe Bay site is N 55° 15.523', W07° 00.710'.

There is a very good maritime museum in Greencastle, which is well worth a visit. But the Tower Museum in Derry has several rooms devoted to *La Trinidad Valencera*, which must be visited. On show are the 10-foot culverin and the 7¼-inch cannon found by the divers on 20 February 1971. Both are outstanding. An excellent exhibit explains the painstaking conservation process every item found under the sea had to undergo.

Site 3: Rossbeg, County Donegal—The *Duquesa Santa Ana*

The place where the *Duquesa Santa Ana* grounded in Loughros More Bay on 28 September 1588 is approximately one kilometre east of the village and harbour of Rossbeg. To reach it drive north from Ardara on R261 signed for Portnoo and Narin. After about 9 km, turn off left for Rossbeg just after the Kilclooney Bridge. The road takes you northwest for about 2 km to a three-road junction. There is a signpost left for Rossbeg 5 km and also a brown sign for the 'Santa Ana Drive'—confirming that you are in the right area. The roads here are narrow, undulating and full of tight bends as they follow a convoluted, rocky and barren landscape. Take it easy!

After 4 km a sign indicates left to 'Tramore Beach—Caravan and Camping Site'. Turn left here but do not take the road up to the caravan park. Stay on the flat and you will reach a small car park at the end where there is room for a few cars. Park here and walk towards the beach through the sandhills.

The beach is an enormous expanse of sand, quite large enough to contain the thousand or so men de Leyva is said to have had in his party at that time. There are outcrops of black rocks at both ends of the beach. The *Duquesa Santa Ana* is said to have come in towards the rocks on the right, and this was where the valiant seamen swam ashore to attach a line when the anchor broke in the storm. The *Duquesa* eventually beached near these rocks, and when the weather calmed down all on board came ashore. De Leyva was hurt in the leg during this operation when they were struggling with the capstan. Most of the survivors would have stayed on the beach, but de Leyva and a small group moved across to Kiltooris Lough and fortified on the island there at its eastern end.

Sandhills are notoriously volatile and change rapidly under stress of wind and rain. Even in the past 30 years there has been a radical transformation. Grass has been stripped off some of the hills perhaps as a result of increased human activity from the nearby caravan park. Sand has actually migrated down to the beach, making it even larger and moving the tideline further out. It can almost be guaranteed, therefore, that the topography of Tramore Beach would have been very different 400 years ago.

The Spanish survivors were in McSweeney Na Doe's country and were perfectly safe from any threat from the English military. He quickly made contact with them, offering all the help he could. It was he who advised them of the presence of the *Girona* near the castle of his younger relative, McSweeney Banagh, only 19 miles away in Donegal Bay. And he accompanied them when they set out to march south to the Harbour of Calabeg. There is a steep mountain pass south of Ardara, but the rest of the journey would have been a reasonably gentle walk down the valley of the Stragar River. De Leyva had to be carried.

The GPS reference for Tramore Beach is – N54° 48.477', W08° 29.944'.

Site 4: The Harbour of Calebeg, County Donegal—The *Girona*

On the main road from Donegal town to Killybegs there are two sharp left turns for St John's Point, one in Dunkineely and the other just through the town. They join after about 1 km and lead down the long narrow peninsula that encloses McSwyne's Bay. At the head of the bay the remains of McSweeney Banagh's Castle still dominates the landscape. Part of one wall is reasonably intact and the remains of other outbuildings can also be seen. Its prominent, raised position must have made it an imposing feature in its day. On contemporary maps it is clearly marked 'Ca. McSwine', and the surrounding countryside 'Mac Swine Bannah'. In the sixteenth century the peninsula was called 'The Rosse' and St John's point was 'Rosse's Point'. Several references in the State Papers to the McSweeneys' part in helping the Spanish are fairly convincing evidence that the *Girona* sheltered here rather than in the modern harbour of Killybegs. It was present for a full six weeks, from 15 September to 26 October. De Leyva and his party would have arrived about 10 October.

The GPS reference for the castle is N54°37.14', W08° 22.808'.

Information from the area was scarce and the only comment about the Spanish camp was that it was 'betwixt the castle and the church'. There is an old church about 1 km north of the castle, but there is also another old friary church, which still survives 3 km to the south at Akle Back. Two roads lead off to the left close together; take the rough track, which goes straight over the hill to the south side of the peninsula. The church is just behind the small harbour.

The GPS reference is: N54° 35.658', W08° 23.554'.

No trace of the two ships that were lost or of the Spanish camp has ever been found, but there has been no systematic search for them either. Robert Sténuit looked in the port of Killybegs but did not find anything. There are topographical clues as to the location of these two ships in the brief reports in the State Papers: 'One of them was cast away a little without the harbour, the other running aground on the shore brake to pieces'. And later: 'Their two ships they burned with powder and great shot because they were driven so far upon the rocks and in dead sand within the same that they were never able to bring them forth again'. No one has so far used these clues to identify the wreck sites, but someone may yet do so.

There is a strong presumption that guns were jettisoned from the *Girona* to make room for as many people as possible, and they might still be somewhere in the bay.

Site 5: Streedagh Strand—*La Lavia, La Juliana and the Santa Maria de Visón*

Eighteen km north of the town of Sligo at the southern end of the village of Grange a large sign points left to 'Streedagh 3 km'. Another, smaller, brown sign is marked 'Spanish Armada 1588, De Cuéllar Trail'. Follow this road for about 1 km and turn right at another 'De Cuéllar Trail' sign. After about another 1 km stop at a stone wall surrounding a memorial in the shape of the bow of a boat. A nearby plaque commemorates the ships and men lost on Streedagh Strand on 21 September 1588. Drive on over the cattle grid and take the road to the right. Follow this road for about 400 metres and turn right again towards the beach, skirting the back bay and crossing another cattle grid. At the end there is a rough car park, which usually has a few visitors. Park here and walk over stone-covered dunes to the beach at Streedagh Strand.

The GPS reference is N54° 19.368' W08° 38.549'.

It would do no harm to remind ourselves of the horrendous scene here on the morning of 22 September 1588. The wreckage of three large Spanish ships and the bodies of about a thousand men were cast up above the tide line and strewn over the two-mile long beach. It was a prospect of complete devastation and an enormous human tragedy, by far the worst of the many disasters caused by the Great Gale.

Instead of returning to the main road take the side road southwest to Raghly Harbour at N54°19.368' W08° 38.549'. From the end of the small quay here you get a good view of the shelter afforded by this north shore of Drumcliff Bay. This is probably where the three Streedagh ships were at anchor for six days between 15 and 20 September 1588. None of the other inlets is deep enough.

Site 6: Aughris Head, County Sligo—Six Armada ships

Return to the main road at Drumcliff where you can visit the grave of the poet W.B. Yeats at Drumcliff churchyard. It seems to attract hundreds of tourists every day. Continue south through Sligo where the road becomes the N4. About 7 km south of Sligo you want to turn west onto the N59 for Ballina, but the road takes you off left, then swings right under the N4. Just past Baltra a brown sign indicates a right turn to Aughris Head and Dunmorran Strand. Follow this small road until you pass Ardabrone Stores on the left. About a third of a kilometre further on the remains of O'Dowd's castle can be seen on the left. The road leads on to a right turn to Dunmorran Strand 2 km, which takes you down to a car park overlooking the strand.

You can now see Aughris Head and the 'open bay in O'Dowd's Country' where six Armada ships were reported as taking shelter on 14 September 1588. They were said to be at 'Aringlas' and the Ardnaglas River empties into the bay about halfway across the strand. This obviously did not offer safe shelter and next day three of them crossed to a better anchorage in Drumcliff Bay east of Raghly Point; the other three sailed north to the Harbour of Calebeg.

The GPS reference for Dunmorran Strand car park is N54° 15.783' W08°43.475'.

___

Site 7: Killala Bay, County Mayo—The *Ciervo Volente?*

In Irish sources there is convincing evidence that an Armada ship was lost in this area, which was described as the Barony of Tirawley. William Burke, the local chieftain, had his home in Ardnaree, now part of Ballina, and one of his gallowglasses, McLaghlan McCabb, killed some survivors as they came ashore. If survivors were able to come ashore in numbers the implication is that the wreck was on a shelving beach, which in turn points to the southern part of the bay, though no trace of a shipwreck has ever been found. The bay itself offers tempting shelter to a ship coasting along the mostly cliff-bound north Mayo coast, and a good place to stop would be just south of Kilcummin Harbour in the northwest of the bay. To reach it take the R314 north out of Ballina, following signs for Killala. Through Killala the road angles northwest for about 4 km when it turns sharp right across a bridge over the River Cloonaghmore. The R314 continues left towards Ballycastle, but take the minor road straight ahead. This soon comes to a crossroads; turn right heading north for about 3 km to Kilcummin Harbour at N54° 16.473' W09° 12.477'. Looking right from the harbour the sheltered bay seems to be the most likely place for an Armada ship to find safe anchorage.

___

Site 8: Inver in Broad Haven—The *San Nicholas Prodaneli*

Return to the R314 and drive west. About 8 km west of Ballycastle the road passes the famous Neolithic site called 'Céide Fields' which can be visited. It is a long drive down towards Belmullet, but at Barnatra a minor road turns right to Inver, about 3 km north. Another small road leads off left down to the shore at Inver, where an Armada ship was wrecked. This was probably the *San Nicholas Prodaneli*, and there is a strong possibility that the *San Pedro el Mayor* may have sheltered near here as well, before departing around 21 October only to be lost in Hope Cove, County Devon, on 7 November. Most of the bays in the Broad Haven region are silted up with dangerous-looking shoals.

Site 9: The Mullet Peninsula, County Mayo—The *Duquesa Santa Ana*

Return to the R314 and continue to Belmullet. The road joins the R313 just east of the town. A feature of this and other parts of the west coast is that they can be designated as Gaeltacht regions. That means areas where residents are encouraged to use Irish as their first language. This affects the visitor only in one respect, which is that road signs, where they are present at all, are exclusively in Irish. In the rest of the country road signs are in both Irish and English. In most places this does not present a difficulty, especially if you are using a good map. In northwest Mayo, however, the roads are tricky, so if you feel you are lost, ask local people for directions; they will always help.

Drive west out of Belmullet and turn south onto the Mullet peninsula just outside the town on the R313. It is about 10 km to Elly Bay where there is a wide pull-in overlooking the bay with tourist information boards and toilet facilities, at N54° 09.740' W10° 05.180'. Elly Bay is where the *Duquesa Santa Ana* anchored from 15 to 23 September 1588, which afforded enough shelter for it to survive the Great Gale on 21 September. Again the inner part of the bay has treacherous shoals and the anchorage would have had to be chosen carefully, possibly in the northern section of the bay. Less than 2 km further south a road turns off right through some new houses towards Tiraun Point. In the past there was a castle or tower house here, but it has now disappeared. According to Gerald Comerford's account de Leyva's party of survivors from the *Rata Encoronada* spent the night camped here on 22/23 September before embarking next morning on the *Duquesa* and setting sail, it was hoped, for Spain, but it returned and was eventually lost near Rossbeg, County Donegal.

Site 10: Fahy Castle, County Mayo—The *Rata Encoronada*

Leave Elly Bay and return to Belmullet. Head east on the R313 to Bangor Erris and turn right on the N59 signed for Westport. Just outside Bangor the road crosses the Owenmore River and about 10 km further on the Owenduff River. Between them the land is covered in heather, bracken and bog with innumerable small lakes and other small rivers. Some historians have assumed that de Leyva and the survivors from the *Rata* marched overland across this ground to reach the *Duquesa* at Elly Bay. One look at the terrain is enough to show that this would have been impossible, especially as the transfer took place in one day—22 September. It could only have been accomplished by boat.

Shortly after crossing the Owenduff River take the minor road off to the right, and in a further 2 km the remains of Fahy Castle can be seen. Another small road brings you down close to it at N54° 02.816' W09° 54.139'. The castle is on ground owned by Mr and Mrs Kevin Moran who live in the nearby house. Please ask permission if you want to visit the castle. You will see that the castle was much too small to house all the 400 plus people in de Leyva's party so they must have camped around it for several days. Looking across to the northwest you will see that Elly Bay is out of sight, hidden behind the Doohooma Peninsula. Distances in Blacksod Bay are deceptively long and the boat trip round to Elly Bay would be all of 20 km, so transferring to the *Duquesa* in a single day would have been a sizeable task requiring several boats, possibly supplied by Richard Burke.

Gerald Comerford's account is very useful in that it supplies dates for all this. But it is confusing too, because he claims to have 'stayed within view of the ship that was at Pollilly by Torrane (i.e. Elly Bay by Tiraun) and the ship that is here', meaning the *Rata* in Tullaghan Bay. The view today northwest from Fahy Castle suggests that is not possible, but perhaps someone else making this pilgrimage will see the answer.

———

Site 11: Clew Bay, County Mayo—*El Gran Grin* and one other ship

From Fahy Castle return to the main N59 and drive south, following signs for Westport. Clew bay is an enormous area. Clare Island with its 1,500-foot high mountain stands guard over the entrance to the bay, and it is 25 km from there to the ports and islands in the eastern end. You get the first sight of it when you reach Mullaranny. The main road turns east here, but to overlook the bay and get a good view of Clare Island go right onto the minor road that skirts the coast of the Corraun Peninsula. Return to Mullaranny and drive east towards Newport.

The eastern end of the bay is densely packed with a large number of small, hump-backed islands. These are sunken drumlins, a relic of the end of the last

Ice Age and similar to the islands in Strangford Lough, County Down. They extend underwater for some distance into the bay and altogether amount to an extreme hazard to ships not familiar with the area. One unnamed ship was lost in the northeast corner of the bay in the district of Burrishoole. Information about it is meagre and is confined to two short reports. One described it as 'having been cast upon the shore at a place called "Borreis", which place belongs to the Earl of Ormond'. The other said that most of the men were lost but that '16 of them came ashore alive with their chains of gold and were apprehended by a tenant of my Lord of Ormonde'. This suggests that it was not wrecked among the islands but on the shore; however, no trace of it has ever been found. The reports were dated on or before 16 September so it was not a victim of the Great Gale.

The other vessel in Clew Bay was *El Gran Grin*, vice-flagship of the Biscay squadron and one of the largest ships in the whole Armada. It was a Spanish galleon manned by a full crew of Spanish soldiers and sailors. It arrived in moderate conditions and anchored safely off the harbour in the southeast corner of Clare Island. It was there for at least six days during which time there were frequent exchanges between ship and shore. It was caught in the Great Gale of 21 September and was destroyed, but again we do not know where. It could have been sunk just outside the harbour or anywhere in the vast expanse of the bay east of Clare Island. Despite much diligent searching nothing has been found.

Clare Island can be visited and it is worth the trip. Drive west from Westport on the R335. The road takes you past the sacred pilgrimage mountain of Croagh Patrick. A short walk up the mountain track to the statue of Saint Patrick gives a superb view of the numerous islands at the head of the bay. Continue to Louisburgh and take the minor road to the right, following signs for Roonagh Quay. At the quay there are usually two ferries competing for your patronage. They are both good modern vessels and either will take you to the island in about 20 minutes. Just beside the harbour on Clare Island the O'Malley Castle still stands relatively intact, and it was here that men from *El Gran Grin* were entertained by Dowdre Roe O'Malley.

Unfortunately the heritage centre on the Island does not yet value its important though brief connection with the Spanish Armada, and there was no information about it on display during 2007. The area round the harbour is known as Faunglas and is undoubtedly the 'Fynglas' mentioned in Fenton's List of Ships. There should be no embarrassment on the island about the report from George Bingham 'The Younger' that the O'Malleys killed up to a hundred of the Spanish survivors. Instead they should celebrate the fact that they hoodwinked an inexperienced member of the English garrison.

Site 12: Northern Connemara—The *Falcon Blanco Mediano*

Return to Louisburgh and turn south on the R335 into the Connemara mountains. At Aasleagh Falls the road joins the N59, which is the main road through Connemara. After Leenaun at the head of Killary Harbour continue another 16 km to Letterfrack. Take a right turn and drive towards Dawros and Tully Mountain, but stay as close as possible to the shore of Ballynakill Harbour. The *Falcon Blanco Mediano* was lost somewhere in this area, apparently after spending some time anchored near Inishbofin, but the exact location of the wreck is not known. The crew seems to have come ashore safely, and about a hundred of them were looked after by Sir Murrough Na Doe O'Flaherty for a short time. At the end of September Sir Richard Bingham visited Galway and demanded that all Spanish survivors should be handed over to him. One of the survivors was Don Luis de Cordoba who was examined before Bingham and gave a long statement which included the sailing directions ordered by Medina Sidonia. All the prisoners were killed on Bingham's orders except for Don Luis de Cordoba and one other, who were later transferred to London.

Inishbofin can be visited by ferry from Cleggan, about 12 km further along the coast.

Site 13: Mace Head, County Galway—*La Concepcion del Cano*

The N59 takes you down through Clifden and bends east again towards Galway City, crossing the heart of Connemara with the imposing mountain range on the left known as the Twelve Pins. About 20 km east of Clifden take the R320 right signed for Carna. At the village of Glinsk you have the option of going on to Carna or taking the minor road right, which stays close to the coast. You are trying to get close to Mace Head. Off the coast is a deep sea inlet called Bertraghboy Bay, which would provide good shelter though it has a narrow entrance. Further round there is quite a large island known as Freaghillaun, and closer to Mace Head another rock named Duirling na Spainneach; both are associated in local tradition with the wreck of an Armada ship. No wreck has ever been found, however. There were only about 20 survivors whom the local chief Tadgh Na Buile O'Flaherty was obliged to surrender to Sir Richard Bingham in Galway. One of the survivors was listed as Don Diego Sarmiento and this has enabled the ship to be identified as *La Concepcion del Cano*, sailing with the Biscay Squadron.

Drive round through Carna and return to the N59. The forbidding landscape in the area, composed mostly of exposed rocks and bogs, looks incapable of sustaining life in the sixteenth century, and it is no surprise that the O'Flahertys here made their living from the sea.

One other Armada ship is mentioned in County Galway. It was anchored for a short time between Barna and Salthill, quite close to the town. Seventy men were sent ashore to try to obtain supplies. When they did not return the Captain decided that it would be safer to put to sea again, so he set sail leaving the 70 men behind. This ship has not been identified and it is not known if it returned safely to Spain.

———

Site 14: Liscannor, County Clare—The galleass *Zuñiga*

Drive east on the N59 towards Galway City, which can now be bypassed using a new ring road. There is a seemingly endless succession of roundabouts, but keep following the signs for Limerick until you can join the N18 south. At Kilcolgan turn right on the N67 heading to Ballyvaughan. From here the road bends south through the region known as the Burren, a word derived from the Irish for 'stony place'. This is a unique geographical area, the most prominent feature of which is the limestone pavements where an extraordinary combination of Mountain, Arctic and Mediterranean plants can be found. Many of them are rare in themselves, but nowhere else in the world can they be found growing together. On the R479 north of Doolin you can stop the car and venture out onto the limestone. The plants of course cannot be touched. Although this provides a brief experience of the Burren, the area has many other fascinating features. It covers the whole of northwest County Clare and would repay an extended visit.

South of Lisdoonvarna take the R478 west towards the Cliffs of Moher—another diversion but worth the stop. There are now elaborate facilities for the tourist here—huge car parks and a modern visitor centre—but they come in droves and have to be catered for. It is a short walk to the top of the cliffs. The highest point is about 600 feet and they are absolutely vertical. Three Spanish Armada ships ran the risk of being caught on this lee shore, but the weather was favourable at the right time and they managed to avoid it. From the top there is a good view of the Aran Islands where at least two Armada ships anchored for a short time before moving down onto the Clare coast.

South of the Cliffs of Moher the R478 cuts inland towards Liscannor, and the remains of Sir Turlough O'Brien's sixteenth-century tower house can be seen from quite a long distance away. The directions in the original State

Paper are specific: '… one ship is anchored in an unusual harbour about a mile westward of one of Sir Turlough O'Brien's houses called Liscannor'. The coast from Hag's Head to Lehinch runs west to east as it forms the northern shore of Liscannor Bay. Turn off the main road near the Rock Shop at signs for Liscannor Mobile Home Park and Castleview Farmhouse. Follow the road down to the seafront as it bends right to the end of a low stone wall overlooking a beach of rough stones. As the road bends away from the sea again a small river comes down the hill and crosses the stones. This is where the men from the *Zuñiga* obtained their fresh water. The ship was anchored just off shore. There was enough shelter in the lee of the Cliffs of Moher for the *Zuñiga* to survive the Great Gale of 21 September 1588 more or less unscathed. It departed two days later in calm conditions with the help of its oars. The area is known as Coolrone and is in fact about 3 km west of Liscannor.

––––

Site 15: Lurga Point, County Clare—The *San Marcos*

This was one of the two ships seen off the Aran Islands, but which later crossed to the Clare coast looking for shelter. Virtually the whole coast is exposed to westerly winds so a safe anchorage was not easy to find. The *San Marcos* was apparently off Quilty, south of Milltown Malbay. Both ships were destroyed in the Great Gale, the *San Marcos* on rocks between Mutton Island and Lurga Point. The main N67 turns inland here and to reach Lurga Point you have to take the minor road right. Although Lurga Point is the name on Ordnance Survey maps, the signpost is marked Seafield Pier and you have to follow this out to the small harbour at N52° 48.517' W09° 29.409'. The rocky islands off shore are an obvious danger, but the wreck site has not been identified in modern times. Further north Spanish Point seems to be a bit of a red herring as there is no information now to connect it to the Armada.

––––

Site 16: Doonbeg White Strand, County Clare—The *San Esteban*

About 12 km further south the *San Esteban* looked for shelter north of Doonbeg village. It too was a victim of the Great Gale somewhere on the White Strand, a semi-circular shelving beach very similar to Streedagh. From Seafield Pier return to the main N67 and drive south. Just before Doonbeg village a right turn takes you down to a car park overlooking the White Strand at N 52° 44.875′ W09° 33.067′. The location of this wreck has never been established, but if the situation at Streedagh is an indication there could still be significant remains somewhere in the bay. Near Doonbeg, a new golf course, designed by Greg Norman, has been built on the dunes north of the village. It is a typical links course similar to Lehinch.

Site 17: The Shannon Estuary, County Clare—*La Anunciada*

From Doonbeg drive south on the N67 to Kilkee, then on towards Loop Head on the R487. Take the R488 left to Carrigaholt. This is where the seven Armada ships on the Shannon first took shelter—on the face of it a good choice in a well-protected bay. But it was shallow at low tide and did not provide good holding ground. They soon moved further east to Scattery Road, west of Scattery Island, probably off Corlis Point, at N52° 06.595′ W09° 30.760′. Drive east from Carrigaholt on the minor road round the coast. Past Doonaha two small roads lead down to the shore; either of them gives a view of the likely anchorage of the seven ships.

Nicholas Cahan in Kilrush made quite a show of denying help to the Spanish, but once they were able to put parties ashore around here they would surely have helped themselves.

La Anunciada was damaged beyond repair and was offered as a bargaining counter to trade for supplies. When this was refused the ship was scuttled and burned, but was hard to sink and drifted ashore somewhere in this area, with the locals swarming all over it, according to Cahan's report.

When an easterly wind came up on Tuesday 20 September, the other six ships took advantage of it to leave the Shannon. Unfortunately next day they ran into the teeth of the Great Gale and two of them were lost in Blasket Sound.

Site 18: Tralee Bay, County Kerry—A small unnamed ship and 24 men

From Tralee take the R558 west towards Fenit. After about 5 km a minor road angles off right to Churchill. Follow this road past the church at the top of the hill and round the back of Barrow Harbour, till you see the sign for Tralee Golf Club. Don't enter the club grounds. A rough track leads you down the side of the Golf Club fence. At a bend near the bottom you get an overall view of Barrow Harbour and the remains of the sixteenth-century tower house where Lady Denny kept the 24 survivors from the small, unnamed ship stranded nearby. The actual site of its shipwreck is not known.

By 19 September these 24 prisoners were reported as having been killed, probably two or three days earlier. This makes them the first Armada survivors to be killed in Ireland. Lady Denny tends to get the blame, but there is a strong possibility that they had been transferred to the English garrison at Tralee, where statements were taken from them and recorded.

_____

Site 19: Blasket Sound, County Kerry—The *Santa Maria de la Rosa*

Blasket Sound is at the very tip of the Dingle Peninsula. It is created by the southeast corner of Great Blasket Island coming close to the coast at Dunmore Head, which is the most westerly point on mainland Europe, at N52° 06.595' W10° 27.924'. This relatively narrow channel is subjected to a three-knot tidal current for most of the day, with only brief periods of slack water. The sound widens further north, but the northwestern approaches to it are impeded by a number of rocky islets and the flat-topped outcrops of Young and Beginish Islands. There is one sandy beach on Great Blasket facing the Sound and it is known as White Strand. It was not the ideal shelter for ships of the Spanish Armada, but two galleons and a patache were there for nine days from 15 to 23 September 1588. The galleons were Martinez de Recalde's flagship, the *San Juan of Portugal*, and Marcos de Aramburu's *San Juan Bautista*. There are four outlying islands—Inishtooskert in the north, Inishnabro and Inishvickillaun to the south of Great Blasket, and the eye-catching conical shape of Teeraght in the extreme west.

On 21 September, at the height of the Great Gale, three of the ships that left the Shannon the day before came into Blasket Sound in some distress. The *San Juan* of Fernando Horra was damaged beyond repair and was abandoned in the sound after an attempt to scuttle her. No trace of its wreck has ever been found so it is presumed that it drifted down into the entrance to Dingle Bay before sinking. One of the new arrivals was another patache captained by Miguel de Aranivar; it returned to Spain. The other ship was the *Santa Maria de la Rosa*, which was dragged down the Sound by the tidal current, crashed into a submerged rock in the narrow channel between Dunmore Head and Great Blasket and sank almost immediately. Over 300 men were drowned; there was only one survivor, a boy said to be the son of the pilot. It is amazing that we have such minute detail of events in Blasket Sound, but it was very well documented in both Spanish and English sources.

From Tralee take the N86 west to Dingle. It is about 80 km through at times dramatic scenery. Dingle is a tourist hotspot so there is plenty of accommodation available. It is a further 16 km on the R559 along the coast through Ventry and around Slea Head before Blasket Sound comes into sight—enjoy the view! In Dunquin there is a Visitors Centre which these days concentrates on the history of the original inhabitants of the islands, probably rightly so, with not very much now about the Armada episode. You have therefore to call to your mind's eye, if you can, those vivid events during nine days of September 1588 and in particular the gale that blew 'with a most terrible fury'. Nor should anyone interested in Armada history forget the summers of 1968 and 1969 when diving teams worked themselves to a frazzle to find and excavate the *Santa Maria de la Rosa.*

Dunquin Pier is about 2 km south of the village and in season two boats offer trips to Great Blasket Island and also around the other islands. The path down to the pier is very steep so you need to be confident you can make the climb back up. On the quayside in 2007 there was still one of the Armada anchors that had been raised in the 1970s. It looks like the *Santa Maria de la Rosa's* sheet anchor.

———

All Ireland's Armada sites are memorable, but which is the most impressive?

Port na Spaniagh at the Giant's Causeway, County Antrim, must come close to the top of the list. Its paralysing, terrifying isolation from which there is no escape still takes the breath away. And we can never forget that Don Alonso de Leyva and 1,300 men died here, so it is in a way a Spanish graveyard, which commands our reverence and respect. When you are there take a moment to remember them.

But nothing can surpass Blasket Sound, County Kerry. It takes the full force of Atlantic weather as it did on 21 September 1588; it can be shrouded in mist, and it can be cut off from the mainland for long winter months at a time, which the islanders frequently had to endure. Even on calm days you can still see the water ripple as the three-knot tide race rips through the channel between Dunmore Head and Great Blasket Island. Its dangers are palpable. Yet there are also days when slack water coincides with the midday sun. Looking out from the shore anywhere from Slea Head to Dunquin, light catches the islands and makes them glow; the sea sparkles, and it is heart-stoppingly beautiful. What a privilege to include such a day in one's life experiences.

PART IV

Appendices

APPENDIX 1

A List of the Ships and Men Lost on the Irish Coast

On 29 September 1588 Geoffrey Fenton, secretary to the Lord Deputy and council of Ireland, sent to the Privy Council in London a list of Armada ships and men known to have been lost in Ireland at that time. There are 17 ships on his list. We can now account for 38 Armada ships that were on the Irish coast or in Irish waters. Not all of them can be identified, not all of them were wrecks, and their fate is not known in every case, but the following is a summary of these ships classified as well as current information will allow.

24 ships known to have been lost in Ireland or in Irish waters

Barque of Hamburg	Foundered at sea off northwest Donegal on 10/11 September. The crew were taken into the *Gran Grifon* and *La Trinidad Valencera*.
Castillo Negro	On 10 September was with the ships off northwest Donegal and could still be seen in calm conditions that evening. There is a strong probability of sea fog overnight, and next morning it had disappeared. It was never seen again and is presumed to have foundered at sea with the loss of all hands.
La Trinidad Valencera	On 14 September came into Kinnagoe Bay, County Donegal, intending to beach, but grounded on rocks about 300 yards off shore at the west end of the bay. After two days it broke up and sank. Most of the crew were brought ashore alive but about 40 were still on it at the time and were drowned.
Duquesa Santa Ana	Entered Blacksod Bay, County Mayo, about 14 September, and sheltered in Elly Bay. On 23 September took on board the men from *La Rata Encoronada* and sailed for Spain.

Owing to calms and southerly winds she eventually sailed north and on 28/29 September was wrecked in Loughros More Bay, County Donegal. All on board landed safely.

La Lavia
La Juliana
Santa Maria de Visón

All three of these ships entered Donegal Bay about 13 September, and on the 15th sheltered in Drumcliff Bay, County Sligo. On 20 September they set sail, but were caught in the Great Gale of 21 September and blown eastwards to be destroyed on Streedagh Strand, County Sligo.

Ciervo Volante

The wreck reported in Tirawley on the north coast of County Mayo has been tentatively identified as the *Ciervo Volante*. The wreck site is not known but is probably somewhere in Killala Bay.

La Rata Encoronada

Entered Blacksod Bay, County Mayo, on 15 September but grounded accidentally on Tullaghan Sand Bank in the eastern end of the bay. The crew came ashore and camped at Fahy Castle near Doona. The ship could not be recovered, but on the 22nd the men transferred to the *Duquesa Santa Ana*.

El Gran Grin

Arrived in Clew Bay, County Mayo, about 14 or 15 September, and found shelter near the southeast corner of the island close to O'Malley's Castle and the harbour. She was there until the 21st when she became a victim of the Great Gale. The wreck site has never been found.

Falcon Blanco Mediano

At first sheltered near Inishbofin Island or Davillaun, County Galway, but was later wrecked in the Great Gale of 21 September somewhere in Ballynakill Harbour. The crew survived and were cared for by Sir Murrough Na Doe O'Flaherty until they had to be surrendered to Sir Richard Bingham in Galway. They were all killed except for Don

Luis de Cordoba. The Armada's sailing directions seemed to have been in his possession.

La Concepcion del Cano The ship wrecked near Mace Head, County Galway, on the rock known as Duirling na Spainneach. There were only about 20 survivors who were also killed in Galway by Bingham.

San Marcos Arrived first at the Aran Islands at the entrance to Galway Bay, but moved to an anchorage on the coast of County Clare. She was wrecked in the Great Gale of 21 September on rocks between Mutton Island and Lurga Point.

San Esteban Was with the *San Marcos* at the Aran Islands and also moved to the Clare coast near Doonbeg. On 21 September she was wrecked on the White Strand; 68 survivors were later killed by the sheriff of Clare on a site near the coast west of Milltown Malbay.

La Anunciada One of the seven ships sheltering in the Shannon Estuary between Carrigaholt and Scattery Island. On 20 September when the other six ships were preparing to set sail, she was unseaworthy, the crew were taken into other ships and she was scuttled. She drifted ashore and was plundered by the local people.

Santa Maria de la Rosa One of the ships that left the Shannon on 20 September, next day she came into Blasket Sound at the height of the Great Gale. She dragged down the sound to the southern end where she hit a rock and sank. All the crew were lost except for one boy.

San Juan (Fernando Horra) Also one of the ships from the Shannon, she entered Blasket Sound about four hours after the *Rosa*, so badly damaged by the Great Gale that she was abandoned and burned. The crew were transferred to Aramburu's *Bautista* and a patache and returned safely to Spain. The remains of the ship have not been found.

La Girona	Entered Donegal Bay on 13 September and sailed into the eastern end of the bay. On 15 September crossed to the Harbour of Calebeg in McSwyne's Bay in the company of two other ships. She survived the Great Gale of 21 September, but was damaged. Don Alonso de Leyva repaired her and she sailed for Scotland on 26 October, but was wrecked near the Giant's Causway on 28 October; 1,300 lives were lost, one of the most costly shipwrecks in the history of seafaring.

A few known wrecks have not been identified

A patache or zabra at Tralee	This is the smallest Armada wreck. It occurred outside Barrow Harbour about 13 or 14 September. Twenty-four of the crew came ashore alive but were later killed, probably in Tralee.
'A Ship at Inver'	This is authentically documented by Gerald Comerford, but he neglected to visit the site. There is some evidence that it could have been the *San Nicolas Prodaneli*.
'… about the islands at Burrishoole'.	This ship was reported as early as 16 September so it was not a victim of the Great Gale. It was in the northeast corner of Clew Bay and was said to be '… cast upon the shore and past recovery so as most of the men are lost … there is come ashore of them 16 persons alive with their chains of gold'. It has been suggested that she may have been the *Santiago* of the Squadron of Hulks.
Two ships with the *Girona*	They were seen to cross Donegal bay with the *Girona* on 15 September, but were wrecked in the Great Gale of 21 September. 'One was cast away a little without the harbour, the other running aground brake to pieces'. The wreck sites have not been found. It is not known if any died in the shipwreck, but all were lost with the *Girona* on 28 October.
At Valencia Island	A ship in 'Desmond' was reported in 'Fenton's List of Ships' at the end of

September. This may have been the *Trinidad* which was with Aramburu's *San Juan Bautista* for part of his voyage in the Atlantic. It coincides with the tradition of a wreck on Valencia Island, but the evidence is very inconclusive.

2 ships lost in Scotland after being in Irish waters

El Gran Grifon This was one of the group of five ships off northwest Donegal on 10 September. It avoided Ireland, stayed at sea during the Great Gale and survived. After making a half-hearted attempt to return to Spain it eventually sought shelter in the lee of Fair Isle on 27 September. She anchored off Swartz Geo hoping to beach there next morning, but was pushed by currents into nearby Stroms Hellier, a steeply sided rocky gully. The crew were able to escape by climbing the masts, which leant against the cliff. Some men died of starvation on the island, but most returned through Scotland to Flanders.

San Juan de Sicilia Also one of the ships off Donegal on 10 September, she ventured into the Inner Hebrides and ended up in Tobermory Bay on the island of Mull. She was there for nearly two months, during which time the local chieftain Donald Maclean supplied food and fresh water. On 5 November the ship sank after an explosion on board following a fire, which appeared to have been started deliberately. Most of those on the ship were lost.

1 ship spent five or six weeks in Ireland but was later lost in England

San Pedro el Mayor On 7 November this ship grounded in Hope Cove, County Devon. The crew came ashore safely and were made prisoners. Three men escaped and later testified that they had spent time in Ireland. The location is not known but may have been Broad Haven, County Mayo.

11 ships survived and left Ireland

Nuestra Señora de Begoña	Entered Blacksod Bay, County Mayo, about 15 September and sheltered somewhere in the south of the bay, probably near Inishbiggle. Left Ireland on 23 or 24 September and returned to a port in Galicia.
Zuñiga	One of the four galleasses on the Armada, she arrived at Liscannor Bay, County Clare, on 15 September and survived the Great Gale apparently undamaged. She left Ireland on 23 September but encountered heavy weather at the entrance to the Channel, and was forced to shelter in Le Havre, where she remained until July 1589 before returning to Spain.
Barque of Danzig	Was one of the ships in the Shannon Estuary, took on board some of the crew of the *Anunciada* and left Ireland on 20 September. She survived the Great Gale at sea and returned to Spain.
San Juan Bautista	Aramburu's ship, arrived in Blasket Sound on 15 September. She lost a few anchors, but survived the Great Gale. Took on board some men from the *San Juan* of Fernando Horra and left Ireland on 23 September. Returned to Santander on 14 October.
San Juan of Portugal (Recalde's ship)	Arrived in Blasket Sound with Aramburu's ship and his own patache on 15 September. Left Ireland on 24 September and returned safely to La Coruña.
Recalde's patache	The tender that accompanied Recalde's *San Juan* and returned to Spain with him.
San Salvador	The ship of Purser Pedro Coco Calderon; was close to the Irish coast sometime between 10 and 14 September, but turned away and never saw Ireland again. She returned safely to Santander.

Ship at Barna

A large, unnamed ship was close to Barna, County Galway. Seventy men went ashore to try to obtain supplies, but were taken prisoner by the citizens of Galway. The captain feared for the safety of the rest of the crew and put to sea. The ship has not been identified and its fate is unknown.

Three pataches

These were part of the group of six ships that left the Shannon Estuary on 20 September. One of them was with the *San Juan* of Fernando Horra in Blasket Sound. It was referred to as 'the ship of Miguel de Aranivar'. Men from the *San Juan* were transferred to it and it sailed for Spain on 24 September. It is presumed to have arrived safely but the fate of the other two pataches is unknown.

Numbers of men lost in Ireland

Calculating the numbers of men lost on the Irish coast is very far from being an exact science. In the Spanish sources there are two different records, one muster taken in Lisbon on 9 May and the other in La Coruña on 13 July. In almost every case they disagree, sometimes profoundly. The *Castillo Negro* is listed at Lisbon as having 313 men; at La Coruña the figure is 203. The *San Pedro el Mayor* had 241 at Lisbon, but only 144 at La Coruña. The second figure corresponds closely to the number of prisoners held at Kingsbridge, County Devon, after the shipwreck. Some ships are missing entirely from the La Coruña muster, presumably because they were still in outlying ports in Galicia at the time.

Spanish musters carry some authority since they form the basis of numbers of men to be paid. But the muster lists account for only soldiers and sailors; supernumeraries are not mentioned and there seems to be no reliable way of estimating them. Apparently some of the higher ranks had an entourage of servants. On the Irish coast and indeed throughout the voyage men were frequently switched to other ships. Another uncertain factor is that crews suffered varying degrees of attrition from enemy action, accidents and sickness.

In Irish and English sources where numbers are mentioned they are obviously approximations, often highly dubious ones especially when large numbers are involved.

Despite the daunting nature of the task, an attempt has to be made to arrive at a figure for the number of men from the Armada who were lost in Ireland.

Barque of Hamburg	0	The crew of 289 in the La Coruña Muster was divided between *La Trinidad Valencera* and *El Gran Grifon.*
Castillo Negro	203	
La Trinidad Valencera	558	Made up of 413 from the La Coruña muster plus 145 from the *Barque of Hamburg.*
Ciervo Volante	171	
La Lavia	302	These three ships are the Streedagh wrecks and total 1,021 men.
La Juliana	412	
Santa Maria de Visón	307	
San Nicolas Prodaneli	294	
La Rata Encoronada	0	The crew of 448 were taken into the *Duquesa Santa Ana.*
El Gran Grin	336	
Falcon Blanco Mediano	103	
Concepcion del Cano	225	This is the only case where the Lisbon and La Coruña musters agree.
San Marcos	386	
San Esteban	274	
Anunciada	0	The crew of 266 were taken into the *SM de la Rosa*, the *San Juan* of Fernando Horra and the *Barque of Danzig*. Those on the *Rosa* were lost in Blasket Sound. Although the *San Juan* was also lost the men were again transferred and along with those on the *Barque of Danzig* returned to Spain.
Santa Maria de la Rosa	412	Made up of 323 from the La Coruña muster plus 89 from *Anunciada.*
Santiago (at Burrishoole)	65	
The Tralee zabra or patache	24	
Duquesa Santa Ana	0	Along with 272 from her own complement she took on board from the *Rata*. These 720 later transferred to the *Girona.*

Girona	1,300	The potential numbers in Calebeg were 1,569, made up of 349 on the *Girona* itself (excluding about 250 oarsmen), plus 272 from the *Duquesa*, 448 from the *Rata* and possibly 500 from the two unnamed ships there. The figure of 1,300 is obviously an estimate, and is possible.
Recalde's *San Juan*	8	Although this ship returned to Spain, eight men were put ashore at Dunquin, County Kerry, and were captured and killed at Dingle.
Trinidad (the ship in Desmond)	241	A ship named *Trinidad* from the Squadron of Castile is listed as missing in the Spanish records.
The unnamed ship at Barna	70	These men were left on shore when the ship departed and were later killed in Galway.
Total	**5,691**	

If an allowance of 5 per cent is made for fatalities during the voyage, that would reduce the total by 284. And a further deduction has to be made for the estimated 500 who escaped to Scotland through the north coast, which leaves 4,907 as the approximate number of Spanish to have died in Ireland.

This is considerably fewer than the figure put forward by many commentators. Fenton's List gave 5,394 and that was before the *Girona* disaster occurred. This calculation does not pretend to be definitive, but it is based on numbers in the official records. (Also an unknown number of Spanish soldiers and sailors, probably not many, survived and lived on in Ireland for several years.)

Men lost in Scotland have not been included in this calculation. About 50 men from the *Gran Grifon* died of starvation on Fair Isle. Probably around 300 out of the original complement of 342 were killed in the explosion or drowned when the *San Juan de Sicilia* sank in Tobermory Bay.

NOTES AND SOURCES

Fenton's List of Ships is referred to in CSPI p. 43; the full list is on MIC 223/51 document NO. 198. Although the calendar gives the number of ships 'drowned and sunk' as 16, the original list on microfilm adds to 17, a slight arithmetical slip on the part of the editor of the CSPI.

The Spanish musters are in Hume, Lisbon on pp 280–283, and La Coruña on pp 339–341.

Sources for the ships in the list are given throughout the text and are not repeated here.

APPENDIX 2

The Escape of Captain Cuéllar

The Beach at Streedagh Strand

Captain Francisco de Cuéllar's first contact with Ireland was when he was catapulted ashore by storm surge during the hurricane force winds of 21 September 1588. The ship he was in, *La Lavia*, was in company with two others, *La Juliana* and the *Santa Maria de Visón*. The bay at Streedagh is shallow and all three had grounded a quarter of a mile or more from the beach, where they were pounded by gale and surf. Cuéllar said that nothing like it had been seen before for in one hour these large ships were all broken in pieces. There were more than a thousand men in them, and he watched as many drowned within the ships. Others threw themselves into the sea but never reappeared. Some found rafts, barrels and pieces of floating timber to hang onto. It was chaos. Cuéllar had to decide what to do. Should he stay with the ship or try to reach the shore? He could not swim, and as far as he could see, one option was as dangerous as the other. On the beach he could see wreckage and bodies already piling up and local Irishmen were 'dancing and leaping with delight at our misfortunes'. They stripped the clothes off all they came across and left them naked.

The remains of his ship were about to sink or be driven ashore in pieces so, along with the Judge Advocate of the fleet, Martin de Aranda, he tried to find floating wreckage that might serve as a makeshift liferaft. One good size part of the ship would have been ideal, but it was attached to the hull by chains and could not be freed. He described how he then kept himself and the Judge Advocate afloat by clinging to a loose hatch cover, though the Judge was soon swept off it to his death. Cuéllar was able to hang on, but as the ship broke up a large piece of timber crushed his legs. Helpless, blinded by pain and sustained only by the instinct for survival, he could do nothing more than hang on and pray for a miracle. How could he possibly get safely ashore from here? But immediately his prayer was answered.

'There then came four great waves one after the other, and without knowing how I did it, nor even being able to swim, I was cast up the beach, where I landed too weak to stand, covered in blood and severely injured'.

The miracle of storm surge!

The Irish scavengers left him alone, probably not having a use for clothing soaked in blood. Hindered by the injury to his legs he could move only slowly, but gradually edged away from the beach, and when darkness fell he had reached a deserted place where he lay down on a bed of rushes. Presently a young Spanish survivor approached him, completely naked, shivering with cold and shock to the extent that he could not speak, even to tell Cuéllar his name.

At about nine o'clock he noticed that the wind had dropped and the sea had gone down. Just then two armed Irishmen came over, one carrying what looked like a gallowglass axe; they were potentially very threatening. Cuéllar and his companion must have felt that they were about to be attacked. But to their surprise they were treated with great kindness. The Irishmen spent some time cutting a large number of rushes and grass and made a bed for them, covering them as well as they could against the cold.

Cuéllar slept for a time, but was wakened at what he reckoned was about one o'clock by the noise of a large number of horsemen going past. He turned to speak to the young Spanish survivor but found that he had died, apparently from shock and exposure, as he seemed to have few physical injuries.

The horsemen were George Bingham and his soldiers. He had been in Tirawley when news of the Streedagh shipwrecks reached him, and he set out right away to get to the scene as soon as possible. The distance he would have had to travel was at least thirty-five miles, and it seems he covered some of it during the night. Cuéllar lay hidden until dawn when he judged it was safe to appear. Bingham's men had already begun their systematic murder of any Spanish survivors they found alive so he could not return to the beach at that time.

The Abbey Church at Staad

Cuéllar describes how he was able to walk only very slowly in search of a 'monastery' of monks where he hoped to recover from his injuries, but does not say how he learned about it. Other Spanish survivors must have been doing the same in the hope of gaining sanctuary. The fact that his leg was injured and as a result he could make only slow progress saved his life. When he reached the Abbey he found it despoiled by Bingham's soldiers, its images burned and destroyed and twelve Spanish victims hanged within the Church. The monks had fled to the mountains.

This was Staad Abbey near the coast only about a mile and a half southwest of the beach at Streedagh, one wall of which still stands. Bingham and his men had violated the sanctuary of a holy place, killed unarmed prisoners and disregarded the convention of lending assistance to shipwrecked mariners. Cuéllar frequently referred to the Irish here as 'salbajes', partly because of their mode of dress, and also because they had robbed the Spanish, but it was English soldiers who killed them and it was the English who, in Ireland, behaved like savages. Any help he had received had come from the Irish, and the lesson he had learned was that he would be safer among them than in surrendering to the English.

This was too close to the beach at Streedagh and still dangerous while George Bingham's party were in the area. Cuéllar could not walk very fast, but he made what haste he could away from the Abbey and down a path that led into a deep wood.

Cuéllar's North Sea ordeal

It was only by chance that Francisco de Cuéllar was on board the ship *La Lavia*. He had been in command of the galleon *San Pedro* of the squadron of Castile, part of the Indian Guard and one of Spain's most prominent fighting ships, which had been fully engaged in all the battles in the English Channel. When the Armada sailed up the North Sea followed by the English fleet and it was clear that fighting had finished, two Spanish ships sailed out ahead of the formation with the intention of stopping to make repairs. One of them was the *San Pedro*. Cuéllar claimed that he had taken a break for the first time in ten days and was not on deck when this happened, but he was accused of disobeying orders and summoned to appear before the Duke of Medina Sidonia on the flagship. He left the *San Pedro* but before he reached the *San Martin* a second message arrived telling him he had been sentenced to death.

Cuéllar was furious. He said he had fought bravely in all the battles and he had done nothing wrong. But he knew whom to blame. It was well known that the Duke had retired to his cabin in despair and was not speaking to anyone. Don Francisco de Bobadilla was the man who gave the orders and everything was arranged by him. On the whole he had served the Armada well, covering for the Duke while he was incapacitated, and supplying much needed coherence to the administration of day-to-day affairs. But in this case he appeared to have exceeded his powers. Formation had been of vital importance during the voyage up the Channel, because it was a way of defending the weaker ships. But in the North Sea it was not so critical, and it was pedantry on Bobadilla's part to make it into a hanging matter.

Cuéllar's status was such that his protests were entitled to be heard, and he was taken to appear before the Judge Advocate of the fleet, Martin de Aranda, who was on *La Lavia*. His case was persuasive enough for the Judge Advocate to stay the execution. Bobadilla was a powerful figure, however, and could not be openly defied, but Aranda had a lawyer's tactical acumen and he devised a way of protecting Cuéllar. He wrote directly to the Duke saying that unless he received a written order from him, signed by his own hand, he would not carry out the sentence. The order for execution was duly rescinded, but he was not restored to his command on the *San Pedro*. He remained under the protection of the Judge Advocate on *La Lavia*.

Cuéllar was not impressed with the seaworthiness of his new ship. She was in the Levant squadron and had been built to the standards of Mediterranean designs. In the first Atlantic storm her seams split and she took on water at such a rate that the pumps were hardly able to cope. She and several other Levant ships fell away from the main fleet. His own ship, the *San Pedro*, was an ocean-going galleon constructed for the Atlantic crossing to the Americas. She survived the storms with no difficulty and was one of the ships to arrive safely back in Santander.

La Lavia was among a group of ships that fell in towards the Irish coast and sheltered in Donegal Bay. Six of them had been sighted off Aughris Head, County Sligo, on 14 September, but next day they moved on trying to find a better anchorage. The *Girona* and two others crossed to the Harbour of Calebeg in Donegal. The other three we now know were *La Lavia*, *La Juliana* and the *Santa Maria de Visón*, all large merchant ships and all members of the Levant squadron. They stayed in the Sligo area and anchored most likely in Drumcliff Bay, probably just off Ardtermon Castle, where Raghly Point provides some protection from westerly winds. Cuéllar says they were little more than half a league from the shore and were there for four days, but were unable to get supplies of food and fresh water.

George Bingham reported that they had a favourable easterly wind on 20 September and they hoisted their sails and put to sea. Cuéllar does not mention this in his account, but his recollections were a year old, and everything was overshadowed by the hurricane force wind that hit them next morning. '… such a great gale arose on our beam, with a sea running as high as heaven that all three ships were driven onto a beach of fine sand …' In fact we now know that they grounded at least a quarter of a mile from the beach; that was why so many of the men were drowned.

The old Irish lady with five or six cows

After leaving Staad Abbey and going about a mile down the path through the woods he met an old Irish woman 'more than eighty years of age' who was driving her cows into the wood to hide them. It appears that Bingham's soldiers had taken over her village, which must have been the village of Grange, about two-and-a-half miles inland from Streedagh and the Abbey. She realized he was one of the shipwrecked Spanish, and according to Cuéllar, said to him 'Tu España?' Her intention was to help him as well as she could, and she was able to convey to him by some means that her village was full of English soldiers and he should stay away from it.

Cuéllar returns to Streedagh Strand

He had eaten nothing for two days and hunger was at the forefront of his mind. The village was closed to him and he had no knowledge of what lay behind it. Best advice would have been for him to go inland, but he decided that if he returned to the beach he had the chance of finding some ship's biscuit or other food. On the way he met two Spanish soldiers; both of them had been stripped naked by the Irish and one had a deep wound in his head. This is one of the few cases where the Irish had inflicted physical injury on any Spanish survivors. They accompanied him back to the beach. It was now three days since the shipwrecks and it seemed that Bingham and his men had left Streedagh either to return to Sligo or to check the hinterland. He claimed that he had killed a hundred and forty Spanish.

They found four hundred dead bodies cast up along the shore, and among them they recognized Don Diego Enriquez. Cuéllar insisted on burying him where he lay, and it may have been at this time he learned of the terrible circumstances of his death. He and three other officers had taken over a chalup, which had a closed deck. They climbed into it and ordered the hatch to be battened down and sealed. It was swept away by a wave and disappeared, but later bobbed up in the surf where it was tumbled around until it rolled up onto the beach. Unfortunately it came to rest upside down with the deck lying on the sand. With all its weight pressing on the hatch, the men inside were unable to break it open. It was not until two days later that the Irish got around to turning it over and opening it. Don Diego Enriquez was only just alive, but he died as soon as he was released; the other three were already dead. They all had the status of 'gentlemen' and had with them 16,000 ducats worth of jewels and money, but it is unlikely that the Irish benefited much from it since there was no cash in the economy of rural Ireland at that time; the clothes would have been more valuable.

Cuéllar just mentions that they then went looking for food, but he does not say that they actually found any; we have to presume they did.

Four Irishmen and a chief

Most of the local population were on the beach gathering anything valuable from the wreckage and from the dead bodies. Four Irishmen came up to them intending to take Cuéllar's clothes; his two companions were already naked. Before they were able to do much harm a man, who must have been a chief, stopped them. He gave Cuéllar and the two naked Spaniards his protection and spent some time in their company. They needed it, as there were so many scavengers about they could easily have been attacked again at any time. He directed them onto a road leading away from the shore to the village where he lived. They were to wait for him there and he would then be able to show them the way to a place of safety.

The road to the chief's village was rough and stony. Cuéllar was barefoot, his leg still hurt from the injury he received while being crashed around in the sea and he had to stop to rest. It would have been unfair to detain his companions who were suffering too; they went on ahead and presumably reached the village. Left alone Cuéllar felt abandoned and depressed. He could only pray to God for help.

Mixed company

Prayer did seem to give him strength and he started walking again, but very slowly. From the top of a low hill he could see some straw huts and headed downhill towards them. The bottom of the valley was densely filled by a wood with thick undergrowth. He had not gone far when another group of four people appeared in front of him. They were a peculiar mixture: an old Irishman, more than seventy years old he thought, two armed men, one English and one French, and a very beautiful young Irish girl. The Englishman must have been a deserter, probably distracted from his duties by the girl. He started to make a show of attacking Cuéllar with a knife, which was parried, but in the end he inflicted another wound on Cuéllar's already injured leg. The old Irishman and the girl intervened and stopped any further violence. They also made sure he had his clothes returned to him, and he retreated into the wood, while the others went back to their hut. The girl, however, had taken a fancy to a vestment containing religious relics. She hung them round her neck asking if she could keep them, because she was a Christian. This prompted Cuéllar's sardonic comment: 'y eralo como Mahoma', 'and that she was—like Mahomet!' Cuéllar would have been looking for the outward appearance of Roman orthodoxy, but even in the late sixteenth century Christianity in Gaelic Ireland still bore the vestige of its origins in the ancient Irish Church.

As Cuéllar sheltered outside the village the Frenchman sent a boy to him with a poultice of herbs to dress his wound and some food in the Irish tradition—butter, milk and oaten bread. Before turning back the boy pointed out the way ahead. He was to go towards some mountains about six leagues distant, where he would find the country of a chief who was a friend of the King of Spain. This was Sir Brian O'Rourke who was apparently already sheltering more than eighty survivors from the shipwrecks. This gave Cuéllar hope and lifted his spirits; at least he was no longer wandering aimlessly. With the help of a stick he began his walk again towards the mountains.

Another village and an Irishman who spoke Latin

That evening he came across a small group of huts. He had reached the stage when he never knew what to expect from the Irish inhabitants, but was pleased to remember that here he came to no harm. One of the men could speak Latin, and Cuéllar drew some comfort in just being able to converse and relate the course of his misfortunes. The man took him to his hut, dressed his wounds, and gave him something to eat and a bed of straw to sleep on. In the middle of the night his father and brothers wakened him as they returned from Streedagh laden with plunder from the ships, but the old man was not unhappy that Cuéllar had been given shelter and well treated.

One of the difficulties in trying to follow Cuéllar's account is to get some idea of the distances he had travelled. It would seem that at this time he was still not very far from the coast if the man's family were able to return to their village after a day's plunder at the beach.

Next morning their hospitality continued. He was supplied with a horse to carry him over some muddy road and a boy to guide him. They had not gone very far when they had to dive for cover as a hundred and fifty horsemen clattered past. This suggests that Bingham's party were still in the area and probably still searching for Spanish survivors.

They were able to resume their journey, but had not gone much further when a party of about forty very rough-looking Irish descended on them. The boy protected Cuéllar as well as he could, saying he was the prisoner of his master. But they beat him with sticks and stripped him of all his clothes. Cuéllar called these men 'Lutherans', meaning Protestants, but it seems unlikely that there would have been English settlers in this area and they would not have been interested in taking his clothes. Possibly they were poor landless Irish who travelled around like gypsies.

The boy was very upset but had to return to his village with the horse, leaving Cuéllar alone, naked and depressed once again. He cut some bracken and found a piece of matting with which to cover himself, but said that he was so dispirited by his unending misfortunes he was just looking for a place to die.

The empty huts beside a lake

He staggered on towards the mountains that had been pointed out to him. When he reached them he says that he found a lake with about thirty huts surrounding it, all apparently empty and deserted. This has been taken to be Glenade Lough about four miles along a steeply sided valley in the Dartry Mountains. It is the only sizeable stretch of water in the area, but would have represented very good progress on Cuéllar's part.

The best and most comfortable looking hut for a night's stay was filled with sheaves of oats, but as Cuéllar settled down he found three men already there; all of them were naked. In their surprise they terrified each other.

Cuéllar cried out an exclamation in Spanish and they responded. They explained that there had been eleven of them who had been stripped of everything they possessed on the shore. Like him they had wandered inland looking for 'a Christian land'. They encountered Bingham's soldiers and eight of their party had been killed, but these three fled into the woods which were so thick that they could not be found. Cuéllar would never have been able to escape through the woods, but earlier that day he had been saved by the alertness of the young Irish boy who knew where there was a crevice to hide them and their horse.

In their excitement they took pleasure in chatting to each other. Cuéllar told them about O'Rourke's village where they could expect to receive help, and they were overjoyed at the prospect of saving themselves. They were amazed too to find that they were with Captain Cuéllar and embraced him warmly. For supper all they could find were some blackberries and watercress.

The oat straw made a comfortable bed with the result that they overslept next morning. They were wakened by voices and a man appeared in the doorway of their hut. Cuéllar thought he was carrying a weapon, but as the men were there to work in the fields it was more likely an Irish agricultural implement of some kind. They held their breath and lay still until the man went out to begin his day's work, which was reaping the oats crop near the huts. The Spaniards decided to stay in hiding. Cuéllar seems to have conjured up a character of villainy for the Irish field workers for which he had no real justification. He called them 'heretic savages' and 'treacherous wretches' and presumed that they came from a place that had inflicted cruelty on the Spaniards, but it is not clear how he came to this conclusion. Maybe it was something about their dress. Anyway the Spaniards remained hidden the whole day until the reapers finished their work and went back to their villages.

They waited until the moon came up before they left the huts and were able to get clear of the area before daybreak.

Rest and recuperation at last

There then followed one of the most important episodes for Cuéllar at this stage of his journey away from the coast. He did not give it the emphasis it deserved, devoting barely a hundred words to it, but it made an enormous difference to his ability to endure the hardships of the remainder of his time in Ireland.

Cuéllar and his three fellow Spanish survivors could make just slow, exhausting progress towards O'Rourke's village, because the terrain was wet and muddy. His injuries were a problem for they delayed everybody.

When they came across another group of huts Cuéllar seemed immediately to be convinced that they were different. He called it a place of safety, where they found 'mejor gente, aunque todos salbajes pero cristianos y caritatibos'—better people, although all savages but Christians and charitable. It would have been good to have a fuller explanation of how this village created such a favourable first impression. Perhaps they were spontaneously welcoming and generous, although still dressed in the Irish style.

Cuéllar's subsequent treatment was certainly in the tradition of hospitality to travelling strangers that was an obligation in Gaelic Irish culture. A man took him to his hut where he, his wife and sons dressed his wounds and looked after him. Cuéllar cursorily tells us that they would not allow him to leave before he was strong enough to continue his journey. Considering the condition he was in, exhausted, starving and wounded, this cannot have taken less than a week, and Cuéllar owed them (and us) a much more magnanimous acknowledgement of his reception here. Possibly he spent a lot of his time sleeping off his exhaustion, but this period was crucial to his survival. Not long before he had been depressed and ready to die. By the time he left this village he was restored in mind and body, and was looking forward to the help he expected to receive from Sir Brian O'Rourke. The three Spanish survivors who had been with him had already moved on. Could this hospitable Irishman have been a minor aristocrat, possibly a junior member of O'Rourke's family?

Disappointment at O'Rourke's village
It cannot have been far to O'Rourke's village around Glenade, and Cuéllar was frustrated to discover that O'Rourke himself was not there. Apparently he had to leave to defend part of his territory that was being attacked by the English. In his absence no one seems to have taken responsibility to care for the Spanish fugitives. Cuéllar says that he found more than seventy of them going about naked and hungry and with injuries that needed attention. The only help he received was when someone gave him a blanket, but it was dirty and swarming with lice. It nevertheless helped him to keep warm.

O'Rourke could not be everywhere and there is no doubt that he had already provided assistance to many Spanish survivors. Reports from spies to George Bingham confirmed that not only did he help them, he also tried to enlist their support in a rising against English occupation. This never had any hope of success as distressed Spanish fugitives were interested only in surviving and getting home. Cuéllar acknowledges that O'Rourke was 'a good Christian and an enemy of the heretics' and he was just unlucky not to find him in his village.

Next morning Cuéllar and about twenty other Spanish survivors went to O'Rourke's house to beg his household to give them something to eat. While they were there he says that news arrived of a Spanish ship on the coast that was going to take any Spanish survivors who had escaped. This was the *Girona* and it had been at Calebeg since 15 September, but the news must have been that it was preparing to leave.

Forced march to the *Girona*

Naturally an opportunity to leave Ireland on a Spanish ship galvanized them into action. Cuéllar and the twenty men with him set off right away to the place they were told the ship was. No mention is made of the other fifty men then in O'Rourke's village, but presumably they would have been advised as well.

Glenade to Donegal is about twenty-five miles, and it would have been another twelve miles or so to the *Girona*'s anchorage at Calebeg. For fit men this would have been at least a two-day trek. He says that they met with many obstacles on the way and the River Erne would have hindered the best of them. Some of Cuéllar's companions apparently succeeded, but he did not. By the time he was writing his account he knew of the loss of the *Girona* and the deaths of nearly everyone on board, and all he could do was thank God for his mercy that he never reached her. Not for the first time his failure to arrive saved his life.

This episode gives us the chance to work out an approximate date for what was happening. We know that the *Girona* sailed from Calebeg on 26 October, so Cuéllar must have been in O'Rourke's village at Glenade about 22 or 23 October. He was shipwrecked on 21 September and he had, therefore, spent a full month covering the twelve or thirteen miles between Streedagh and Glenade. We do not know at what point he gave up on his attempt to reach the *Girona*, but the likelihood is that he did not actually get very far, because the next part of his narrative takes place around the western end of Lough Melvin, southeast of Bundoran.

The disguised priest

Cuéllar describes how he was now lost and confused. He struggled along a track in what he hoped was the right direction, when he came across a priest dressed in secular clothes. He said that this was the custom in that kingdom to prevent the English from recognizing them. This was more likely a Franciscan friar as many of them were serving among the Irish people. Cuéllar always drew comfort from being able to converse in Latin and the priest was also pleased to meet a Spanish survivor and learn of the shipwrecks. He shared his food with Cuéllar, and told him about an Irish chieftain who always maintained his independence from the Queen of England at his castle and among the mountains behind it. It was supposed to be six leagues distant, but his estimates of distance do not correspond to the geography of the area. Six leagues from Bundoran (Bundrowse in old papers) would take you to Donegal Town and it is fairly certain Cuéllar did not walk all the way there and back. His recollection of the size of the countryside here must have been influenced by the amount of effort he had had to exert to cover it. He was being directed to Rossclogher Castle at the western end of the southern shore of Lough Melvin, the home of the chieftain called McClancy (or in some documents McGlannagh), just four miles from Bundoran and only two miles from Kinlough. The outstanding feature of Rossclogher Castle was that it was on an island in the Lough and was virtually impregnable. Before he could get there, however, he had one more hardship to endure.

The inharmonious blacksmith

This tale is so peculiar, so improbable, that it could almost have been conceived in a bad dream. He says that as he went along he met a savage who tricked him into going to his hut in a deserted valley. There he was told he must stay for the rest of his life and learn his trade, which was that of a blacksmith. It seems Cuéllar was to attend to the bellows. Blacksmiths develop their muscles and strike an imposing figure, and Cuéllar did not dare to refuse to work with him in the forge. He says he was there for more than eight days and was always careful not to annoy the wicked blacksmith or an accursed old woman he had as his wife.

Work in a blacksmith's forge is among the most physically demanding that it is possible to imagine, and yet we are asked to believe that Cuéllar was able to stick it for more than eight days, despite all the injuries he had suffered. Also he was a man in his fifties, not exactly apprentice material. It is fairly certain that the blacksmith could not speak Latin so how did he propose to communicate with his new slave?

But then his good fairy intervened in the form of the priest returning that way, surprised to see him detained against his will and forced to work for this savage. He gave the blacksmith the edge of his tongue and assured Cuéllar that he would ask McClancy to rescue him. Sure enough next day four of McClancy's men arrived along with a Spanish soldier and they took him off to Rossclogher Castle. It seemed that ten escaping Spanish survivors were already being sheltered there.

A happy ending! But had he been eating too many mushrooms?

At Rossclogher Castle

Cuéllar's recollection was that he spent three months at Rossclogher, but it cannot have been as long as that. Allowing for three or four days returning from the attempt to reach the *Girona*, and another nine days in the captivity of the blacksmith, he must have arrived at Rossclogher about 8 or 9 November. He later tells us that he left on the tenth day after Christmas, which would be 4 January 1589 in the Old Style calendar, or 14 January in the Gregorian calendar, meaning that he had been there for just a few days longer than two months. It was still a long stay and his health benefited from it.

On his arrival he was half naked, covered only by straw, but he was given a blanket of the kind they used themselves, and this was how he dressed while he was there. McClancy was very welcoming and the women of the castle took a great interest in his welfare. McClancy was very much the man in charge, however, and Cuéllar referred to him as his 'master'. He was greatly impressed by McClancy's wife who was 'very beautiful in the extreme and especially kind to me'. This expression of admiration has been seen as somewhat more lavish than was, perhaps, necessary in the circumstances, and it has stimulated a few fertile imaginations to invent an intimate relationship between Cuéllar and McClancy's wife. Unfortunately there is no additional evidence for it, and readers must judge for themselves whether or not these words betray a lingering emotional involvement.

Cuéllar did seem to spend time with her, and he describes how on one occasion they were sitting in the sun together along with some of her friends who asked him about life in Spain and other countries. Presumably the conversation was in Latin. It led on to Cuéllar reading their hands and telling their fortunes, which was an immediate hit with both men and women. He had a gift for improvising what he called 'a hundred thousand absurdities', and it soon got out of control for they pestered him all hours of the day. On the other hand he appreciated the irony that after the many life-threatening situations he had just come through, he could thank God he now had to endure 'nothing worse than to be a gypsy among savages'. It had gone far enough, however, and McClancy had to order them not to bother him any more.

News reached Rossclogher that the Lord Deputy, William Fitzwilliam, had set out from Dublin with seventeen hundred men to begin his journey into the north. Rumours flew ahead of him about the terrible punishments he was inflicting on any Spanish survivors he found and on Irish people who had sheltered them. The English were coming and McClancy, in a great rage, had to decide to move all his people and cattle to safety in the mountains. Cuéllar was invited to accompany them, but with the remaining eight other Spanish fugitives he asked to be allowed to stay in the castle and resist any attempted assault by the English. Nine against seventeen hundred was not as hopeless as it sounds, because Rossclogher Castle, being on an island, was highly defensible. The nearby ground was marshy so that artillery could not be moved onto it, and without artillery Cuéllar calculated the English could do very little. They armed themselves with six muskets, six arquebuses and other small arms together with boatloads of stones and provisions for six months. McClancy insisted that they would defend his castle to the death and not surrender it for any false promises.

The situation was a stand-off. English soldiers could do nothing but shout threats at one moment and offer safe passage the next. They apparently had two Spanish prisoners whom they hanged, but gained nothing by it. The Spanish returned the verbals with defiance. After seventeen days the siege was brought to an end by the weather; heavy snowstorms descended on the area and the Lord Deputy was forced to withdraw.

At the end of December the Lord Deputy sent an account to the Privy Council in London of his journey into the north. It began on 14 November and he records that he arrived back in Dublin on 2 January 1589—seven weeks and one day. By 18 November he was in Athlone, and from there he says they went to Sligo where they joined with Bingham's men. He described the scene at Streedagh; the 1,200 bodies had been buried but the wreckage was still strewn along the shore—'as great a store of timber than would have built five of the greatest ships I ever saw, and some such masts for bigness and length I never saw any two could make the like'. He said he travelled to Bundrowse and then on to Ballyshannon on the Erne. Although it was only three or four miles out of the way he never mentions a siege at Rossclogher Castle. There is nothing unusual about that. On the occasions when it is possible to crosscheck details in official documents, it is no longer surprising to find that unfavourable events are simply not reported. The Lord Deputy knew quite well that there was no way he could say his whole force had been defied for seventeen days by nine Spanish fugitives without making himself look a fool. He did report that O'Rourke, O'Hara, McGlannagh, Maguire and others had taken their people and cattle into the mountains and woods, which was true, but only part of the story. Fitzwilliam bore his grudges deeply and stored up vengeance to be exacted later. He vowed he would return.

News of the English humiliation soon spread and McClancy came down to reoccupy his castle. He was ecstatic that his home had been preserved, declared his lasting friendship and offered the use of all his possessions to Cuéllar and his fellow Spanish. The local subordinate chieftains also came round to do the same. This overflowing gratitude began to worry Cuéllar especially when McClancy offered him one of his sisters 'para que me casase con ella'—that I should marry with her! He tried to put things in perspective by pointing out that what he really wanted was a guide to take him to a place where he could embark for Scotland. McClancy would not give him leave to depart, saying that the roads were not safe. This was partly true since the Lord Deputy and his escorts were not far away, but Cuéllar suspected that his actual intention was to keep him there to act as his personal guard. This was confirmed when one of McClancy's sons told him that he was to be kept there until the King of Spain sent his soldiers, because in the long run he knew he would be defenceless against the English garrisons. Cuéllar had to protect himself, however, and he arranged with four other Spanish fugitives to leave Rossclogher secretly two hours before dawn on 14 January 1589. He says he travelled through the mountains and deserted places, which would seem to indicate that they went northeast through Fermanagh and Tyrone rather than along the coast to Donegal town and up the Barnesmore Gap to Ballybofey and Strabane, a well frequented route.

On the north coast

Cuéllar recalls that they were twenty days on this journey to the north coast, which meant they arrived there on 3 February. But he says nothing about how they sustained themselves on the way. In the depth of winter they could not have lived off the countryside so they must have found some people to give them shelter and food. He claims he found the place where Don Alonso de Leyva perished, but Port na Spaniagh at the Giant's Causeway is so remote it is hardly likely that he dragged himself out to it. If he had he would surely have given a vivid description of such a dramatic place. More probably he came across an inhabited area around the Bushfoot and been told of the *Girona* disaster. Why he did not make contact with the Macdonnells of Dunluce is a mystery. Even if he had to wait for a ship to Kintyre he would have got one eventually. All he says is that he went among the huts of some savages there who told him there was no ship to take him to Scotland. Then he had news of a chieftain in a nearby territory who had some boats that were about to sail. This was O'Cahan whose home was at Castleroe on the west bank of the Bann opposite Coleraine about nine miles west of Bushfoot.

Cuéllar now began to complain again about the wound in one of his legs. He said he could hardly move because of it, and consequently he found the boats had left two days before he arrived. We had not heard about his leg wound for some time and it seemed that he had recovered from it. There were two periods of convalescence one of which, at Rossclogher, lasted two months, and after that he undertook the walk to the north coast—a distance of not less than a hundred miles. This walk might have reopened his wound but he did not complain about it until he had to do the nine miles from the Bushfoot to Castleroe.

He wandered about O'Cahan's village until he was more or less adopted by some Irish women who took him to their huts in the hills. They tended his wound and looked after him for a month and a half, by which time it had healed again. It was now the end of March or the beginning of April, and

Cuéllar was ready to make another attempt to persuade O'Cahan to ship him to Scotland. He returned to Castleroe, but O'Cahan refused to speak to him, pleading that he had promised the Lord Deputy not to entertain any more Spanish survivors in his territory. An English garrison were stationed close to the village so he would have been in some danger, but it so happened that most of the soldiers and O'Cahan's fighting men were, at this time, away invading a neighbouring territory.

Cuéllar was able to move freely about the village and soon found some extremely beautiful girls, with whom he became very friendly. He says he went to their house sometimes 'a conbersacion y parlar'—for conversation and talk. He makes it sound like a literary debating society, but we cannot help noticing his partiality for beautiful Irish girls. One evening when he was there two young English soldiers came to visit. One was a sergeant who knew about Cuéllar, but he seemed to be able to talk himself out of immediate danger by convincing them that he had already been captured in the group from the *Trinidad Valencera*. He had to admit that he was Spanish, which would have been obvious in his voice whatever language they were using. The sergeant told him that he would have to go with them to Dublin, and that they would provide a horse to carry him since he could not walk. He agreed to wait while the Englishmen consorted with the girls. Their mother signed to him to escape through the door, which he did he says 'with great haste leaping over ditches and penetrating thick undergrowth until he lost sight of O'Cahan's castle'. This does not sound like someone crippled by a leg wound, but adrenaline can work amazing remedies in extreme situations.

Cuéllar's narrative on the north coast has mysterious, unexplained gaps and imprecise descriptions that make it difficult to interpret where he actually was. At nightfall he says he came to a very large lake, on the shores of which were a herd of cows. But there are no large lakes in the area west of the Bann, unless this was just a flooded field. Two young boys were moving the cattle to higher ground where their parents were taking refuge from the English. They treated him with much kindness and he stayed with them for two days. One of the boys went down to O'Cahan's village to pick up news of what was happening. Apparently the two Englishmen were going about in a great rage still searching for Cuéllar, and when he heard this he realized he would have to leave the area completely.

Next morning he headed off west to make contact with a bishop who was living in retirement on the shores of the Foyle. This was Redmond O'Gallagher, the Catholic Bishop of Derry, and he had already helped survivors from the *Trinidad Valencera* after they had been attacked by members of an English force under the Hovenden brothers at Castle Burt. Cuéllar's newly found fitness enabled him to cover the twenty miles to the

Foyle in a day, and he was overjoyed to find the bishop and kiss his hand. While this was certainly one option open to him, we cannot help wondering why he never seems to have made contact with the Macdonnells of north Antrim. He would surely have been well received at Dunluce Castle, and further east they had another home near Ballycastle, from both of which they had regular contact with Kintyre. They were already reputed to have shipped about five hundred Spanish survivors to Scotland. Going west looks like the wrong direction.

There were twelve other Spanish fugitives staying with the bishop and they were treated with sympathy and generosity. Mass was said daily for them. They had to wait six days while a boat was arranged and stocked with provisions for the journey, which would normally take two days. The bishop warned them to take care and be patient in Scotland, because the people were mostly Protestant and there were few Catholics. Cuéllar was immensely impressed by Redmond O'Gallagher, calling him an honourable and just man; he prayed that God might hold him in his hand and deliver him from his enemies.

Scotland

Cuéllar was a bit shocked by the boat that was going to undertake an open sea crossing. He called it 'una pobre barca'. It must have been an Irish curragh, which might have looked less elegant than its Mediterranean counterpart, being made of a timber frame covered in cowhides, but it was a well-proven design that had served the trade with Scotland for centuries. Saint Brendan had sailed to the Americas in one nearly a thousand years before.

His luck with the sea continued to be bad. He and seventeen others left the shores of Lough Foyle at dawn one day, which must have been in early April 1589. Before evening they were hit by a southerly gale that carried away the sail and forced them to run before it. Cuéllar says they were driven to Shetland, which they reached at dawn next day, but a day's sailing even in a southerly gale cannot have taken them further than the Inner Hebrides. Islay was about 75 miles away; Mull would have been 120 miles and might have been remotely possible, but Shetland was out of the question and was another example of Cuéllar's ignorance of the geography of this part of the world. They spent two days here making 'the miserable boat' fit for sea again, and three days later arrived in Scotland. There is no indication of where they made landfall, but the Ayrshire coast would have been the most logical place.

Scotland was a disappointment. Cuéllar expected that Spanish fugitives would be treated well, given clothes and shipped to Spain, but he found that they were largely neglected. There were still several hundred other Spanish survivors in the Edinburgh area waiting to be shipped to safety. He claimed that he was there for six months, but it was probably a bit less than that. During this time they were left to wander around as naked as they had been in Ireland. He had a poor opinion of King James, calling him a nobody—'no es nada', who had neither the authority nor the dignity of a king. James VI was still at this time only twenty-two years old. He became king while just a baby and Scotland had been ruled by a council of noblemen who were accustomed to exercise what political power there was. Some of the noble families were Catholic and they provided help and comfort to the Spanish, for which Cuéllar expresses great appreciation. But Protestants were in the majority and were unsympathetic. From them he says they received a lot of name-calling and if any Spanish survivor answered back they would attack and kill him.

Eventually they managed to send a letter to the Duke of Parma asking for King Philip's help to get them home, and a Scottish merchant living in Flanders was contracted to supply four ships and victuals for the voyage. Parma had apparently agreed to pay him five ducats for every Spanish survivor he delivered safely to Flanders. It must have been about the beginning of September 1589 that they embarked and set sail for Dunkirk on these four ships.

The voyage to Flanders

Their troubles were far from over, however. Firstly they were forced by bad weather to put into Great Yarmouth for shelter, with the distinct prospect of being made prisoners. This did not happen, but it is not completely clear how they managed to get away with it. Cuéllar says in his narrative that they were 'carrying passports from the Queen of England, by which we were assured of safe passage from all the armies and navies of her country and coasts'. This is a clumsy literal translation, but it is also almost certainly untrue, or at best a misinterpretation of events.

Another version of what might have happened appears in Hakluyt's *Voyages*. He says 'they passed touching at Yarmouth on the coast of Norfolke, and were there stayed for a time untill the Councel's pleasure was knowne; who in regard of their manifolde miseries, though they were enemies, wincked at their passage'. This is such a superb example of the colourful language used by Elizabethans one has to hope that it is true. It is not improbable either. About six hundred prisoners being held in Devon were on the point of being repatriated. Spanish prisoners held in England were sheltered, fed and clothed and treated better than anywhere else.

Treachery on the coast of Flanders?

Surely Cuéllar had now overcome all obstacles in the way of his safe return. On 22 September 1589, however, the four small ships arrived off the bar at

Dunkirk to find Dutch flyboats waiting for them; apparently they had been there for a month and a half. He was convinced that this was treachery, but it is difficult to see on whose part. The merchant who arranged the crossing would be paid only for Spanish survivors delivered safely, and he was about to lose his valuable ships, so he had no interest in setting up an ambush. The English had their opportunity at Great Yarmouth and did not take it. Somehow the Dutch seemed to have learned of the voyage, possibly from trading ships plying back and forth from Edinburgh. Or they may just have been blockading an enemy supply port: six weeks is a long time to wait for a tip-off to be realized. They had many scores to settle with Spanish invading armies; this was their chance and they took it.

Two of the four Scottish boats were destroyed by Dutch gunfire. Cuéllar was in one of the other two, which got away and ran for the shore, but they were soon grounded in the shallows. They broke up in the surf, and Cuéllar then found himself in the same plight on the coast of Flanders as he had suffered at Streedagh Strand, County Sligo, almost exactly one year earlier— he was cast up on the shore hanging on to planks of wood. Some soldiers helped him, but he had to endure the indignity of arriving in Dunkirk wearing only his shirt. Even at that he was lucky for he saw nearly all the men with whom he had been travelling killed. He claimed that he was one of only three left alive.

Cuéllar completed his memoirs in the city of Antwerp on 4 October 1589— an incredible tale of survival in a seemingly endless succession of life-threatening disasters and one fit to rank among the greatest escapes in history.

Postscript—Cuéllar's view of life in Gaelic Ireland

Buried in his narrative Cuéllar gives his impression of life in Gaelic Ireland. He places it within the context of his stay at Rossclogher Castle, and that may have been when he had time to reflect on his surroundings rather than be preoccupied by mere survival. But it has special value to Irish history as an independent and impartial perception of the remnant of ancient Ireland that still existed at the end of the sixteenth century. It is, therefore, worth while to take it out of its chronological place in the narrative and look at it separately. He writes:

It is the custom of these savages to live like the wild beasts among the mountains, which are very rugged in that part of Ireland where we were lost. They live in huts made of straw. The men are all well built with handsome features and limbs, and are as swift as the deer. They eat only once a day and that is at nightfall, their usual meal being oaten bread and butter. They drink only sour milk for they have nothing else. They do not

drink water, though theirs is the best in the world. On feast days they eat
some half-cooked meat without bread or salt; that is their usual custom.

Huts were made of woven withies covered with straw. They were moveable
and suited the pattern of life of pastoral people. The sour milk they drank is
known as buttermilk, which is exactly the opposite of what its name implies,
being the residual liquid after butter has been extracted. It is used in baking
Irish bread and was widely drunk on its own until recent times. There is no
explanation for the supposed neglect of water: although they ate only once a
day they would still have needed to drink frequently throughout the day.

They dress in their normal habit of tight trousers and short coats made of
coarse goat hair, over which they wear a sheepskin mantle. Their hair
hangs down to their eyes. They are great walkers and well used to hard
work.
      They carry on constant warfare with the English that occupy a local
garrison on behalf of the Queen, against whom they defend themselves
and never allow them into their territory.
      The land here (that is Rossclogher Castle and south of Lough Melvin)
is always flooded and marshy. All this area is more than forty leagues in
length and breadth.

His estimate of the size of McClancy's territory is spectacularly wrong. Forty
leagues is 120 miles so he implies that it covered the whole of northwest
Ireland. Forty square leagues, or 120 square miles, is still far too large. Ten
miles by twelve miles would impinge on O'Rourke in the south and Maguire
in the north. Cuéllar's estimates of distance can be taken as overestimates in
every case.

The main ambition of the people is to be robbers and plunder one
another. Hardly a day passes without a call to arms among them, for as
soon as they learn of cattle or anything valuable in a nearby village, they
'go Santiago' in the night and attack and kill each other. The English
garrisons get to know who has stolen the most cattle, and descend upon
them to carry away their plunder, leaving them no alternative but to retreat
to the hills with their wives and cattle for they have no other property—
neither furniture nor clothing. They sleep on the ground on freshly cut
rushes, full of water and ice.

It must have been a surprise for Cuéllar to find that neighbouring villages
were constantly at war with each other. The tradition of cattle raiding went

back into the mists of very early history. The subject of Ulster's great epic poem 'The Táin' is a cattle raid. In the Old Testament 1 Chronicles Ch. 7 verse 21 tells how the people of Garth, who were born in the land, killed the sons of Ephraim, because they came down to steal their cattle. Change the names and it could be rural Ireland even as late as the sixteenth century. Cuéllar laments the lack of law and order, and without it people cannot begin to accumulate wealth. The apparent participation of English garrisons in rustling was in fact the collection of the Queen's rent in the form of 'rent beeves' as there was no money in the system and no other property of value. To Irish farmers it was stealing just the same.

> Most of the women are very beautiful, but badly dressed. They wear nothing but a chemise covered by a blanket and a linen cloth on their head folded several times and tied in front. They are great workers and housekeepers in their own way.
>
> These people call themselves Christians. Mass is said among them, regulated in accordance with the orders of the Church of Rome, but almost all their churches, monasteries and hermitages have been torn down by English garrisons and by those of this country who have joined them and are as bad as they are.

It would appear that mass was said even when ordained clergy were not available in remote areas. Possibly itinerant priests left a container of consecrated host for this purpose. The refinements in education, art and religious observance which evolved in the monasteries of the ancient Irish Church in the first millennium are missing here. But the people seem to be content and not in the least sorry for themselves. This was the remnant of a very old civilization by which many people had lived for thousands of years.

> In short, in this kingdom there is neither justice nor reason, and each person does as he pleases.
>
> These savages showed us favour, because they knew we had come against the heretics and were their great enemies. If they had not guarded us as well as they did themselves none of us would still be alive. We had to be grateful to them for this, although they were the first to rob us and strip to the skin all those who came ashore alive.

Cuéllar accurately sums up the response of the Irish people to the arrival of the Spanish. They were the first to rob them of everything they possessed, but they did not kill them and, within the constraints of their basic poverty, helped them when they could.

The fate of the Irish chieftains

McClancy and O'Rourke were heroically implacable in their opposition to English occupation. Their willingness to give assistance to Spanish survivors was only part of their unequal struggle. Eventually it cost them their lives. Sir Richard Bingham as President of Connaught was determined to subdue their territories and impose the structure of English civil administration on them.

At Easter 1590 George Bingham attacked McClancy's stronghold. McClancy tried to escape by swimming, but a shot broke his arm. When he was brought ashore Bingham killed him, severed his head and sent it to Dublin. The remorseless Bingham was proud of himself. He called McClancy 'the best killed man in Connaught a long time … an arch-rebel who never lived dutifully one day in all his life and never paid Her Majesty one penny of rent for all the lands in his country'. He was able to ignore the absurdity that it had been McClancy land for many generations.

McClancy was O'Rourke's right-hand man. Without his support O'Rourke felt exposed to the advancing English garrisons, and he decided he would move to Scotland to try to enlist the help of the Scottish King. Reports suggest that he was asking for King James' mediation to secure a pardon for him from Queen Elizabeth, but that would have been out of character. King James delivered him instead to his fate in England, and on 2 November 1591 he was indicted for high treason. Within a few weeks he was executed at Tyburn. At his request he was hanged in the Irish tradition using a withy instead of a rope of English hemp.

Bringing modern social reform to a remote area of independent people was a task requiring sensitive and sympathetic handling. Bingham, the Flail of Connaught, was not the right man for the job. It is no wonder that he generated hatred and bitterness that lasted hundreds of years. And it is poignant to think that the immediate reason for the deaths of two Irish chieftains was because they aided the shipwrecked Spanish.

NOTES AND SOURCES

Cuéllar's original manuscript is in the Colección Salazar, no. 7, folio 58, in the Royal Academy of History in Madrid. It is a matter of debate to whom it was addressed. Some commentators have suggested that it was to King Philip, but one guess being as good as another, my instinct is that it was sent to the Duke of Parma. It was printed in Spanish in C.F. Duro *La Armada Invencible* (Madrid 1884–1885), and reproduced in P. Gallagher and D.W. Cruickshank *God's Obvious Design* (London 1990) and on the Internet. There have been several English translations since the 1890s. H. Allingham and Robert Crawford *Captain Cuéllar's Adventures in Connaught and Ulster* (London

1897) is now available on the Internet. I have also referred to the translations by Frances Partridge in Evelyn Hardy *Survivors of the Armada* (London 1966) and Jim Stapleton *Sligo to the Causeway Coast* (Sligo 2001). In chopping back and forth between the original Spanish and the various translations I have inserted, for better or worse, my own interpretation in some places.

The original text reads more or less continuously with only a token gesture towards punctuation. All the currently available translations make an attempt to relieve the eye by applying modern standards of paragraphing and punctuation. The narrative is, however, composed of a sequence of many separate episodes, and in an effort to make them more digestible I have divided them into sub-sections each with a title of its own (though unfortunately not titles imaginative enough to give sub-editors sleepless nights). Knowing how fallible one's own memory can be, allowance has to be made throughout for the fact that this is not a diary. Cuéllar was writing up to a year after the events he describes, and his appreciation of the passage of time, the distances travelled and the general geography of northwest Ireland are sometimes bizarre. But by relating the dates of known events from external sources a tentative timeframe can be superimposed.

Some information from Irish sources has been added in the appropriate places. For example George Bingham's part in the killing of survivors at Streedagh is from microfilm copies of State Papers in the Public Record Office reference MIC 223 reel 51, document numbers 237 to 240. And the sighting of six ships off Aughris Head on 14 September is on the same microfilm, document number 77.

The additional information about the escape from Great Yarmouth is in Hakluyt's *Voyages*; in the Everyman Edition it is in volume 2, p. 399. This is part of an unusual account of the Armada by a Dutch writer, Emanuel van Meteran, originally in Latin but presumably translated by Richard Hakluyt.

The date of Cuéllar's letter is 4 October 1589 and this is of course from the New Style calendar. Dates from Irish and English sources have been adjusted to make them agree with New Style dating. There is one slight complication. When he says that he left Rossclogher Castle ten days after Christmas, we have to presume that Christmas was celebrated locally on the basis of the Old Style calendar. Ten days after Christmas would be 4 January 1589 Old Style, which had to be changed to 14 January 1589 to make it conform to New Style.

APPENDIX 3

The Diary of Marcos de Aramburu

The account of what happened to Marcos de Aramburu, Inspector General and Paymaster of the Galleons of Castile, sailing with the Vice-Flagship (the San Juan Bautista*) for which he assumed responsibility.*

On Thursday night 25 August 1588, in latitude more or less 59°N, 60 leagues to the west of Ireland, it was getting dark, the wind was southeast, we were in company with many ships of the Armada and, just before nightfall, it became misty. We sailed with the two mainsails during the night, as the wind was fresh and all the other ships were on the same sail. The night was very misty and we saw neither ship nor lantern.

The morning of 26 it was still foggy. We found that our fore mainsail was damaged so that we were forced to lower it in order to be able to navigate. Since it was raining and it took a lot of work, we were delayed until about an hour after midday. Some ships passed us close enough to be seen, and in the afternoon we saw the Flagship with some other ships on our prow to the southwest and somewhat to windward. There were more ships to the south, two leagues away, with both mainsails and the top yards set fairly high as the sea and the weather would allow no more. We followed them.

That night [26/27] about the fifth watch the wind changed to the south, the southwest and even as far as north northeast. I gave orders to set course to the ssw so that, if the Armada did not change course, I reasoned we would meet them and, if it did change, then we would be on the same course.

And so at dawn on 27 we saw some ships to the west to windward sailing together, and, although we pressed on all day as fast as we could out to sea to ssw, we could gain nothing on them, because they too were doing the same. At nightfall the wind was westerly, as it had been all day, and we were overtaken by the ship *Trinidad*. We discussed with them what was the best we would be able to do, and we came to the opinion that we should continue on the same course as it was the most suitable for our voyage, and the Armada could hardly do other than sail from the north. On the same course another ship appeared to windward but we were not able to recognize her. From dusk right through the night [27/28] we pressed on with both mainsails, changing course to sse close to the wind, as there was nothing better we could do.

On the morning of 28 we found ourselves alone with the *Trinidad*, the weather was overcast and dark, but we held the same course till nightfall s¼se. Not another sail did we see. When night fell the wind began to drop and passed through sw to south. Taking soundings we found ourselves in 120 brazas with a gravel bottom and we steered w¼sw at midnight.

At dawn on 29 the wind began to freshen from the south with heavy seas, mists and rain. We continued on the same course [w¼sw] with the mainsails lowered until night, and all through the night until dawn on 30.

On the morning of 30 the wind dropped and, with a very heavy shower as the wind died, the sea moderated. All the rest of the day the wind stayed light NE but with clouds building up from the sw. At dawn the ship *Trinidad* had gone, although last watch before daybreak she had been there, following our lantern, and the previous evening at dusk she had been only half a league from us. Taking a reading of the sun today we were in latitude 58°N, 95 leagues from the coast of Ireland, in 125 brazas, a rocky bottom without sand or gravel.

On 31 a wind sprang up from the south and we steered wsw until 4 o'clock in the afternoon, when the course came round to ssw.

On the afternoon of 1 September we tacked again to sw. The sea was rough, the wind SE and there was a lot of mist.

The morning of 2 September the *Trinidad* appeared three ship lengths off our stern, but with the fog we lost sight of it again almost at once. We held the same course and waited for about half an hour, but as she did not appear, we got under way with the mainsail. In the afternoon it cleared up a bit, and we sighted her sailing from NE about a league away. We turned over towards her, and she told us she had to stop because she was taking a lot of water forward. Presently she set sail again, and a gentle wind sprang up from SE. We steered sw¼s with seas running from sse. Then two hours after dark the wind veered through south round to NW very strong, and stayed like that till dawn on 3 September, when it became calm until the afternoon

On 3 and 4 September we sailed courses between SE and ssw; the latitude reading was 56½°N, 120 leagues from the coast of Ireland. [This latitude reading must be a mistake—Medina Sidonia was at 58°N and Aramburu recorded 56½° again on the seventh after four days sailing courses between wsw and sse. It is probably best to take it that he was at the same latitude as the Duke and that this was a transcription error.]

On 5 September we continued on the same course until nightfall with a moderating wind, and we sailed with it ws¼w with heavy seas and a strong wind. [On 6] at 2 o'clock in the afternoon, after we had a heavy squall, suddenly the seas calmed and the wind changed to wNW. The sea continued to moderate and we headed sse.

On 7 we continued on the same course with the same wind. We were able to take an accurate latitude and found we were in 56½°N. At 4 o'clock in the afternoon the wind came round to sw with a gentle sea.

On 8, the day of Our Lady, the day dawned with the wind and the sea the same as the previous afternoon. The latitude was taken in 55°N, and we were sailing on a heading SE¼s.

On 9 we took the latitude in 54°N, 100 leagues from the land of Ireland, running with a moderate sw wind easing gradually; the course was SE¼S.

On 10 we held the same course with a light wind: we did not take a latitude reading.

On 11 two hours before dawn we sighted land. We were on a fresh sw wind steering SE. Because the weather was misty, we did not see it until we were only one league from it. Some of us thought it was the Island of Drosey [Dursey] and others the Isles of Quelmes [the Skelligs]. The pilot was of the opinion it was the islands Bull and Cow, 8 leagues from the Cape. We turned out to sea with a ssw wind and headed west. At 4 o'clock in the afternoon the wind began to freshen and the seas to rise.

On 12 we kept heading out to sea with the same wind and sea conditions, and at 5 o'clock in the afternoon it began to blow from the south with great strength, which by the night had become a very heavy storm with very rough seas and sea mist. The ship *Trinidad* had joined us. It had both mainsails furled; from midnight onwards we were unable to see it although we showed our lantern signal.

On 13 at dawn the wind veered to NW and the seas began to go down; we steered S¼SE.

On 14 we continued on the same course with the same wind and at midday to leeward we saw a big ship and a patache sailing together. We began heading over towards her, and by dusk we were within a league of her, but since it was dark we could not follow her. We showed our lantern the whole night in the hope that she would see us.

On 15 we continued heading south on a westerly wind. Two hours before dawn we sighted, to windward and to the north of us, a ship displaying lights, and another to leeward of us which had no lights. We suspected that they were the same ships we had seen the previous day, and that they were standing away from land, of which we were also afraid. For the rest of the time until daybreak we carried on the same course. At dawn we sighted on our prow two large islands, and away to port, to the east, the mainland. As we could not go on we turned NW. Fleeing from there we came across the same two ships which we now recognized were the flagship of Juan Martinez de Recalde and a patache, towards which we turned on a crosswind. We did not recognize what land it was, nor know what to do, but we saw Juan Martinez being able to double one of the islands by another piece of land in front of him, and turn onto an easterly course. We fell in to windward of him and were able to follow him, imagining that he had some knowledge of this place. He kept on towards the mainland and got into the Port of Vicey through an entrance between low islands no bigger than the length of a ship. He dropped anchor and we behind him, and after us came the patache, which was carrying a Scotsman who had been taken into it after the Duke had captured his ship. Today we saw another ship to leeward of us close to the mainland. God help him find a way out for he was in great danger.

On 16 Juan Martinez gave us two cables and an anchor, since we had only one cable which was in the sea, and I gave him an anchor of 30 quintals, which was useless for us, but of which he had the greatest need.

On 17 Juan Martinez sent over a longboat with 50 soldiers to look for a landing place. They took a linguist to treat with the Irish for supplies of water, of which we had great need, and for some meat. They found nothing except wild cliffs beaten by the seas, and about 100 soldiers marching along the cliffs carrying a white flag with a red cross. It was suspected that they were Englishmen, and that eight men, whom Juan Martinez had sent ashore on 15 in a chalup to reconnoitre, must have been captured or had been lost in the sea.

On 18, 19 and 20 we remained in this port without being able to sail. Juan Martinez himself managed to get some water but I, without a batel or a chalup, could do nothing. He got little and that with much effort.

On 21, in the morning, it began to blow from the west with a most terrible fury. It was bright and with little rain. Juan Martinez's ship dragged anchor over on top of us, he put out another anchor and cable, and, having already hit us astern shattering our lantern and breaking the rigging of the mizzen mast, he regained control of his ship. At midday the ship *Santa Maria de la Rosa* of Martin de Villafranca came in by another entrance somewhat nearer the mainland from the northwest. Coming in he fired a piece as if asking for help, and further on he fired another. All her sails hung in pieces except for the fore mainsail. She came to a stop with one anchor, which was all she had, and, with the tide coming in from the southeast, she held steady for a while. At 2 o'clock the tide turned and she began to swing on her anchor and dragged to within two cable lengths from us, and we dragged with her. We could see she was going to sink any minute. They tried to hoist the fore mainsail but she went down right away with every man on board, not a soul was saved, a most extraordinary and frightening thing. We were dragged over on top of her in great danger ourselves. Thanks be to God we were held by an anchor with only half a cross piece which Juan Martinez had given us with a cable. As we came to a stop the ship swung and we recovered the other anchor. We found that it came up with only the cross piece and half the shaft, for the rest had broken, and the cable had been frayed by the rocks over which we were [anchored for 4 days]. At this moment the ship of Miguel de Aranivar also came in.

This same afternoon at 4 o'clock the *San Juan* of Fernando Horra came in, her mainmast gone, and as she came in her fore mainsail ripped to pieces. She dropped anchor and stopped. With the fierce weather we were not able to hail her or give her any assistance. On the morning of 22 he launched his chalup and sent over to let us know what he needed. It was obvious his situation was hopeless, and Juan Martinez agreed that I should take on board everybody in the company of Gonzalo Melendez, and that those from the company of Don Diego Bazan should be divided between the pataches; [so Miguel de Aranivar's ship was a patache]. I urged him that we should get away quickly because of my shortage of supplies. Without a boat I had no chance of getting fresh water, and the bread and other things he had given us were being used up. I wanted him to set fire to the *San Juan* [of Fernando Horra] and let us sail away. As will be seen, he wanted to save the artillery from her and make every effort to save the ship, but it proved to be impossible. And so he publicly gave me permission to make my way back to Spain.

On the morning of 23 September we sailed from Vicey on a light easterly wind. But, as we left the harbour, we had hardly gone two cables when the wind fell calm and the current began to drive us onto the island, so that in a short time we would have been lost. Then the wind picked up again and we were able to continue sailing with the current towards the rocky islets, which were in a line to the north of us. Again the wind dropped and the tide, which was coming in, kept moving us towards the land to the north between four islands and the rocky islets. Before nightfall we cast anchor with only one cable, which was all we had. One hour later, after dark, the wind began to blow from the SE and the ship began to drag towards the islands, which are so rocky that no one sailing onto them could be saved. We swung round on our cable and, lifting the anchor, we set sail, commending ourselves to the Lord. We had no idea whether there was a way out but, with the night so dark and cloudy, we were forced to take the risk. First we tried to make our way out to windward of the rocky islets but were prevented by the current, which rather would have carried us to destruction. We turned and tried again for an opening between the islands. The wind was becoming quite fresh with a swell, a lot of cloud and showers. Thanks to our Lady, in whom we placed our trust, we managed to get out this time. Sailing all through the night to the west, we found that by morning we were 8 leagues from land.

On 24 September 3 hours after daybreak a great storm sprang up from the southeast with heavy rain and rough seas. Thank God it lasted only 2 hours. We feathered our sails and lay to. Almost at once the wind veered westerly and, with the big seas, we took a pounding and a lot of damage on the prow. We were not able to set sail until the afternoon when, with a moderating wind, it became possible. Next day [25] at dawn we found ourselves off the entrance to the port we had just left, 3 leagues out to sea in calm conditions.

During the morning of 25 the wind came round to SSE and S. We set course to the west to take advantage of the wind and double the Cape of Drasey [Dursey Island]. We sailed that day and all night till, next morning [26], we reckoned we were 10 leagues out to sea.

On 26 the wind came round to WSW and SW, strong with big seas moving us along at good speed on the course SSE, sometimes SE¼S, until we judged we had doubled the Cape of Drosey (sic) and we were north/south from there about 14 leagues.

On the morning of 28 [should be 27?] the wind came round to S and SSW. We changed course to W then to WNW. In the middle of the night [i.e. early on 28] such a great gale blew up from NW, with such violent seas and rain that our fore mainsail ripped to pieces; nothing was left of it. We lowered the mainsail, but were not able to take it in, and the ship began to roll badly. As a result, the guns that were stowed below, the ballast, pipes of wine and coils of rope, all shifted to the port side. At the same time we were engulfed by three huge waves which hit us amidships and we thought we were lost. We attached a boneta to the shrouds of the foremast and commended ourselves to God and his Blessed Mother. With it the ship began to handle reasonably well, and we were able to manage in that way for the rest of the night until the following morning.

From the morning of 29 the wind gradually dropped and, because of the heavy seas, we continued sailing towards the southern quarter until the afternoon, when we were able to fix up an old fore mainsail which we had made ready. The night was quite calm with not much wind and, sailing until morning [30] on the course SE¼E, we worked all day putting the ship in order.

On 30 we carried on with the task of making repairs, getting the topmast aloft and restoring the ship. It remained calm until dark when the wind became light NW all through the night. We maintained a southerly heading until morning [1 Oct] without putting up the main topsail, because the weather became threatening, the seamen were sick, and it was doubtful if they could have taken it in again.

During 1 October we sailed on in the same way. At midday a reading of the sun showed we were in 48¼°N.

From 2 to 7 October we continued sailing in reasonable weather and at dawn on 8 we sighted land which we reckoned to be the Cape de Peñas off Torres [just west of Gijon]. A fresh easterly wind came up and we sailed with it till next morning.

On 9 the wind veered to the west. We turned towards land, to what we identified as Rivadeo, because it was our intention to make for La Coruña. The wind kept getting stronger and presently it veered to NW fresh. We stood out to sea all that night.

On 10 October a great westerly gale developed, which damaged our main topsail and the main foresail, and broke the shrouds and the cables of the mainmast on the port side, so that the mainmast itself began to give way. This was during the night and at dawn [on 11] we hove to, reinforced the mainmast shrouds and refitted the foremast. We threw overboard the main topmast, the lateen yard and other things as the ship was being strained, and we were in the most serious plight.

During 11 October we headed back towards the land, and next morning [12] we sighted Los Arrocles, 14 leagues from Santander on the Galicia side.

On 12 we ran the whole day on a very fresh wind making for Santander. We arrived off the harbour there three hours after nightfall, firing guns periodically and sticking close to the coast, but no help came. It became calm and we turned out to sea.

At dawn on 13 we found ourselves off Santoña, but because of the bad state we were in, all we could do was ask for help by firing guns. No one heeded us. At 3 o'clock in the afternoon the wind came round SE, fresh but without rough seas, and two hours after nightfall, we arrived and anchored at the entrance to Santander.

On the morning of 14 October we entered port and anchored in safety, for which we give thanks to God, and for finding in port the Flagship and a good portion of the Armada.

Colec. Sans de Barutell Simancas art. 4. numero 946.

Published in Spanish in C.F. Duro, *La Armada Invencible*, VOL. II, document number 178. Translated by Paul Russell-Gebbett, Professor of Spanish at Queen's University Belfast from 1970 to 1986.

APPENDIX 4

Irish History

The Spanish Armada's contact with Ireland was a dramatic but very brief episode that left scarcely a ripple on the surface of the course of Irish history. In reading about it in contemporary documents, however, we are confronted by apparent anomalies and complex relationships that the general reader cannot be expected to understand and which therefore demand some kind of explanation. For example we encounter chieftains of traditional Irish territories bearing titles of English nobility, such as Sir John O'Doherty on the remote peninsula of Inishowen and Sir Brian O'Rourke from the hills of Leitrim, who nevertheless would have been proud to call himself a rebel against English rule in Ireland. Conversely in a corner of County Kerry the local landowner was obviously English, Sir Edward (and Lady) Denny. What was going on? How did Irish history evolve into such a complicated state of affairs?

There can be few subjects more written about than Irish history. One eminent history has a bibliography that runs to 35 pages, and it deals with only a limited period! The subject continues to receive attention from the most distinguished scholars, whose intimate knowledge of the details of Ireland's past is staggering. It is therefore almost impossible to give a quick tour of Irish history without offending practically everybody. Genuine historians with a sensitive disposition should perhaps look away now!

It is possible to distinguish three main groups of people living in Ireland in the sixteenth century. The most numerous were the Gaelic Irish, also called the Irish and sometimes the 'mere' Irish by the haughty Normans. The Normans invaded Ireland in the twelfth century and embarked on a campaign of conquest that was almost but not quite successful. Over the period of 400 years they changed. At first they were called the Anglo-Normans, then the Anglo-Irish, and later the Old English. The New English were the sixteenth-century undertakers and adventurers who tried to take advantage of opportunities offered by the plantations of Leix and Offaly, Munster, and later Ulster. Subsidiary to these three, the Scots of the Inner Hebrides and Ayrshire had, from ancient times, regular communication with and settlements on the north and east coasts of Ulster. From the thirteenth century Scottish mercenary gallowglasses served in the forces of many families throughout Ireland, and in places formed settlements of their own.

The Vikings who came to Ireland in the ninth and tenth centuries were nearly all Norwegian. They came first as raiders but then as settlers, founding trading towns along the coast such as Wexford, Waterford, Cork, Limerick, Galway and of course Dublin. Later some Danes relocated from the north of England to settle in the south and east. They retained their identity and were referred to as Ostmen.

Foreign invaders who were conspicuous by their absence were the Romans. In bypassing Ireland they left an undisturbed backwater where Galapagos type isolation allowed the evolution and preservation of a uniquely introverted society.

Gaelic Ireland

The origins of Gaelic Ireland are obscured by the lack of written history. The Irish language did not begin to be written down until the seventh century, and even then it was confined to the scholar monks in the monastic communes where Latin biblical texts and commentaries were at first annotated, and then transcribed in Old Irish. Once they mastered the capacity to express aspects of life in written Irish there followed an unprecedented explosion of vernacular literature greater than in any other European country at that time. There was a rush to record what had for generations been oral tradition kept alive by Irish scholars, bards, brehons and storytellers. Every culture values its origins and annals were produced that tried to recapture memories of a heroic past with great battles, legendary deeds, endless genealogies and saints' lives.

Modern historians wrestled with this mass of information, trying to extract genuine history from what obviously was composed of a great deal of mythology. The same problem confronts students of Homer and the Old Testament. Finding history in mythology was given the name Euhemerism, and was valued as an alternative to genuine history when an authentic record was missing. An enormous amount of work went into tracing genealogies and interpreting what the annals, saints' lives and bardic poems seemed to be saying about the possible origins of Gaelic Ireland. By the middle of the twentieth century this appeared to have been brought to some kind of agreed resolution.

It was concluded that Gaelic Ireland was the product of probably three or four waves of migrations from the Celtic tribes of middle Europe who brought Iron Age technology to Ireland in the final three hundred years or so BC. Traces were found of Celtiberian origins as well, called Milesian. All this was worked out to an elaborate degree and everyone was satisfied with a view of Ireland that gave it a European Celtic identity. This seemed to be supported by the work of philologists who discovered elements of Indo-European languages in Old Irish.

It should be noted, however, that the word 'Celtic' did not appear in any Irish literature of the first millennium, and in fact was not used in Ireland until the seventeenth century. 'Celtic' in the European context came from the Greek word 'Keltoi'. It was applied to tribes who were just outside the northern fringe of the 'civilized' Mediterranean world, stretching from the Scythians and Parthians in the east around the Black Sea, to the Dacians in the Danube valley and the Germanic and Gallic tribes in the west. They were by no means homogeneous and the word Keltoi seems to have served as a catchall definition of semi-civilized neighbours. It was not complimentary and meant literally 'barbarians'. 'Celtic' is used today to include people from Ireland, Scotland, Wales, the Isle of Man, Cornwall and Brittany. It is perfectly valid to express in this way a recognizable affinity within this group, but it does not automatically imply a connection with the original Celtic tribes of middle Europe.

In the 1990s archaeologists became involved with the initial objective of finding physical evidence to determine whether Ireland was connected to the Hallstatt or the La Tène Celtic cultures of central Europe. To everyone's astonishment no connection with either could be found. At first the fault was thought to be in the archaeology, but gradually other options had to be considered. It was clear that Ireland had imported Iron Age technology, but there was no evidence of waves of migration of people from central or northern Europe.

All this is fairly recent, but a growing body of opinion is coming to the conclusion that the Iron Age people of Ireland were Irish—the same people who had been there all along, back through the Bronze Age at least as far as the Neolithic. The introduction of farming is generally thought to have involved a progressive increase in population in Europe, which led to expansion into previously empty or sparsely occupied territory, and this could explain the origin of most of the inhabitants of Ireland. It could also account for the Indo-European component in the Irish language.

The implications of this are enormous. If it proves to be right it would mean that Gaelic Ireland was much older than had previously been thought, possibly as early as 3000 BC. It was in the third millennium BC that the great megaliths were built; they in turn imply economic surpluses, which could only come from farming. It is early days yet for history to come to terms with such a huge shift in the perspectives of Ireland's past, but it offers a solution that appeals to logic in a way that theoretical waves of migration never quite satisfied. Ireland's outstanding historical scholars will no doubt enlighten us in the years to come.

It is enough for now to know that in the sixteenth century the Gaelic Irish people had been there for a very long time. They were by far the most numerous of the different groups and can claim to be the indigenous population. After the sixteenth century the structure of their society broke down in the aftermath of the Elizabethan conquest, but the ordinary people were still there. And their descendants still are today, even after traumatic intervening experiences which included famine and mass emigration.

The unique feature of Gaelic Irish society was its structure. It was intensely aristocratic, greatly favouring the elite family of each territory. They had an entourage of clients who worked the land and a household that included bards, brehons, storytellers and musicians, monks, abbots and warriors. But the majority of the population were landless slaves and labourers. The aristocratic family unit was supreme, and was known as the *derbfine*, which was strictly defined as the descendants to the fourth generation of a previous chieftain or king. Since they tended to have large families both in and out of wedlock, all of whom were acknowledged, the *derbfine* could amount to hundreds of people. The family assembly met to elect and inaugurate the king and his tanist, and they alone had the power to dispose of any property. Ireland had about sixty such 'countries' in the sixteenth century, but in the previous centuries there had been hundreds of them. There was a continuing struggle among neighbouring territories for dominance and the exaction of tribute. A cattle raid was the standard opening move in a contest to establish superiority, and normal political activity amounted to the expansion or contraction of neighbouring territorial entities.

In Gaelic Ireland there was no perception of Ireland as a unified nation state, which all the petty kingdoms could willingly serve. The notional title of High King was never filled, but was in any case thought of not as a potential government of Ireland—rather as an overlordship attracting tribute from as wide an area as possible. The political horizon for most Gaelic lords was the limits of their own territory and, although they accepted the distant overlordship of the papacy in religion and the Angevin kings in politics, they expected to be left alone to conduct the affairs of their territory in the way they had always done. Gaelic Irish society has always been cellular.

There may be a temptation to think of Gaelic society as 'primitive'. It was certainly archaic, but within the compass of its everyday activity it was in fact highly sophisticated. Irish law was not just a legal system; it was a code of conduct for every conceivable aspect of life. The tradition of oral learning was enormous and the bards provided the function of news distribution as well as epic poetry and historic tribal traditions. The rules of hospitality were respected and observed.

The problem for Gaelic Ireland was that it had not adjusted to the outside world and sooner or later it was bound to crash in on them. It was on a dead end road and the sixteenth century marked the end of that road. Sixty independent Gaelic lords needed to act as one to defend Ireland from colonial encroachment and this was beyond them.

The Irish Church

Christianity had a profound effect on Gaelic Ireland. It was embraced with enthusiasm nearly everywhere, although traditional pagan practices and superstitions found a way of being accommodated in the new religion.

At first an orthodox church organisation was established with a regular structure of dioceses and parishes administered by the normal appointments of bishops and priests. But this did not fit with the cellular structure of Irish society, and each territory quickly evolved its own religious community. They were referred to as monasteries, but were not like the monasteries of the second millennium, which were sponsored by religious orders. They were in effect religious and educational communes staffed by abbots and monks and, like everything else in Gaelic Ireland, possessed by the aristocratic families of each individual territory.

The family provided land for building the monastery and also the farms for its sustenance. A successful monastery became a status symbol and families sought to attract outstanding educational and religious figures. A founding saint was essential, and Ireland acquired a sainthood numbering well over two thousand. These were strictly Irish saints; none of them was officially canonized. Some were based on historical people, many were purely mythological, but all were credited with miraculous powers and heroic achievements. Two positions of authority connected with the monastery, which were unique to Ireland, were coarb and erenagh. They were appointed by the family and were the means by which the family exercised its jurisdiction over the monastery. Coarb was the successor of the founding saint. Erenagh was the family representative who was responsible for maintenance of the buildings and for efficient running of the farms. There was not much room for outside interference.

Some monasteries flourished greatly and became religious and educational centres of international reputation. They attracted students and monks from far afield and exported talented and inspiring Christian leaders all over Europe. They also attracted artists and craftsmen who produced beautifully illuminated gospels and a rich store of gold, jewel-encrusted church artefacts. There was some rivalry among the monasteries and they were not above having violent confrontations.

The Irish Church was famously in dispute with Rome over a number of issues. The one most frequently referred to was the calculation of the date of Easter; another was the form of the tonsure. The Roman Church struggled to achieve uniformity throughout its many disparate congregations, but it was forced to extend a measure of tolerance to some eccentric situations, which Ireland undoubtedly was. The date of Easter was a technicality that consumed a lot of heat and energy at the time, and has received too much attention ever since.

Problems with the calendar were not confined to the western churches. Every civilization from China and India in the east to Central America in the west tried to reconcile the ever-present lunar monthly cycle with the more elusive solar yearly cycle. Since they were virtually irreconcilable, calendars in the ancient world were all inherently inaccurate. Even today the involvement of the lunar cycle in determining the date of Easter feels unsatisfactory and must some day be changed. It seems therefore, in retrospect, to be an unlikely subject for fundamental disagreement within the early Christian Church. It is unconnected with biblical authority or essential matters of faith. In the end it came down to insistence on obedience rather than overwhelming weight of argument.

The real difficulty was the organization of the Church in Ireland. The Irish aristocracy had interposed its authority and, while its influence was benign and even generous, it deprived Rome of the chain of command it normally expected to exercise through its bishops and clergy. It was in the community monasteries that religious activity took place and their organization was distinctly Irish. Women were an intrinsic part of the life of the monasteries, both as wives and office bearers. Religious and secular appointments in the commune were often the hereditary preserve of a branch of the ruling family specializing in ecclesiastical affairs without even the pretence of having them endorsed by Rome.

Blatant disregard for the requirements of clerical celibacy and the simultaneous holding of two or more benefices were officially regarded as abuses, but they were such an integral part of life in the Irish Church that they continued for centuries more or less unchallenged. Added to that the virtual impotence of the episcopacy to do anything about it meant that sooner or later the papacy would have to insist on reform.

Reform began from within as two synods around 1150 established diocesan episcopacies and introduced new religious orders from western Europe. The great Saint Malachy (the first Irishman to be officially canonized) brought the Cistercian order to Ireland and founded the new monastery at Mellifont as a totally Gaelic community. In the thirteenth century, however, Cistercian houses of English origin came into conflict with Gaelic traditions and were forbidden by their statutes to receive native Irish as monks.

The effect of the reforms was limited; in many ways it did not change the church in Gaelic areas at all. A regular parochial system was introduced giving bishops the power to make or approve clerical appointments, and the payment of tithes was made obligatory. But in practice a custom evolved to make payments to the bishops as fees for the approval of family members as nominees to clerical offices, and rents were paid by erenaghs for the church lands. An obligation to entertain the bishop and his party was often commuted to a money payment; indeed many bishops refused to go into Gaelic areas where conditions were uninviting and where they were sometimes physically abused.

A device had been found to acknowledge papal supremacy and give the outward signs of regular parochial organization, while at the same time enabling the church in Gaelic areas to continue as before. Clerical celibacy was still ignored and ecclesiastical branches of ruling families still exercised hereditary rights over clerical appointments. This situation continued unchanged into the sixteenth century.

The Normans

The reforms proposed for the Irish Church did not come soon enough or go far enough to satisfy the papacy, and in 1155 Pope Adrian iv issued the papal bull *Laudabiliter*. In it he officially claimed papal overlordship of Ireland, denounced the current state of the Irish Church and commissioned King Henry ii to take on the task of bringing conventional organization and observance to Ireland. The project was seriously discussed in council at Winchester but was violently opposed. What profit could there be for an Angevin King, with pressing affairs in France and England, in trying to solve the problems of an island outside the familiar civilized world and without even an organized national government? It was given a definite 'no'; *Laudabiliter* was shelved and forgotten for sixteen years.

In 1166, internal rivalries in Leinster led to Dermot Mac Murrough being exiled. He looked for support and found it eventually in Richard Fitzgilbert of Wales, known ever since as 'Strongbow'. They put together an army and landed in Waterford in 1170 intending to march on Dublin. Henry ii had to face the prospect of Strongbow extending the power and influence of the Welsh Geraldines, thereby posing a challenge to his authority in England and Wales. Strongbow and his allies had to be stopped, and in 1171 Henry brought a professional army over to Ireland. With little opposition he soon received the submissions of Strongbow, his Irish confederates and the townsmen of Dublin, Wexford and Waterford.

Henry had been sucked into Irish affairs most unwillingly and for solely political reasons. For authority he eventually fell back on *Laudabiliter*, but might the authority it conferred be regarded as having lapsed on his refusal to carry it out in 1155 or 1156? Adrian IV had died in 1159 and Henry was temporarily out of favour with the current pope, Alexander III, over the murder of Thomas à Becket in Canterbury Cathedral. At this stage the legality of Henry's invasion of Ireland was questionable to say the least. He must have been unsure of it himself or he would not have sought Alexander's later approval.

It was a critical landmark in the course of Irish history, because for centuries thereafter England's claim to govern Ireland was based on Henry II's papal commission. *Laudabiliter* never appeared as documentary proof, although some claimed to have seen it. Alexander later approved by letter Henry's actions in Ireland, but it was very much after the event, and it might be disputed whether legality could be conferred retrospectively. Whether Henry II's invasion of Ireland was actually legal at the time is a question that a constitutional lawyer might enjoy putting to the test.

The synod of Irish bishops naturally welcomed Henry's intervention since his religious objective was to restore power to the episcopacy, and he did take his religious obligations seriously. His title, by the way, was to be 'Lord of Ireland' not King.

The Normans, nevertheless, were here!

The colony

Normans were energetic colonists. They had imposed their form of society on Anglo-Saxon England a hundred years earlier, and started out to do the same in Ireland at the end of the twelfth century. They built castles and employed what for Ireland were advanced military tactics using cavalry, archers and mailed foot soldiers. A population explosion in Europe and England, a result of long periods of warm weather and good harvests, provided a steady stream of new colonists to take up tenancies in the Irish baronial estates. Prominent names associated with the Norman Conquest appeared at this time: Fitzgeralds in Kildare and Munster, Butler in Ormond, de Courcy and later de Lacy in Ulster, de Burgo in Connaught and eastern Munster and Prendergast in Wexford. In the early days of the colony they were referred to as Anglo-Normans. They spoke French or a northern dialect of French called *langue d'oïl*, and this was the language used in official documents.

A number of Irish lords grew in strength and importance. The O'Briens in Thomond, the O'Connors in Connaught and Ofaly, O'Neill in Ulster and MacCarthy in Desmond were strong enough to offer opposition to Norman encroachment.

As in England the Normans had an exaggerated self-esteem and they quickly relegated the native Irish to a despised underclass. In 1185 Geraldus Cambrensis wrote a *History and Topography of Ireland* after a relatively brief visit. It would have been a valuable document in many ways, because it is a very good, very early survey of the natural environment, especially of birds and animals. When it came to the Irish people, however, his comments are extremely uncomplimentary, and this has earned him an infamy that discredits him irredeemably in the eyes of every Irish person. Some examples of what gave so much offence are:

> ... although they are fully endowed with natural gifts, their external characteristics of beard and dress, and internal cultivation of the mind, are so barbarous that they cannot be said to have any culture.

(It is strange that the conventions of dress in Ireland should so annoy the Norman temperament. Centuries later they were still objecting to it.)

> They are wild and inhospitable people. They live on beasts only, and live like beasts ...
>
> This is a filthy people, wallowing in vice. Of all peoples it is the least instructed in the rudiments of the Faith. They do not attend God's church with due reverence.
>
> Moreover, above all other peoples they always practise treachery. When they give their word to anyone, they do not keep it, although they are very keen that it should be observed with regard to themselves.

He describes some objectionable conduct that is so outlandish as to be obviously untrue, and this raises the question of how much of his account was anecdotal and how much personal observation.

Without taking every detail at its face value it is still clear that the Normans did not admire the native Irish! They certainly took very seriously their mission to conquer and reform Ireland.

Up to about 1250 the conquest was largely successful, and the colony had steadily increased in size until they had a strong presence nearly everywhere except northwest Ulster. The first weakness in the colony seemed to be that supplies of new colonists began to dry up. Ireland was not as big as England, but it was bigger than they thought, and there were just not enough people to complete the conquest. From this time onward the colony was on the defensive.

The colony was weakened by other factors. Interaction between the colonists and the native Irish gradually changed the character of the Norman areas. Several leading Normans married Irish women and the Irish custom of fostering was introduced. Children were brought up to speak Irish. Differences were noticed and the distinction was made between 'English blood' and 'English born'.

The best interests of the colony began to diverge from the wishes of the English government, which often wanted to use Irish finance and manpower to support their military adventures. Henry III minted £50,000 of new coinage in Dublin and transferred all of it to London. The same situation was to alienate the American colonies five hundred years later. It was about this time that it became appropriate to refer to the 'Anglo-Irish' as opposed to the 'Anglo-Norman'.

The original aim of the colony had been to integrate the Irish into Norman society. By the end of the thirteenth century the opposite was taking place: the colonists were beginning to absorb Irish ways.

The fourteenth century

The first quarter of the fourteenth century marked a serious decline in the economic fortunes of the whole of western Europe. A very rapid change of climate set in that signalled the end of the Medieval Warm Period, which for about five hundred years had brought increases in agricultural production and in populations. Economic surpluses all over Europe had promoted investment in great projects such as cathedrals and churches. In those days global warming was good; global cooling was to be dreaded. A succession of cold, wet summers from 1315 to 1317 led to famine and disease. These were the opening shots in what was to become known as the Little Ice Age, from which we are only just now emerging. Plague epidemics became a recurring threat; the Black Death in 1348–1350 was merely the worst of them. The population declined by as much as a third, and a severe economic recession began that was to provide the context within which everything else took place in the history of the next 300 years.

In Ireland the bad weather of 1315 was accompanied by a serious invasion attempt by Edward Bruce and 6,000 men from Scotland. His more famous brother, Robert the Bruce, was fighting a war of independence against the English and this was mostly a diversion tactic. Edward had himself crowned 'King of Ireland' at Dundalk on 1 May 1316. He wandered the country throwing his weight about, winning several battles but achieving nothing like a conquest, and was eventually killed in battle in October 1318. It was a sideshow.

The Statutes of Kilkenny

It is generally acknowledged that the Statutes of Kilkenny were a failure, but they serve as a clear illustration of the degree by which the Anglo-Norman colony had decayed from within and the strength that Gaelic Ireland had regained. Thirty-five acts were passed in 1366–1367 under the initiative of Lionel, Duke of Clarence, who had been sent to Ireland to halt the alarming decline in the colony. The preamble to the statutes sums up the extent of this deterioration and indeed the deterioration in the general well-being of Ireland in the middle of the fourteenth century:

> Whereas at the conquest of the land of Ireland, and for a long time after, the English of the said land used the English language, mode of riding and apparel, and were governed and ruled, both they and their subjects according to English law, in which time God and holy Church were maintained and themselves lived in due subjection. But now many English of the said land, forsaking the English language, manners, mode of riding, laws and usages, live and govern themselves according to the manners, fashion, and language of the Irish enemies; and also have made divers marriages and alliances between themselves and the Irish aforesaid; whereby the said land and the liege people thereof, the English language, the allegiance due to our lord the king, and English laws are put in subjection and decayed, and the Irish enemies exalted and raised up, contrary to reason.

So there you have it. The Irish language was being used instead of English, modes of riding and dress were Irish, English law was giving way to March law and Brehon law, and intermarriage was taking place. Later, objections were raised to children being fostered in the Irish tradition, learning the Irish language and customs as a result. Practices in the Gaelic Church gave particular offence and it was decreed:

> … that no Irishman of the nations of the Irish be admitted into any cathedral or collegiate church by provision, collation, or presentation of any person, nor to any benefice of Holy Church amongst the English of the land.

This emphasized that there were differences between the Anglo-Norman church and the church in Gaelic Ireland.

The tide was running against the colony. Numbers were greatly reduced by the Black Death and later plagues, by many colonists returning to England, and by those who remained, adopting Irish habits of life. It was said that they 'became more Irish than the Irish', but that is not strictly true. One thing the leading colonists were not going to do was endanger the security of their property by adopting the Irish method of succession by tanistry. They wisely adhered to the English law of succession by primogeniture. As other colonists gave up, the great Anglo-Irish lords consolidated their estates until they controlled vast areas of the south and west. The Fitzgeralds of Kildare, the Butlers of Ormond and the Fitzmaurices of Desmond were so powerful they were referred to as 'magnates'. The purely English colony contracted to an area around Dublin and Drogheda, made secure by ditch and palisade, and called the Pale.

The fifteenth century was distorted by continued economic recession. The English treasury could not afford the money or the manpower to attend to Irish affairs; consequently large parts of the countryside fell into waste and churches and public buildings decayed. England was preoccupied by conflict between the rival houses of York and Lancaster and had little alternative than to allow the strongest faction among the magnates to control the government in Dublin. This turned out to be the Earl of Kildare, and his descendants more or less ruled Ireland as justiciar or Lord Deputy until 1534. A two-year interval from 1494 to 1496 saw the advent of Sir Edward Poynings and the passing of the famous 'Poynings' Law'. This established the superior rights of the English crown over the parliament in Dublin. It came into being as a short-term safeguard against dissident Yorkists using Ireland as a base for rebellion against Henry VII, but it remained in effect for nearly three hundred years and was felt as an instrument of oppression over the parliament of Ireland.

The sixteenth century

In 1515 an anonymous correspondent submitted a document to King Henry VIII which he called the 'State of Ireland and Plan for its Reformation'. It occupies more than thirty pages so a few extracts will have to convey its message.

Of the situation in Gaelic areas he writes:

There reigneth more than 60 chief captains that liveth only by the sword, and obeyeth to no other temporal person, but only to himself that is strong: and every of the said captains maketh war and peace for himself and obeyeth to no other person English or Irish except only to such as may subdue him by the sword.

His description of the tradition of succession by tanistry is:

The son of any of the said captains shall not succeed to his father without he be the strongest of all his nation. He that hath the strongest army and hardest sword among them hath best right and title, and by reason thereof there be but few of the said regions that be in peace within itself.

A graphic explanation of the origins of continuous warfare that debilitated many Gaelic areas!

He also describes 30 'great captains of English noble families that followeth the same Irish order and keepeth the same rule'.

English settlers it seems were no better off:

All the English folk of the said countries be of Irish habit, of Irish language and of Irish conditions except in the cities and walled towns. And for the more part they would be right glad to obey the King's laws, if they might be defended by the King of their Irish enemies.

The correspondent goes on at length about the evil of extortion that is carried on by the Irish nobles under the tradition of 'coyne and livery'. He says 'What common folk in all this world is so feeble, so greatly oppressed and trod under foot with so wretched a life as the commons of Ireland'. It makes sense that the people treated as slaves and labourers in Gaelic Ireland were not happy about it.

About the condition of the Church he paints a very depressing picture:

The prelates of the Church and clergy is much cause of all the misorder of the land, for there is no archbishop nor bishop, abbot nor prior, parson nor vicar nor any other person of the Church, high or low, great or small, English or Irish, that useth to preach the word of God saving the poor friars beggars. The Church not using its premises is much cause of all the said misorder.

It is a momentous phrase: 'the poor friars beggars'. It shows the impact that the Franciscans made and the service they delivered to the common people. There has been at least the suspicion that the church in Gaelic Ireland served only the aristocratic elite and that the common people were not able to share in the sacraments and offices. Most church buildings were small and appeared to be unlikely to accommodate the whole population. It might also explain the perpetuation of pre-Christian superstitions throughout the countryside.

Even allowing for some exaggeration and for the fact that no one person could exhaustively survey the whole country, this report to King Henry comes across as reasonably authentic. The main point is that the system was letting the country down. The Gaelic lords had too much power, they were not constrained by laws that protected the common people, and they dissipated the country's resources in constant warfare. The system killed initiative when the energies of all the people were needed most. Having said that, it has to be acknowledged that a good leader is not dependent on a good system, and in some places an outstanding chieftain was able to rule his territory peacefully and justly. But this was the exception. Ireland had the best farmland in Europe, but was not exploiting it.

Finally both the Gaelic and Anglo-Irish lordships still had no perception of Ireland as a nation state. This would have been an achievable goal at the time given the shortage of money and other resources that England was able to devote to the task of governing Ireland. Throughout the sixteenth century they continued to operate on a shoestring and managed to get away with it. If the Irish lordships had worked together there is no doubt that they would have been able to defend themselves against further colonial intrusion.

Several milestones were passed in the 1530s and 1540s that marked the stages by which the Tudors tried to modernize Ireland. It is referred to as the Tudor Conquest, but it was not a military operation. Henry VIII is at times portrayed as a bit of a bumbling fool mainly because of his contorted matrimonial machinations, but he had learned how to be an astute politician, and he also had radical ideas for reform, which he was able to implement through legitimate parliamentary procedures. Although most of them did not come to fruition in Ireland until the reign of Elizabeth, the process was started under Henry.

The end of the Kildare hegemony

England had more or less left Ireland in the charge of the Earls of Kildare for the previous fifty years except for the short interval of Poynings' Parliament. The great Garret More had died in 1513 and been succeeded by his son Garret Óg. Henry began to feel dissatisfied about his lack of control over Ireland and in 1529 appointed his son Duke of Richmond as lieutenant, together with a council of English officials, including Archbishop John Alen. He was signalling that henceforth he wanted Ireland to be governed by Englishmen appointed by him, thereby reducing the standing of Garret Óg.

Internal plotting undermined the council and in 1532 Henry reappointed Garret Óg, but Garret was soon suspected of using the king's artillery for the defence of his own castles. He was arrested and taken to the Tower. He died of natural causes in December 1534, but a rumour that he had been executed prompted a reckless gesture from his 21-year-old son known as Silken Thomas. It was hardly a rebellion, but he too was arrested and later executed at Tyburn. The experiment of having an Irishman, even one of Anglo-

Norman descent, in the position of Lord Deputy was over and would not be repeated.

The Act of Supremacy 1534

The effect of the Act was to make the monarch of England, in this case Henry VIII, supreme head of the Church in England instead of the pope. Henry intended this as a sort of technical adjustment, leaving England Catholic but without the pope. He was not a Lutheran, and the Catholic sacraments and Latin Mass were to continue to be celebrated as before. In less than fifteen years, however, what emerged was a new church. Under Edward VI the Church of England became Protestant with married clergy, a new Book of Common Prayer and a new structure of liturgy and theology.

In Ireland separate legislation was required. Henry issued 'Ordinances for the Government of Ireland' to make the Act of Supremacy effective immediately. The Council in Dublin was to set aside papal jurisdiction over episcopal appointments, which would come instead from Canterbury. In 1536 the 'Reformation Parliament' met in Dublin to pass into law the body of legislation covered by the Act of Supremacy in England. This was forced through despite opposition from a group of lower clergy in parliament known as the clerical proctors, who held it up for more than a year. Patrick Barnwell and some others were courageously outspoken, but the provisions were enacted. It should be remembered, however, that Dublin's writ did not run outside the Pale and so the effects were not felt in the rest of the country for a considerable time.

Although the Church of Ireland officially became the established Church, the country as a whole was instinctively Catholic. The Anglican clergy were not equipped to deliver pastoral care to an Irish-speaking population, and in any case many clergy left their impoverished benefices unattended. For a crucial fifty years or so there was no incentive for traditional Catholics suddenly to become Anglican and this is when the pattern of religious loyalties was set for centuries to come.

One of the other Acts of the Reformation Parliament was to change Henry's title from 'Lord of Ireland' to 'King of Ireland'. This was not just a courtesy; it was necessary to institute the principle of English law that the Crown acting through Parliament was the ultimate landowner.

The dissolution of the monasteries

The Act of Supremacy gave Henry VIII jurisdiction over monastic institutions as part of the Church and one of his first actions was to confiscate monastic property to the benefit of the Crown. This is not the place to debate its justification or otherwise. It happened and was accompanied by much unsightly vandalism to nobody's credit. The buildings, with some exceptions, were of less significance than the landed property, which was extensive and now became available for grants to what was hoped would be more productive tenants.

In Ireland only those monasteries and friaries within the Pale and in some towns were immediately involved. In the Gaelic and Anglo-Irish areas of the west and north the procedure took more than a hundred years. Some Franciscan communities continued their ministry clandestinely and earned popular admiration. In 1542 the first Jesuits arrived, determined to promote their mission, but formed the impression that many leading citizens were ready to accept the situation so long as they could continue with their regular Catholic form of worship.

As in England the resettlement of monastic land benefited some already wealthy landowners: the Butlers of Ormond did particularly well. But large amounts of monastic land also contributed to schemes for new settlers.

Surrender and Regrant

It seems Henry VIII himself thought up the idea of Surrender and Regrant. It was mentioned first in the 1520s as a possible way of dealing with Cormac MacCarthy, Lord of Carbery. It did not begin to be implemented until 1541, and it is certain that no one at that stage foresaw the profound effect it would ultimately have on Irish society. Military conquest was rightly seen to be out of the question. It would have been impossibly expensive, even if it could physically have been achieved, given that there were more than sixty separate virtually independent petty kingdoms, each with its own army, and with many of them set in impenetrable local terrain of bog and woodland. Henry described the only tactic open to him as 'sober ways, politic drifts and amiable persuasions'. He came up with Surrender and Regrant as one of his amiable persuasions, which became the cornerstone of the Tudor Conquest.

The way it worked was that the Gaelic chiefs had first of all to 'come in' to the Lord Deputy or one of his officials and offer their submission to the King's authority. This was taken to be a surrender of their territory. It was then immediately granted back to them so that they had the security of royal acknowledgement of possession of their land. They were required to pay what was little more than a nominal rent to the Crown.

Since they were in exactly the same position as they had been before there seemed to be no strenuous objections—well not quite 'exactly'. What followed was an unforeseen chain reaction that was as radical in its ultimate outcome as a revolution. In effect they now held their land from the Crown; they were subject to, and entitled to the protection of, English law. They had the right of access to the King's courts and, to provide that, the framework of English social order had to be established—a process known as 'shiring'. Counties were created as administrative units with sheriffs, coroners and justices of the peace appointed as servants of the Crown.

As the Irish chiefs now became important landowners they were eligible for titles that reflected their status. Some became Earls, others Barons and Knights, which brought with it the entitlement, duty even, to sit in the Irish parliament.

Under English law each of the Gaelic Irish chiefs now had personal title to the land which in Irish tradition had previously belonged to the *derbfine*. The property now passed to the next generation by primogeniture instead of by the Gaelic tradition of tanistry and election in a family assembly. This gave the ruling chieftain security of possession but at the same time downgraded the other members of the family. It could be argued that this was a good thing since it eliminated the excuse for endless succession warfare that everywhere undermined Gaelic society. The rest of the family could not be alienated, however, especially since each branch was often the specialized expert in such subjects as law, the Church, medicine, music or estate management. Adjustments had to be made. Some Gaelic lords unnecessarily went through traditional inauguration ceremonies as well, and continued to apply Irish law in dealing with vassal subgroups, freeholders and professional servants. Important members of the family were sometimes given English titles of lesser rank.

In the years after 1541 Surrender and Regrant seemed to be widely taken up, but only slowly and sporadically implemented. O'Donnell of Donegal became the Earl of Tyrconnell. In County Clare Murrough O'Brien went to the extent of writing to Henry and travelling to Greenwich to accept the English title Earl of Thomond, with baronies and knighthoods devolving to close family members. When the Armada ships arrived in 1588 Sir Turlough O'Brien was the family landowner in Ibrecane, Boetius Clancy was County Sheriff and Nicholas Cahan was Coroner, evidence that the apparatus of the English legal system was in place in County Clare.

Surrender and Regrant became the main instrument by which Gaelic Irish society was brought to an end. Almost as a side effect, as it evolved it gradually separated the Irish Chiefs from their traditional extended families and reduced the old Gaelic society to an anachronism.

It is almost certain that this was way beyond the result envisaged by Henry VIII when it occurred to him in the 1520s. It was a complete accident!

Plantation

The concept of plantation evolved at first as a method of dealing with the problem posed by the O'Mores of Leix and the O'Connors of Offaly. They were too close to the Pale for comfort yet were protected by seemingly impenetrable terrain. They regarded it as their inalienable right to raid into the Pale and plunder its wealth. Attempts to subdue them by force of arms were never a lasting solution. Their territory was said to be 'more easily won than kept. Out of these wastes, in small numbers or great, the rebels issued into the heart of the Queen's County and thence into every part of the Pale adjoining, spoiling the same at pleasure …'

Queen's County was named after Mary Tudor and it was she who devised the plan to confiscate to the Crown the eastern parts of these native Irish territories and grant them to a number of English settlers. It was a carefully worked out scheme as to the number and size of the estates to be granted, and the obligations on the settlers to erect stone houses and provide a given number of armed men to the Lord Deputy when required. Garrison fortresses were erected which became Philipstown and Maryborough.

The plans were enacted by parliament in 1557 just a year before Mary died, but it was a long time until they began to be carried out. Mary was replaced by Elizabeth, and she extended them further to include the area west as far as the Shannon. Even by the end of the century they still had not been fully completed.

Mary had established the principle, however, that where there was perceived to be rebellion, 'Confiscation and Plantation' could follow. It was also applied to large tracts of land associated with the monasteries as the dissolution progressed across the country. As an instrument of colonization this was a good deal harsher than Henry VIII's 'amiable persuasions'.

The Munster Rebellion

Rebellion in Munster was centred on the Anglo-Irish lordships, and when it came it was consequently more serious. Elizabeth had set up presidencies to govern Connaught and Munster. It proved to be more difficult to shire the Anglo-Irish areas than the Gaelic ones, because the Anglo-Irish lords were so powerful. The presidencies were supposed to force the reforms through and extend the structure of English law into very large parts of the country.

In Munster the Earl of Desmond had a vision of his great estates being taken over by government officials. He created formidable obstructions to the efforts of the presidency and was sent to the Tower. His cousin James Fitzmaurice took over the running of the estates and, like Desmond, was determined to protect their lands. In 1569 he began a revolt which seemed to be going nowhere until he attacked and burned the English garrison at Kilmallock. The president, Sir John Perrot, captured Fitzmaurice and forced a submission out of him in humiliating circumstances. This only added fuel to

Fitzmaurice's grievances, which became centred on religion. He began to call his conspiracy 'The Catholic League' and in 1575 left for Europe to gather support for a religious crusade against the Protestant occupation of Ireland. He was a charismatic character and succeeded in getting papal backing for a small force of three hundred or so Italians and Spanish, who landed with him at Dingle in 1579. Within a month, however, he was killed in a pointless skirmish near the Shannon. (His son Maurice Fitzgerald was with the Spanish Armada, but died at sea on the *Duquesa Santa Ana* just before it entered Blacksod Bay.)

In September 1580 a second papal force landed on the Dingle peninsula, this time at Smerwick on the northern coast, where they occupied an old fort. After a siege they surrendered, but were murdered by the Lord Deputy, Lord Grey de Wilton. Technically all this amounted to rebellion, but it never seemed to pose much of a threat. Although he really achieved very little, the name Fitzmaurice is still revered as a symbol of resistance. The Earl of Desmond had been released from the Tower, and although he was not a natural soldier he eventually joined the rebellion only to be killed in battle in November 1585.

The great Geraldine family of Desmond was thereby virtually extinguished. In 1586 parliament passed an act of attainder against them. Their lands were thus confiscated and a process of Plantation was begun. The estates were huge, more than five million acres, and although there were many acquisitive New English keen to profit by the venture, they hardly began to fulfil the planting conditions. It was many years before the Plantation of Munster made much headway.

One disillusioned planter who was obviously an idealist lamented:

Our pretence in the enterprise of plantation was to establish in these parts piety, justice, inhabitation and civility with comfort and good example to the parts adjacent. Our drift now is, being here possessed of land, to extort, make the state of things turbulent, and live by prey and by pay.

Another correspondent writing in 1588 was one of the failures:

I fear some of the greatest undertakers are discouraged in the action with the sight of this rude and tottering uncertain state ... so impossible is it to draw honest English inhabitants to this waste country ... to the dismay of many adventurers who expect money, and this country yieldeth only meat.

There was no cash in the economy of the Irish countryside; even the rent collected for the Queen was referred to as 'rent beeves'.

There are few tidy conclusions or happy endings in Irish history. At the end of the sixteenth century Gaelic Irish society was being worn away. A culture that had survived for perhaps 4,000 years was unable to resist the feudal and post-feudal world that was flooding in. It might have been an anachronism, but for the Gaelic Irish people it had provided a degree of stability and security. There was not much wealth even for the aristocracy, but there was no joy for them either in the harsh realities of the new order. The only comfort was provided by mendicant friars who shaped the religious loyalties of the common people for the next 300 years.

The year 1588 fell in the middle or towards the end of the middle of the transition between the old and the new order. A chief like Sir John O'Doherty had accepted a title of English nobility, but his people still lived according to the old Gaelic traditions. In Mid-Ulster Hugh O'Neill had become Earl of Tyrone, but he was not chieftain of the O'Neills; under the old Gaelic system that title belonged to Turlough Luineach O'Neill who absolutely refused to accept an English title. In a transition period any mixture between old and new is possible and can be expected. The change was being forced through in a way that left the people of Ireland feeling oppressed, especially in the west and northwest, which is the area where most of the drama of the Armada was played out.

The Anglo-Irish for the most part gradually settled down as the landed gentry. Many of the Gaelic Irish lords did the same and thereby helped to change their traditional society forever. The poor Irish were therefore deprived of their patronage and left with nothing to take its place.

The New English were hungry for land, and the plantations supplied opportunities for their energy and enterprise. They were joined by a group known as the 'servitors' who came to Ireland as soldiers but expected to receive grants of land as their reward. Some were very large grants indeed.

In the first years of the seventeenth century Scottish settlers arrived in south Antrim and north Down. They were private venture economic migrants, not connected with the later Plantation of Ulster. They were 'covenanters' who later formed the nucleus of the 'Presbyterian' church in Ireland. They worked hard and built a community. As non-conformists they too were oppressed by the penal laws and in the eighteenth century many left Ireland for the New World.

Could Ireland peacefully accommodate such diverse population groups?

NOTES AND SOURCES

There has been a huge effort in the twentieth century to interpret the contents of early Irish literature and to extract from it 'proof' of Ireland's mid-European Celtic ancestry. The works of T.F. O'Rahilly *Early Irish History and Mythology*, Dublin 1946, and T.E.G. Powell *The Celts*, London 1958 are impressive, and it seems a shame to question them. The doubts cast by archaeology are raised in Barry Rafferty *Pagan Celtic Ireland*, London 1994, and developed by Barry Cunliffe in *The Ancient Celts*, Oxford 1997.

The significance or otherwise of the Irish language as evidence of early Irish history is discussed in Colin Renfrew *Archaeology and Language, The Puzzle of Indo-European Origins*, London 1987. Without being convinced himself, he seems to reveal that less is known about the languages of the Continental Celts than of the Insular Celts, and that the presumed connection between them through the old theory about Brythonic and Goidelic having continental origins is now on shaky ground. By finding Indo-European connections in the Irish language he does more to associate it with the spread of farming in the third millennium BC than with the Iron Age.

The Irish Church in the first millennium is most satisfactorily described by Kathleen Hughes in *The Church in Early Irish Society*, London 1966, and (with Ann Hamlin) in *The Modern Traveller to the Early Irish Church*, London 1972. Dáibhí Ó Cróinín's *Early Medieval Ireland 400–1200*, London 1995, is a beautiful book and includes a comprehensive survey of the Irish Church through which it is possible to appreciate the unique position it occupied in western Christendom. John R. Walsh and Thomas Bradley *A History of the Irish Church 400–700 AD*, Dublin 1991, reveals the intense spiritual motivation that energized the Irish Church at that time.

There is no quicker way to give offence in Irish History than to try to explain the 'one church' thesis. The church of the first millennium was unorthodox in its organization and practice, but there was only one. After the Norman invasion a church organization was established that complied with the conventions of the rest of western Christendom and served the Anglo-Norman population. As we have seen, a device was found to integrate the Gaelic Church through acknowledgment of episcopal authority, but in practice its idiosyncrasies continued. The Statutes of Kilkenny made a clear distinction between 'Ecclesia inter Anglos' and 'Ecclesia inter Hibernes', and barred Gaelic clergy from access to 'any benefice of Holy Church amongst the English'. An independent observer could be forgiven for concluding that he was witnessing what were de facto two churches serving two very different congregations. It appears, however, that it was in everyone's interest to maintain the 'one church' thesis. This could be done by pointing to the fact that, after the twelfth century, papal supremacy was acknowledged in authorizing appointments to the sees in all areas. In the Gaelic Church this was usually no more than an endorsement of the candidate from the ecclesiastical branch of the ruling family, but the semblance of one unified Church could be maintained. Indeed while Gaelic Irish society retained its ancient structure the Church in Gaelic areas had no alternative other than to adapt to it.

After 1534 the church in Anglo-Irish areas became the Anglican Church and, therefore, Protestant. Surely this was the opportunity to recognize that there were now two churches. But no! The Anglican Church was resolute in claiming its heritage in the early Irish Church. As part of 'one church' it could continue to derive its patrimony from Saint Patrick and the other Irish saints. The Gaelic Church after the sixteenth century quickly became a bastion of Catholic orthodoxy, bearing little or no resemblance to the church that for centuries had been run by coarbs and erenaghs and hereditary ecclesiastical families. Through the continuity of its connection with the papacy it could also claim the heritage of the early Irish Church. It would be pleasing if all Christians were indeed of 'one church' so—let it continue!

The Norman invasion and the evolution of the colony are a huge subject covered by an enormous literature. The following were most helpful: Edmund Curtis *A History of Ireland*, London 1936; A.J. Ottway-Ruthven *A History of Medieval Ireland*, London 1968; J.F. Lydon *The Lordship of Ireland in the Middle Ages*, Dublin 1972; Francis John Byrne *Irish Kings and High-Kings*, Dublin 1971. And from the Gill History of Ireland series, Michael Dolly *Anglo-Norman Ireland*, Kenneth Nicholls *Gaelic and Gaelicised Ireland in the Middle Ages*, and Margaret MacCurtain *Tudor and Stuart Ireland*, published in Dublin in 1972, are all useful.

The report on the state of Ireland is from the State Papers Henry VIII, volume II part III 1515 entitled 'The State of Ireland and Plan for its Reformation'. The quotations from the disillusioned Munster planters are in CSPI p. 52 and p. 62.

Apologies are freely offered for the intrusion of eccentric interpretations. None of the above authors should be blamed.

SELECT BIBLIOGRAPHY

As I have previously stated I tried to work mostly from original sources with the intention of producing an independent interpretation of four-hundred-year-old evidence. But naturally I am indebted to several authors whose specialized knowledge and experience were essential. I have not used many of the histories produced in the middle of the twentieth century, mainly because I found myself arriving at rather different conclusions. This bibliography is, therefore, correspondingly short, since it is confined to those works directly related to specific incidents in the text; it does not set out to provide a reading list of the wide range of publications available on the subject of the Armada.

Contemporary Sources

Calendar of State Papers Ireland—Elizabeth VOL. 137, August 1588–September 1592 (London, 1885).

'Calendar of Letters and State Papers relating to English Affairs Preserved in or Originally Belonging to the Archives of Simancas VOL. IV. Elizabeth 1587–1603', Martin Hume (ed.) (London, 1899).

J.K. Laughton (ed.), 'State Papers Relating to the Defeat of the Spanish Armada in 1588', two volumes (The Navy Records Society, 1894).

Public Record Office, microfilm copies of original documents September and October 1588, stored under the reference number 223, reel numbers 51 and 52.

Acts of the Privy Council of England VOL. XVI (Norwich, 1898).

Other Published References

Steven Birch and D.M. McElvogue, *The International Journal of Nautical Archaeology* (1999), 28. 3. An interim report on the three Spanish Armada transports lost off Streedagh Strand, County Sligo.

Stephen Budiansky, *Her Majesty's Spymaster* (New York and London, 2005).

K.S. Douglas, H.H. Lamb and C. Loader, 'A Meteorological Study of July to October 1588: The Spanish Armada Storms' (Norwich, 1978).

K.S. Douglas, 'Navigation: the Key to the Armada Disaster', *Journal for Maritime Research* (Greenwich, 2003).

C.F. Duro, *La Armada Invencible*, two volumes (Madrid, 1884–1885).

C.O. Erickson, 'An Incipient Hurricane near the West African Coast', *Monthly Weather Review*, February 1963.

Niall Fallon, *The Armada in Ireland* (London, 1978).

P. Gallagher and D.W. Cruickshank (eds), *God's Obvious Design* (London and Sligo, 1990).

Winifred Glover, *Exploring the Spanish Armada* (Dublin, 2000).

W. Spotswood Green, 'The Wrecks of the Spanish Armada on the Coast of Ireland', *The Geographical Journal*, VOL. XXVII, May 1906.

Richard Hakluyt, *Voyages* (Everyman Edition, London, 1907).

Evelyn Hardy, *Survivors of the Armada* (London, 1966).

Irish Law Reports, VOL. 3, pp 413–42, 26 July 1994 and 29 June 1995.

Colin Martin, *Full Fathom Five: Wrecks of the Spanish Armada* (London, 1975).

Colin Martin and Geoffrey Parker, *The Spanish Armada* (London, 1988).

Paula Martin, *Spanish Armada Prisoners* (Exeter, 1988).

Garrett Mattingly, *The Defeat of the Spanish Armada* (London, 1959).

Herrera Oria, *Armada Invencible* (Valladolid, 1929).

Geoffrey Parker, 'Diary of a Soldier', etc., *The Mariner's Mirror* (August 2004).

Jack Scoltock, *We've Found a Cannon* (Coleraine and Ballycastle, 2003).

Robert Sténuit, *Treasures of the Armada* (London, 1972).

David Waters, *The Art of Navigation in England in Elizabethan and Early Stuart Times* (London, 1958).

Sidney Wignall, *In Search of Spanish Treasure: A Diver's Story* (London, 1982).

INDEX